核心素养导向的
高中英语思维型课堂
教学实践

黄 焱 / 著

中国文联出版社

图书在版编目（CIP）数据

核心素养导向的高中英语思维型课堂教学实践/黄
焱著. — 北京：中国文联出版社，2023.6
ISBN 978-7-5190-5211-9

Ⅰ.①核… Ⅱ.①黄… Ⅲ.①英语课—课堂教学—教
学研究—高中 Ⅳ.①G633.412

中国国家版本馆CIP数据核字（2023）第096708号

著　　者　黄　焱
责任编辑　刘　旭
责任校对　秀点校对
装帧设计　刘贝贝　李　娜

出版发行　中国文联出版社有限公司
社　　址　北京市朝阳区农展馆南里10号　　邮编　100125
电　　话　010-85923025（发行部）　　010-85923091（总编室）
经　　销　全国新华书店等
印　　刷　北京四海锦诚印刷技术有限公司

开　　本　710毫米×1000毫米　　1/16
印　　张　16
字　　数　271千字
版　　次　2023年6月第1版第1次印刷
定　　价　58.00元

前 言

FOREWORD

《普通高中英语课程标准（2017年版）》细化了中国学生发展核心素养的教育方针，凝聚了英语学科的核心素养。学科的核心素养是指学生通过学科的学习而逐步形成的关键能力、必备品格与价值观念。英语学科的核心素养主要包括语言能力、文化意识、思维品质和学习能力。将思维品质作为一个显性目标提出来是我国英语课程建设史上前所未有的举措。培养思维能力，这才是英语教育的根本。关于思维品质的培养，在中国英语语言环境背景下，阅读和写作是促进思维品质提升的最有效途径。同时，思维品质的培养需要深度学习的支撑，所以，阅读和写作教学要在深度学习理念的指导下进行。学生没有深度学习，就不可能提升素养。指向素养的学习，一定是有深度的。

本书共分四章内容。第一章介绍阅读能力的培养策略。高中英语教材是英语课程资源的核心，所选的阅读文本涉及各类话题，语言真实，表达地道，能开阔学生视野，拓展学生思维方式，是一个丰富的英语素材库。在这个章节中，通过大量的文本分析案例和文本结构思维图，帮助一线教师分析了解文章结构和提炼积累语言表达。单元阅读教学设计侧重落实学生思维能力的训练，为实际教学提供一定的借鉴。第二章介绍写作能力的培养策略。写作，究其实质就是一种逻辑表达。写作和思维也是密不可分的。写作能力的提高必须依赖于学生的"认识能力"和"语言文字表达能力"两个方面的因素。语料库的积累是学生写作思维培养的基石。为此，本章精选了创新型单元学案集、语境记忆单词文本资料、高考原题改编资料。在积累大量语言素材的同时，通过对句子、段落和语篇的仿写、创写等途径来实现语用知识的迁移，提升学生的写作能力。第三章介绍校本课程建设。自主开发的合美英语校本课程作为学校英语学科课程的重要补充，凸显人文关怀。其中英语诗歌鉴赏选修课程系列，精选具有代表性的不同风格的中外诗歌。以欣赏为主，通过读、悟、述、品、评、诵和仿，引领学生走进诗歌的境界，去感悟体验诗歌的韵律之美、形式之美、内容之美。第四章主要是教学论文，内容涉及阅读与写作教学、教学策略、学习策略等方面。

在本书付梓之际，要感谢深圳市坪山区教育局为坪山区名师成长搭建的工作室平台以及为名师著作出版提供的经费支持；也要感谢我的单位坪山高级中学为工作室的运行发展提供良好的条件保障和经费支持。

目 录
CONTENTS

上篇　指向素养的学习

下篇　课例研究与反思

第四章　教学论文

上 篇

指向素养的学习

第一章　阅读能力培养策略

自新课程改革以来，核心素养成了新时代教育改革的重要内容。学科核心素养是学科育人价值的集中体现，是学生通过学科学习而逐步形成的正确价值观念、必备品格和关键能力。英语学科核心素养主要包括语言能力、文化意识、思维品质和学习能力。

1. 语言能力

英语语言能力构成英语学科核心素养的基础要素。英语语言能力的提高蕴含文化意识、思维品质和学习能力的提升，有助于学生拓展国际视野和思维方式，开展跨文化交流。

2. 文化意识

文化意识体现英语学科核心素养的价值取向。文化意识的培养有助于学生增强国家认同和家国情怀，坚定文化自信，树立人类命运共同体意识，学会做人做事，成长为有文明素养和社会责任感的人。

3. 思维品质

思维品质体现英语学科核心素养的心智特征。思维品质的发展有助于提升学生分析和解决问题的能力，使他们能够从跨文化视角观察和认识世界，对事物做出正确的价值判断。

4. 学习能力

学习能力的培养有助于学生做好英语学习的自我管理，养成良好的学习习惯，多渠道获取学习资源，自主、高效地开展学习。

英语学科核心素养的落实是目前基础教育阶段英语课程与教学改革的重要任务，基于学生核心素养的学习不是简单学习，而是深度学习。

随着基础教育体制改革的深化，课堂教学改革是学校教育改革与发展的核心议题。历经20年的课程改革，虽然在学习方式、教学模式上有所改变，出现了项目式学习、翻转课堂、小组合作学习、研究性学习、社会综合实践等各种教学模式，但实践证明这些教学模式也隐藏着教学形式化、课时冗余化、内容零散化、学习浅层化等种种问题。为了解决上述教学实际中存在的问题，深度学习、单元教学越来越引起教师的关注。《普通高中英语课程标准（2017年版）》中进一步体现了深度学习的重要性。它提出高中英语教学要围绕学生的核心素养即语言能力、文化意识、思维品质和学习能力四个关键素养来进行。深度学习和单元教学既是深化教育教学改革过程中学者需要关注的内容，也是全面提高教育质量实践中教师需要面对的问题。那么，怎样理解单元教学和深度学习，怎样理解两者之间的关系，怎样设计单元中的核心任务才能实现深度学习等问题，仍然是教师教学实践中亟待解决的困惑。只有厘清上述问题，才能使教学实践更符合教学规律，促进学生核心素养的发展。

在整个单元教学中，阅读能力的培养至关重要。教育部文件指出英语阅读是发展语言能力、思维品质和学习能力的主渠道，也是实现课程学科素养目标的重要保障。普通高中英语课程标准倡导指向学科核心素养的英语学习活动观和自主学习、合作学习、探究学习等学习方式。学生是一个积极主动、独立的生命体，所以我们不仅要关注高认知，还要关注知识习得的过程。阅读教学就是在深度学习理念指导下进行的。学生没有深度学习，就不可能有素养。指向素养的学习，一定是有深度的。

一、国内外有关深度学习的研究

国外对于深度学习的相关研究起步较早，主要关注深度学习的内涵以及深度学习的学习策略研究，这也是国内相关研究的理论基础。Liz Grauerholz（2001）认为深度学习应该是整体性的学习，与浅层学习的表面性和碎片化不同，深度学习更加注重整体。 国内学者张浩、吴秀娟（2012）指出深度学习应该是一种带有主动性质、批判性质的学习，是认识学习本质的一个过程。通过对知识信息进行深度加工，对复杂的概念进行深度理解，对其内在含义深度掌握，对个人知识体系进行主动构建，从而促进高级思维能力的培养和发展。

国内外学者在研究过程中还发现深度学习是一个十分复杂的过程，要实现深度学习，还需要进行更多的实践，需要许多外部条件的支持。Alison Rushton

（2005）认为利用形成性评价，进行有层次的评价和引导，可以促进深度学习的实现。Lecun Y., Bengio Y., Hinton G.（2015）提出深度学习的达成，由引导者来实现，同时，虚拟的学习环境、思维导图等的有效运用，可以为深度学习提供有效的保障，以达成学习的深层次理解和思考。国内学者郭华（2016）认为："深度学习是在教师引领下，学生围绕具有挑战性的学习主题，全身心积极参与、体验成功、获得发展的有意义的学习过程，并具有批判理解、有机整合、建构反思与迁移应用的特征。"王静（2014）提出了构建认知结构、思维结构、动作技能以及情感结构的深度学习多维评价体系，分析和阐述了这些不同领域中深度学习可能实现的学习目标。

本章以高中英语阅读教学为切入点，针对在深度学习视角下培养学生阅读能力的方法和策略进行研究，以期为提升英语教学质量和效果提供参考价值。

二、阅读课堂中读写实践的整合机制

1. 文本结构的剖析与模仿

文本的结构是文章的"骨架"，是作者为表现主旨而对写作材料进行构思安排的结果，是文章部分与部分、部分与整体之间的内在联系和外部形式的统一，是行文思路的具体体现。阅读时把握了文本的结构，才能真正理解文章。同样，写作时只有把握好了文本的结构，整体谋篇布局，才能真正做到思路清晰、行文流畅。所以，阅读和写作有机结合就能相得益彰。

通过阅读文本教学，我们关注结构分析，从解读标题、辨别文体、浏览首句、概括每段主旨、关注过渡与衔接等入手，梳理文章内部段与段、层与层之间的关系以及段落与语篇之间的结构层次。这些过程都可以为写作打好基础。有了对文本结构的剖析，积累语言素材和写作素材，据此学生对文章的整体结构进行模仿，从模仿到熟练、再到创新，从而完成整个写作过程。这样，在模仿中激发写作灵感，激活创新思维，逐步使学生由被迫作文向自觉、自愿作文过渡和转变，并最终形成"我手写我心"的自如的写作能力。

2. 围绕文本主题激发和提升学生思维

阅读教学除了对文本信息的准确解读，还从思维的深度上引领学生认识和评价文本，使文本的解读更加多元。我们借助阅读，一方面读出语言、内容、结构，另一方面围绕文本的某个主题来激发和提升学生的思维品质，进行写作的输出。写什么、怎么写很重要，但"为什么这么写"更重要。每个文本都有很多思想的激发点，把文本中体现思辨的因素挖掘出来并利用好来实现思想、态度、情感和价值观等目标。

3. 话题语言的提炼与积累

高中英语阅读教材是英语课程资源的核心，涉及各类话题，语言真实，表达地道，能开阔学生视野，拓展学生思维方式，是一个丰富的英语写作素材库。通过阅读文本教材，引导学生做好核心话题语言素材的提炼和积累，并创设真实语境，在分析、概括、提炼的基础上将这些素材转化为写作内容，让学生能学以致用。

三、英语阅读教学改进行动——文本解读

阅读是获取知识最直接、最有效的方法。阅读从某种意义上说是写作的"彩排"，它是一种很好的语言输入。阅读材料能为写作提供"彩排的道具"。阅读材料其实就是一种很好的范例。合理有效地利用教材阅读文本，在很大程度上能有效地达到输入和输出的结合。每篇课文都能作为培养学生作文的创造思维的一个支点，如何激活学生创造思维，撬起作文教学的这个"地球"，方式方法很多，只要用心去做，学生的作文思维就会得以强化，作文能力就会提高，肯定能写出富有创意的好作文来。所以说，要切实提高学生的思辨能力和写作水平必须经过系统的训练，而抓好阅读教学是其中重要的一个环节。文本信息和目标语言是阅读课堂教学活动的基点。文本解读不仅要做到多层次、多角度，更要考虑学生主体，将文本内容转化为学生的学习经历。具体表现在：

文本解读维度	What	语篇的主题和内容
	How	文体特征、内容结构、语言特点
	Why	语篇的深层含义，作者或说话人的意图、情感态度或价值取向

资料来源：《普通高中英语课程标准（2017年版）》，第59页。

根据上表，阅读教学绝不能简单地处理成做几个表层的阅读理解题，而应该是对语篇资源价值和思想内涵做进一步的挖掘。阅读教学的目标定位是培养和提高分析语篇、解决语篇问题的能力，增强语言综合运用能力。课题组对阅

读课进行精心研讨，确定了文本解读的基本模式。

1. 文本解读的四个层面

（1）内容层面——理解文本表层信息：向学生提问文本直接陈述的事实与观点。

（2）结构层面——理解信息点间的相互联系：理解作者为证明自己观点所选用的例子以及理解分析作者的结论从何而来。

（3）思维层面——理解观点思想：理解文本主旨；理解词汇句子等在文中的特殊含义；分析作者观点、思想和态度。

（4）语言层面——学习目标语言：阅读教学中语言处理从话题、功能和修辞等视角进行。

基于此，通过大量的课堂实践，摸索出阅读课教学模式，具体如下：

Step 1 Brainstorming for their own different ideas about what aspects should be included in the passage.

Step 2 Reading for structures, cohesion and coherence of the passage.

Step 3 Reading for languages related to the specific topic.

Step 4 Viewpoints exchange and discussion.

Step 5 Imitating writing.

2. 阅读材料的文本分析

笔者选取人教版Book 5& Book 6两本书侧重训练学生从"内容结构"和"语言"两个层面对阅读材料进行文本分析、自主学习，以此训练学生的思维和帮助学生积累词汇句型。其内容设计着眼于培养学生的注意力、观察力、记忆力、想象力、思维力。这套"习案"发挥了学生的主体作用，促进了智力发展。

Book 5 Module 1 Reading 文本分析

British and American English

Words, words, words

①British and American English are different in many ways. ②The first and most obvious way is in the vocabulary. ③There are hundreds of different words which are not used on the other side of the Atlantic, or which are used with a different meaning. ④Some of these words are well known —Americans drive automobiles down freeways and fill up with gas; the British drive cars along motorways and fill up with petrol. ⑤As a tourist, you will need to use the underground in London or the subway in New York, or maybe you will prefer to get around the town by taxi（British）or cab（American）.

内容结构层面	第①句是段落的中心句，是一个总体陈述。第②③句是逐层论述第①句。第④⑤句都是例子来说明第③句表现在单词方面的差异
语言层面	短语： fill up with get around 句式： ...and ...are different in many ways. The first and most obvious way is ...

Chips or French fries?

①But other words and expressions are not so well known.②Americans use a flashlight, while for the British, it's a torch. ③The British queue up; Americans stand in line. ④Sometimes the same word has a slightly different meaning, which can be confusing. ⑤Chips, for example, are pieces of hot fried potato in Britain; in the States chips are very thin and are sold in packets. ⑥The British call these crisps. ⑦The chips the British know and love are French fries on the other side of the Atlantic.

内容结构层面	第①句是本段的中心句，后面的第②③句都是举例说明第①句。第④句是一个过渡句，后面第⑤—⑦句是举例说明第④句
语言层面	短语： queue up stand in line 句式： 句子，+ while +句子 For example， 句子

Have or have got?

①There are a few differences in grammar, too. ②The British say Have you got ...?while Americans prefer Do you have ...?③An American might say My friend just arrived, but a British person would say My friend has just arrived. ④Prepositions, too, can be different: compare on the team, on the weekend（American）with in the team, at the weekend（British）. ⑤The British use prepositions where Americans sometimes omit them（I'll see you Monday. Write me soon！）.

内容结构层面	第①句是本段的中心句，后面的第②③句都是举例说明第①句。第④句也是一个中心句，后面第⑤句是举例说明第④句
语言层面	短语： compare...with... 句式： There are a few differences in ... ..., too, can be different.

Colour or color?

①The other two areas in which the two varieties differ are spelling and pronunciation. ②American spelling seems simpler: center, color and program instead of centre, colour and programme. ③Many factors have influenced American pronunciation since the first settlers arrived four hundred years ago. ④The accent, which is most similar to British English, can be heard on the East Coast of the US. ⑤When the Irish writer George Bernard Shaw made the famous remark that the British and the Americans are two nations divided by a common language, he was obviously thinking about the differences. ⑥But are they really so important？ ⑦After all, there is probably as much variation of pronunciation within the two countries as between them. ⑧A Londoner has more difficulty understanding a Scotsman from Glasgow than understanding a New Yorker.

内容结构层面	第①句是本段的中心句，阐述在spelling和pronunciation两个方面的区别。后面的第②—⑤句都是举例说明第①句。第⑥句是一个过渡句，起到自然转换话题的作用。其中使用了过渡衔接词but。通过最后⑦⑧两句可以推断出这个问题的答案，推出作者的意图
语言层面	短语： differ in be similar to think about after all 句式： The other two areas in which ...differ are ... After all, ... Sb has / have more difficulty doing sth

Turn on the TV

①Some experts believe that the two varieties are moving closer together. ② For more than a century communications across the Atlantic have developed steadily. ③Since the 1980s, with satellite TV and the Internet, it has been possible to listen to British and American English at the flick of a switch. ④This non-stop communication, the experts think, has made it easier for British people and Americans to understand each other. ⑤But it has also led to lots of American words and structures passing into British English, so that some people now believe that British English will disappear.

⑥However, if you turn on CNN, the American TV network, you find newsreaders and weather forecasters all speaking with different accents — American, British, Australian, and even Spanish. ⑦One of the best-known faces, Monita Rajpal, was born in Hong Kong, China, and grew up speaking Chinese and Punjabi, as well as English.

⑧This international dimension suggests that in the future, there are going to be many "Englishes", not just two main varieties. ⑨But the message is "Don't worry." ⑩Users of English will all be able to understand each other — wherever they are.

内容结构层面	第①句和第⑤句都是陈述观点，第②③④句进一步论证观点，表明英式和美式英语逐步同化。第⑥句However的使用以及第⑦句都是用来体现出第⑧句中的this international dimension。最后一段第⑧—⑩句体现出作者的观点Users of English will all be able to understand each other—wherever they are，这也正是全文的中心
语言层面	短语： at the flick of lead to turn on grow up as well as 句式： Some experts believe that... The experts think...has/have made it easier for sb to do... ...so that... However, ... One of the best-known faces, sb, was born ...and grew up speaking... ...suggests that...

Book 5 Module 2 Reading 文本分析

The Human Traffic Signal

1. _____

① At 3500meters, La Paz, in Bolivia, is the highest capital in the world. ②Life is hard at high altitude, and the mountains make communications difficult. ③Many roads are in bad condition and accidents are frequent. ④One road in particular, which goes north from La Paz, is considered the most dangerous road in the world. ⑤On one side the mountains rise steeply: on the other side there is a sheer drop, which in places is hundreds of metres deep. ⑥Although there is not a lot of traffic, on average, one vehicle comes off the road every two weeks. ⑦The drop is so great that anyone inside the vehicle is lucky to survive.⑧In theory, the road can only be used by traffic going uphill from 8 in the morning，and by traffic coming downhill from 3 in the afternoon. ⑨But in practice, few drivers respect the rules.

内容结构层面	第①②③句介绍La Paz的地理位置以及当地的路况。词汇the highest, hard, difficult, in bad condition, frequent 说明了当地路况的险峻。第④⑤⑥⑦⑧⑨句是例证。列举了其中一条最为险峻的道路。文中通过the most dangerous road，rise steeply，a sheer drop以及第⑥⑦句足以证明这条道路的危险。第⑧⑨句是起到引出下文的作用，与第2段的第一句自然衔接
语言层面	短语： make sth difficult in bad condition on average in theory in practice respect the rules 句式： ...is the highest...in the world. One road in particular, which..., is considered the most dangerous... Although...，... ...is lucky to survive. In theory, ... But in practice，...

2. _____

① But thanks to one man, the death toll has fallen. ②Timoteo Apaza is a gentle 46-year-old man who lives in a village near the most dangerous part of the road, known locally as la curva del diablo（the Devil's Bend）.③Timoteo has an unusual job—he is a human traffic signal. Every morning he climbs up to the bend with a large circular board in his hand. ④The board is red on one side and green on the other. ⑤Timoteo stands on the bend and directs the traffic. ⑥When two vehicles approach from opposite directions they can't see each other, but they can see Timoteo. ⑦Timoteo is a volunteer. ⑧No one asked him to do the job, and no one pays him for it. ⑨Sometimes drivers give him a tip, so that he has just enough money to live on.⑩But often they just pass by, taking the human traffic signal for granted.

内容结构层面	第①句是本段的中心句，而且下文中主人公Timoteo名字出现了5次。所以我们可以推出下文主要是描写Timoteo以及他所做的事情。根据上下文我们不难发现第⑩句中的"the human traffic signal"指的就是Timoteo。读完整段，我们自然就理解了段落中第③句作者为什么认为Timoteo做了一份"unusual"的工作
语言层面	短语： thanks to be known as pay sb for sth live on 句式： ...is a ...man who... ..., known as... ..., but/ and... ..., so that... ..., taking sb/sth for granted

3. _____

① So why does he do it? ②Before he volunteered to direct the traffic, Timoteo had had lots of jobs. ③He had been a miner and a soldier.④Then one day while he was working as a lorry driver he had a close encounter with death. ⑤He was driving a lorry load of bananas when he came off the road at a bend and fell three hundred metres down the mountain. ⑥Somehow he survived. ⑦He was in hospital for months. ⑧Then, a few years later, he was called out in the night to help pull people out of a bus which had crashed at la curva del diablo. ⑨This last experience had a profound effect on Timoteo.⑩He realised that he was lucky to be alive himself, and felt that it was his mission in life to help others. ⑪ And so every morning, week in, week out, from dawn to dusk, Timoteo takes up his place on the bend and directs the traffic.

内容结构层面	第①句 "So why does he do it？" 是本段的中心句。下文从第②— ⑩句采用了举例说明的方法来回答这个问题。第②—⑧句是讲述经历，第⑨ ⑩句是表明这段经历对他的影响。叙述经历或故事所以使用了过去时态或过去进行时。最后一句表明Timoteo已经把指挥交通看成了自己每天要做的事情，成了一种习惯，所以使用了一般现在时
语言层面	短语： work as have a close encounter with be in hospital have a profound effect on week in, week out from dawn to dusk take up 句式： Before sb did sth, sb had had done sth Sb was doing sth when... This ...experience had a/ an...effect on... Sb realised that...

Book 5 Module 3 Reading 文本分析
The Steamboat

There was a big storm after midnight and the rain poured down. We stayed inside the shelter we had built and let the raft sail down the river.Suddenly, by the light of the lightning, we saw something in the middle of the river. It looked like a house at first, but then we realised it was a steamboat.It had hit a rock and was half in and half out of the water.We were sailing straight towards it.

"It looks as if it'll go under soon. " Jim said, after a couple of minutes.

"Let's go and take a look. " I said.

"I don't want to board a sinking ship." said Jim, but when I suggested that we might find something useful on the boat, he agreed to go. So we paddled over and climbed on to the steamboat, keeping as quiet as mice. To our astonishment, there was a light in one of the cabins. Then we heard someone shout, "Oh please boys, don't kill me! I won't tell anybody！"

A man's angry voice answered, "You're lying. You said that last time. We're going to kill you."

When he heard these words, Jim panicked and ran to the raft. But although I was frightened, I also felt very curious, so I put my head round the door. It was quite dark, but I could see a man lying on the floor, tied up with rope.There were two men standing over him. One was short, with a beard. The other was tall and had something in his hand that looked like a gun.

"I've had enough of you. I'm going to shoot you now. " this man said. He was obviously the one who had threatened the man on the floor. And it was a gun he had in his hand.

"No, don't do that. " said the short man, "Let's leave him here. The steamboat will sink in a couple of hours and he'll go down with it."

When he heard that, the frightened man on the floor started crying."He sounds as if he's going to die of fright！ " I thought, "I have to find a way to save him！ "

I crawled along the deck, found Jim, and told him what I had heard."We must find their boat and take it away, then they'll have to stay here. " I said.

Jim looked terrified."I'm not staying here. " he said.But I persuaded him to help me, and we found the men's boat tied to the other side of the steamboat. We climbed quietly in and as we paddled away we heard the two men shouting.By then we were a safe distance away.But now I began to feel bad about what we had done. I didn't want all three men to die.

内容结构层面	1. 文章标题的解读：整个文章以steamboat 为主线故事情节按照find a steamboat—board a steamboat—see what happened on a steamboat—take the steamboat away这个线索发展。 2. Part1: find a steamboat 段落中使用了大量描写天气的词句：a big storm，poured down，lightning。表现出当时天气的恶劣。 另外，还有一些描写船的词句：It had hit a rock and was half in and half out of the water. ...as if it'll go under soon. Part 2: board a steamboat paddled over，climbed on to，keeping as quiet as mice 这些词句反映出当时作者很小心翼翼。 Part 3: see what happened on a steamboat 本段运用了语言、动作和内心变化描写，从中可以看出每个人物各自的性格特征，而这正是学习本段的重点。 The man tied: frightened. The short man: not that cruel. The tall man with a gun: cruel, aggressive. Author: brave, curious, clever, helpful. Jim: terrified. Part 4: take the steamboat away 介绍作者做了什么，重点关注动词。 通过文章最后一句，可以设计对后面的故事情节进行续写，既可以培养学生的想象能力，又可以训练学生的写作能力
语言层面	短语： take a look keep as quiet as mice to pne's astonishment be tied up look terrified persuade sb to do feel bad about 句式： it looks as if...

Book 5 Module 4 文本分析

The Magic of the Mask

①Think of carnival, and you think of crowds, costumes, and confusion.②The sounds and sights change from one country to another but the excitement is the same everywhere.

内容结构层面	本段的关键词carnival，作者用crowds, costumes和confusion 形象地概括出carnival 的特点。第②句中重点突出but后面句子中的excitement is the same。这句要关注连词but 的使用，从change from one country to another 和the same 可以推断出转折关系
语言层面	句式： Think of ... and you think of... ...but...

① "Carnival" comes from two Latin words, meaning "no more meat".②In Europe, where it began, carnival was followed by forty days without meat, as people prepared for the Christian festival of Easter.③People saw Carnival as a last chance to have fun at the end of the winter season.④Having fun meant eating, drinking, and dressing up.

内容结构层面	第①句介绍carnival名字的来源；第②句介绍carnival的时间；第③和④句是对carnival 特点的概括，所以这段我们可以了解到carnival 的基本信息
语言层面	短语： come from prepare for have fun at the end of dress up 句式： ..., meaning... People see ...as a last chance to do. Doing sth meant doing...

①The most famous carnival in Europe was in Venice.②At the beginning, it lasted for just one day.③People ate, drank, and wore masks.④As time passed, however, the carnival period was extended, so that it began just after Christmas.⑤For weeks on end people walked round the streets wearing masks, doing what they wanted without being recognized.⑥Ordinary people could pretend to be rich and important, while famous people could have romantic adventures in secret.⑦<u>Many crimes went unpunished.</u>

内容结构层面	第①句是中心句，介绍Venice的carnival。第②—⑦句按照时间线索进行介绍，使用了at the beginning—as time passed—for weeks等词汇介绍carnival in Venice 的进展。第⑦句是承上启下，说明下一段中政府采取的措施
语言层面	短语： at the beginning last for for weeks on end pretend to be in secret go unpunished 句式： The most adj.+n. is ... As time passed, ...so that... Ordinary people...while famous people...

①The government realised that wearing masks had become a problem. ②Their use was limited by laws, the first of which dates back to the fourteenth century.③Men were not allowed to wear masks at night; and they were not allowed to dress up as women.④In later times more laws were passed.⑤People who wore masks could not carry firearms; and no one could enter a church wearing a mask.⑥If they broke the laws, they were put into prison for up to two years.⑦Finally, when Venice became part of the Austrian empire, at the end of the eighteenth century, masks were banned completely, and carnival became just a memory.

内容结构层面	第①句是本段的中心句子，同时从意义上承接上一段的最后一句。第②—⑦句按照时间顺序，分别从the fourteenth century—in later times—at the end of the eighteenth century具体介绍政府采取的措施以及对应的影响，所以本段的学习要提示学生关注时间
语言层面	短语： date back to be not allowed to do dress up as break the law be put into prison up to 句式： The government realised that... ..., the first of which dates back to... Sb are not allowed to do... If ..., ...

①But in the late 1970s the tradition was revived by students.②They began making masks and organizing parties, and threw bits of brightly coloured paper （called coriandoli ）at tourists.③The town council realised that carnival was good for business, and the festival was developed for tourists.

内容结构层面	第①句是本段的中心句，使用but 表明与上一段构成转折关系。这句中心句中的关键词是revived。第②句具体介绍what students did to revive the tradition。第③句介绍政府对此做法的态度
语言层面	短语： in the late 1970s throw sth at sb 句式： Sb began doing... Sb realised that...

①Today, carnival in Venice is celebrated for five days in February.②People arrive from all over Europe to enjoy the fun.③Hotels are fully booked and the narrow streets are crowded with wonderful costumes.④German, French and English seem to be the main languages. ⑤But the spirit of Venice carnival is not quite the same as the great American carnivals.⑥ If the key to Rio is music and movement, then in Venice it is the mystery of the mask.⑦As you wander through the streets, you see thousands of masks—elegant or frightening, sad or amusing, traditional or modern—but you have no idea what the faces behind them look like.⑧Nobody takes them off.⑨If the masks come off, the magic is lost.

内容结构层面	第①句是本段的中心句，today承接上文，介绍现在carnival 的相关情况。第②③④句都是分层论述。第⑤句是一个过渡句，由but 引出Venice carnival和the great American carnivals的差异。第⑥句回答了what is the spirit in Venice。后面第⑦—⑨句进一步介绍mask 的神秘，突出了mask 在Carnival in Venice 中的重要地位
语言层面	短语： be crowded with the key to have no idea come off 句式： ...is not quite the same as... As you wander through..., you see... You have no idea what...

Book 5 Module 5文本分析

A Life in Sport

①They called him the prince of gymnasts.②When he retired at the age of 26, he had won 106 gold medals in major competitions across the world.③They included six out of seven gold medals at the 1982 World Championship, and three at the 1984 Olympics in Los Angeles（as well as two silver and a bronze）. ④Li Ning was the best. ⑤When sports journalists met in 1999 to make a list of the greatest sportsmen and sportswomen of the twentieth century, Li Ning's name was on it, together with a footballer Pelé and boxer Muhammad Ali. ⑥But even though he had won everything it was possible to win in his sport, Li Ning retired with the feeling that he had failed. ⑦ He was disappointed because he had not performed well in the 1988 Seoul Olympics.

内容结构层面	整个段落分为两个层次。第①—⑤句是第一层次，其中第①句是中心句，关键信息是the prince of gymnasts. 接下来②—⑤句通过例子和数据来证明他是the prince of gymnasts 这一事实。第⑥句中使用but 引出李宁在退役时对自己的表现并不满意。第⑦句是对第⑥句的补充说明
语言层面	短语： at the age of make a list of 句式： it was possible to do... When sb did...at the age of..., sb had done... Even though ..., ... Sb did with the feeling that... Sb was adj.（disappointed...）because...

①But it was this sense of failure that made him determined to succeed in his new life.②A year after his retirement, Li Ning began a new career— as a businessman. ③But he didn't forget his sporting background. ④He decided to launch a new brand of sportswear, competing with global giants like Nike and Adidas.⑤ He made the unusual choice, for a Chinese person, of choosing his own name as the brand mark. ⑥The bright red logo is made up of the first two pinyin letters of Li Ning's name, L and N.

内容结构层面	第①句是一个过渡句，承上启下。关键词在于a new life。根据下文可以了解到所谓的新生活就是创办了自己的运动品牌。"his new life"与"a new career"相呼应。 第③句中因前面提到他想当商人，但没有忘记自己的运动员背景，所以使用了衔接词but。 第⑤句中注意选词，使用了"unusual"。根据第⑤句中"choosing his own name as the brand mark"看出这个品牌的独特之处。第⑥句是对第⑤句的补充说明
语言层面	短语： (be) determined to do compete with make the unusual choice be made up of 句式： It was sth that made sb ... Sb decided to do..., competing with... Sb made the ...choice of doing...

①Li Ning's sports clothes came onto the market at just the right time. ②The number of young people with money to spend was on the increase — and sport had never been so popular. ③ Li Ning's designs were attractive, and they had a major advantage over their better-known rivals — they were cheaper. ④A pair of Nike trainers, for example, could cost up to five times as much as a similar Li Ning product. ⑤ Success for Li Ning was guaranteed, and it came quickly.

内容结构层面	这个段落是分—总的结构。第⑤句是中心句，其中success 是关键词。前面4句话都是举例论证李宁品牌的success. 从时机（came onto the market at just the right time）、消费情况、与同品牌竞争的优势三个方面解释了李宁品牌为什么会成功。其中第④句中用了for example 举例进一步解释第③句
语言层面	句式： The number of ...was on the increase. ...had a major advantage over... Success for ...was guaranteed

①In just a few years, Li Ning won more than fifty percent of the national market.②Today a Li Ning product is purchased every ten seconds.③But the clothes are not only worn on the athletic strack or the football pitch.④If you go into a school or university anywhere, the chances are you will see students in Li Ning tracksuits with the familiar logo. ⑤The company has also grown internationally. ⑥The Spanish and French gymnastics teams wear Li Ning clothes, while Italian designers are employed by the company to create new styles. ⑦Whenever Chinese athletes step out onto the track during the 2008 Olympics, they will be wearing Li Ning tracksuits.

内容结构层面	这一段虽然没有明显的中心句，但是不难发现这几个句子的相似之处，都是在说明Li Ning clothes 的影响。比如：第①句中的....won more than fifty percent of the national market；第②句中的 "every ten seconds"；第③句过渡句引出第④句进一步说明李宁品牌的推广和流行；第⑤句中的关键词是internationally，后面第⑥⑦句是一个例证，说明了公司的国际性，在国际上的重要影响力
语言层面	句式： If..., the chances are... ..., while... Whenever..., ...

①But Li Ning's goal when he retired was not to make money. ②His dream was to open a school for gymnasts. ③He was able to do this in 1991. ④Since then, he has continued to help young people to achieve their sporting ambitions. ⑤Like Pelé and Muhammad Ali before him, who have worked with the United Nations children's rights and peace, Li Ning has discovered that the work of a great sportsman does not finish when he retires from the sport. ⑥It starts. ⑦And if you are a great sportsperson, anything is possible, as Li Ning's advertising slogan says.

内容结构层面	第①句过渡句，引出第②—④句介绍了李宁完成的梦想以及继续要实现的梦想。通过第⑤—⑦句我们可以学习到李宁的精神—anything is possible！
语言层面	短语： achieve one's ambitions retire from 句式： One's goal when...was not to do... One's dream is to do... Since then, sb has done... And if..., anything is possible, as sb says

Book 5 Module 6文本分析
Saving the Antelopes

①On a freezing cold day in January 1994, Jiesang Suonaudajie found what he was looking for—a group of poachers who were killing the endangered Tibetan antelope. ②Jiesang knew he had to move quickly. ③ He shouted to the poachers to put down their guns. ④Although surprised, the poachers had an advantage—there were more of them. ⑤In the battle which followed Jiesang was shot and killed. ⑥When his frozen body was found hours later, he was still holding his gun. ⑦He had given his life to save the Tibetan antelope.

内容结构层面	本段详细介绍了Jiesang拯救藏羚羊的故事。包含了记叙文的几大要素。时间：On afreezing cold day in January 1994；人物：Jiesang and a group of poachers；起因：a group of poachers were killing the endangered Tibetan antelope；结果：Jiesang was killed。 通过本段的学习，让学生掌握描写一个故事情节的时候，人物、起因、经过和结果四要素必不可少
语言层面	短语： shout to sb put down hold one's gun give one's life 句式： On a freezing cold day in January 1994, sb found what... Sb shouted to sb to do... Although +adj.（surprised...），...

①At the beginning of the twentieth century there were millions of antelopes on the Qinghai-Tibetan Plateau.②By the 1990s the number had fallen to about 50, 000. ③ The reason is simple: the wool of the Tibetan antelope is the most expensive in the world. ④It is soft, light, and warm—the ideal coat for an animal which has to survive at high altitudes. ⑤A shawl made from the wool（known as "shahtoosh", or "king of wools" in Persian）can sell for five thousand dollars.⑥For poachers the profits can be huge.

内容结构层面	第①②句是陈述藏羚羊数量不断减少的客观事实。第③句是本段的中心句，从冒号后面到第⑥句都是分析原因。第⑥句是总结
	
	the wool: the most expensive
	{ the ideal coat
	  a highly-cost shawl
	     ↓
	  for the huge profits

语言层面	短语： (be) made from 句式： By+时间, the number had fallen to... Sth, known as..., +v....

①Often working at night, the poachers shoot whole herds of antelopes at a time, leaving only the babies, whose wool is not worth so much. ②The animals are skinned on the spot and the wool taken to India, where it is made into the shawls. ③From there, it is exported to rich countries in North America and Europe. ④The business is completely illegal—there has been a ban on the trade since 1975. ⑤But in the 1990s the shawls came into fashion among rich people. ⑥A police raid on a shop in London found 138 shawls. ⑦About 1，000 antelopes—or 2 percent of the world's population — had been killed to make them.

内容结构层面	第①②③句详细介绍poachers 捕杀和贩卖藏羚羊的过程，使用了shoot，be skinned，taken to，be exported to等词汇。第④句是对前三句的一个总结。第⑤句中使用but，因为a ban 与came into fashion 构成转折关系。第⑥⑦句中都用到具体的数据（138，1000）来说明为制造披肩杀害了很多藏羚羊这一事实。正是披肩的流行才导致那么多的藏羚羊被杀害
语言层面	短语： at a time on the spot be made into come into fashion 句式： Often working…, … …, where定语从句 There has been a ban on…since…

①In the 1990s the Chinese government began to take an active part in protecting the antelopes in the Hoh Xil Nature Reserve—the huge national park in the Qinghai-Tibetan Plateau，which is the main habitat of the antelopes. ②Over the next ten years about 3，000 poachers were caught and 300 vehicles confiscated. ③Sometimes there were gunfights, like the one in which Jiesang Suonandajie was killed.

内容结构层面	本段主要是介绍政府采取的措施以及成效。第③句可以看出与捕猎者的斗争非常艰巨，伤亡也很严重
语言层面	句式： Sb began to take an active part in doing… Sometimes there were sth, like the one in which…

①But today the government seems to be winning the battle. ② The number of poachers has fallen. ③The small group of officials who work in the reserve are helped by volunteers who come from all over the country, and who are ready for the difficult conditions of life at 5，000 metres. ④Meanwhile, in those countries where the shawls are sold, police are getting tough with the dealers. ⑤International co-operation seems to be working. ⑥Since 1997 the antelope population has begun to grow slowly again.

内容结构层面	第①句是本段的中心句。首先使用but 是体现与上文的一个逻辑衔接。第②句是对第①句的补充说明。后面第③—⑤句详细介绍采取的应对措施。从volunteers, police, international co-operation三个方面分层论述，中间运用了meanwhile 过渡衔接词。第⑥句进行总结，介绍成效
语言层面	短语： be ready for get tough with 句式： ...seem to be doing... Sb who...are helped by volunteers who... Meanwhile, ... Since+时间, sb have/ has done...

Book 6 Module 1文本分析

How Good Are Your Social Skills?

Have you ever crossed the road to avoid talking to someone you recognize? Would you love to go to a party and talk confidently to every guest? Do you want to make more friends but lack the confidence to talk to people you don't know? And are you nervous about the idea of being at a social event in another country? Don't worry —we can help you!

You needn't worry about situations like these if you have good social skills. And they are easy to learn. People with good social skills communicate well and know how to have a conversation. It helps if you do a little advance planning.

Here are a few ideas to help you.

Learn how to do small talk

Small talk is very important and prepares you for more serious conversations. Be prepared! Have some low-risk conversation openers ready.

Think of a recent news story—not too serious, e.g. a story about a film star or sports star.

Think of things to tell people about your studies.

Think of "safe" things you can ask people's opinions about—music, sport, films, etc.

Think of topics that you would avoid if you were talking to strangers—and avoid talking about them! That way, you don't damage your confidence!

Develop your listening skills

Listening is a skill which most people lack, but communication is a two-way process—it involves speaking AND listening. Always remember—you won't impress people if you talk too much. Here are some ideas to make you a better listener:

DO

Show that you are listening by using encouraging noises and gestures—smiling, nodding, saying "uh—huh" and "OK", etc.

Keep good eye contact

Use positive body language

Ask for more information to show your interest

DON'T

Look at your watch

Yawn

Sign

Look away from the person who is talking to you.

Change the subject.

Finish other people's sentences for them.

Always remember the words of Benjamin Disraeli, British Prime Minister in the 19th century: "Talk to a man about himself and he will speak to you for hours!"

Learn the rules

If you go to a social occasion in another country, remember that social rules can be different.In some countries,for example, you have to arrive on time at a party; in other countries, you don't need to. In addition, you need to know how long you should stay, and when you have to leave. Some hosts expect flowers or a small gift, but in other places, you can take things, but you needn't if you don't want to. Remember also that in some countries, you mustn't take flowers of a certain colour, because they're unlucky. In most places, you don't have to take a gift to a party—but find out first!

内容结构层面	通过Here are a few ideas to help you.这个过渡句引出下文，分别从learn how to do small talk; develop your listening skills; learn the rules 这三个大方面提供建议。 此外，在分层论述的时候同样沿用过渡句的写法。所以，这是一篇非常好的写作范例，值得学生借鉴。它能有效帮助学生学习中心句和过渡句以及如何围绕中心句展开论述
语言层面	短语： avoid doing lack the confidence to do be nervous about worry about prepare sb for sth look away from on time find out 句式： You needn't worry about situations like these if you have good social skills. Here are a few ideas to help you. Be prepared! Have some low-risk conversation openers ready. Here are some ideas to make you a better listener. In addition,...

Making friends in the USA

①In the USA, conversation is less lively than in many other cultures, where everyone talks at the same time.②When someone talks, everyone is expected to listen, no matter how dull the person's speaking may be.

① If you're not sure what to talk about, you can ask what people do.② We're defined by our jobs and we're usually happy to talk about them, unless you're a spy!

①Some people say that Americans talk about their feelings more than Asians, but are more secretive about factual matters.②You can safely ask questions about families, where you come from, leisure interests, as well as the latest movies. ③We're interested in people's ethnic background too. ④But it's best to avoid politics, religion and other sensitive topics.

内容结构层面	第1段中，第②句点明了作者的观点。 第2段中，第①句是本段的中心句。 第3段中，第①③④都是表达观点的句子。 第②句是对第①句的进一步举例说明
语言层面	短语： at the same time be expected to do be secretive about be interested in 句式： Some people say that... But it's best to do...

① A highly personal conversation can take place after a very short period of knowing someone, but this doesn't mean that you're close friends, or the relationship is very deep. ②But a lot of people are very friendly and hospitable, and the famous invitation "If you're ever in Minneapolis/ San Diego/ Poughkeepsie, do call by and see us！" is never made without a genuine desire to meet again.

内容结构层面	这两句话的主题是a highly personal conversation，介绍了a highly personal conversation的特点
语言层面	短语： take place a genuine desire to do 句式： But this doesn't mean that...

①But while few Americans will worry about the questions you may ask, particularly if you clearly show you're aware of cultural differences, they may hesitate before they ask you similar questions.②In fact, it's a sign that they don't wish to violate your private life. ③So, many Americans will talk about safe topics because they don't dare to be too curious or personal, but will happily talk about more private matters if you take the lead.

内容结构层面	这一段要特别注意句子之间的关联衔接。第①句中的but承接上一段，句子的观点是they may hesitate before they ask you similar questions。第①句举例说明，第②句是对第①句的补充说明，解释为什么人们会犹豫。第③句中使用so，表明是对整个段落的一个总结
语言层面	短语： be aware of take the lead 句式： But while..., ...（while 表"尽管"） In fact, it is a sign that... ...because...

①Generally we dislike arguments, and we avoid topics which lead to disagreement. ②It's easy to return to discussing the weather: "Do you like the USA? How do you like the weather？" or making compliments："What lovely flowers and what a beautiful vase！" "That's a fabulous dress you're wearing." You should accept compliments graciously and say "Thank you！"

内容结构层面	本段是典型的总—分结构。第①句是中心句
语言层面	短语： lead to disagreement make compliments 句式： Generally we dislike ...and we avoid topics which ... It's easy to return to ...

①There are a couple of dangerous topics of conversation: age and money.②Age is not treated as something very special, unless someone is very old："Isn't she wonderful for her age！" and there are no special rules or signs of extra respect for elderly people.③Anyway, Americans always want to look younger than they really are, so don't expect an accurate reply！

④Income is a very private matter and you'd do well to avoid asking how much people earn, although some people may not only be open about it, but show off their wealth. ⑤We don't ask how much things cost, either.

⑥But what we don't like is silence, and almost anything is better than the embarrassment of a quiet party and silent guests.

内容结构层面	第①句是中心句，第②③句从age角度介绍，第④⑤句从money 角度介绍。第⑥句是一个总结，告诉人们相互交流的时候最怕沉默，要打破僵局
语言层面	短语： a couple of be treated as show off 句式： There are a couple of dangerous topics of conversation... What we don't like is ... Anything is better than...

Book 6 Module 2文本分析
语篇A

①The elder stateswoman of British fantasy literature is J.K.Rowling, the gifted creator of Harry Potter. ②Joanne Rowling's roots are in the southwest of England, where she grew up. ③But the idea for Harry Potter came to her while she was on a delayed train between Manchester and London.④She wrote down her ideas on the back of the envelope.⑤She then went to teach English in Portugal, where she continued to add flesh to the bones of the first Harry Potter story. ⑥But her name is forever associated with Edinburgh in Scotland, where she lived and developed the format for the whole series of seven books.

内容结构层面	第①句引出主人公，第②③④⑤⑥句详细介绍她的创作思路来源。其中特别关注but连接词的使用
语言层面	短语： grow up add sth to sth be associated with 句式： 句子，the gifted creator（同位语） 句子，where 定语从句

①There are many anecdotes about how, in 1990, J.K. Rlowling began the first draft of Harry Potter and the Philisopher's Stone. ②She had the extra burden of looking after her baby daughter while she worked, and because she was too poor to own a typewriter, she wrote by hand. ③She spent many hours over a single cup of coffee in a warm cafeteria in Edinburgh because she had no money to pay for the heating at home.

④Success was not swift and Rowling might have given up. ⑤But she was stubborn and overcame all the difficulties. ⑥It was only in 1997 that she completed the first Harry Potter story, which, because the publishers in the USA requested an adjustment to the title, was known as Harry Potter and the Sorcerer's Stone.

内容结构层面	第①句介绍了她的成绩。第②③句详细介绍了Rowling 如何努力写小说。其中第④⑤句表明了Rowling 能成功的原因：being stubborn and overcoming all the difficulties。最后一句第⑥句介绍她努力后取得的成绩
语言层面	短语： have the extra burden of... look after by hand pay for give up overcome all the difficulties be known as 句式： ..., because... It was only in +时间+ that+ 句子（强调句）

①Rowling always intended that her output would be a book every year until she had finished the series. ②In fact, it took her about ten years to complete. ③But after the first book, the success of each of the following titles was automatic. ④The fifth book, The Order of the Phoenix sold about seven million copies the day it was published.

内容结构层面	本段第①②句介绍Rowling耗费的精力。第③句用But引出她取得的成绩，第③④句是举例说明
语言层面	短语： in fact 句式： Sb always intended that... It took sb some time to do... n.，同位语，+v.+ the day +从句

①Rowling's style has been a target for some criticism, but what makes the books so important is that, because they appeal to readers of all ages, they create a special literary bond between parents and children. ②In an age of computer games and television programmes, it is also claimed they are responsible for a renewed interest in reading. ③Harry Potter has even become part of the school curriculum, much to the pleasure of the schoolchildren.

④And the Harry Potter effect is not just restricted to the English-speaking world. ⑤Rowling's books have been translated into more than 55 languages, and it has been estimated that more than 250 million copies have been distributed around the world.⑥In 2005 it was estimated that Rowling had accumulated more than one billion dollars on deposit in her bank.⑦ She has thus attained the status of being the first writer to become a billionaire.

内容结构层面	本段使用举例说明的方法具体介绍了Rowling和她作品的影响和成绩，具体表现如下：第①句中they appeal to readers of all ages, create a special literary bond between parents and children；第③句 has even become part of the school curriculum, much to the pleasure of the schoolchildren；第⑤句 have been translated into more than 55 languages；第⑥句had accumulated more than one billion dollars；第⑦句being the first writer to become a billionaire。所以例子足以证明她的成绩和影响，直击主题

续　表

语言层面	短语： appeal to sb of all ages in an age of be responsible for much to the pleasure of... be restricted to be translated into 句式： what makes sth so important is that... it is also claimed that... it has been estimated that... sb has thus attained the status of being the first man to do...

语篇B

①One of the most famous fantasy stories of the twentieth century is the trilogy The Lord of the Rings by J.R.R. Tolkien. ②All three parts of the story have been made into very successful films. ③The story takes place in a world called Middle Earth.④Humans are only one of the creatures who exist at this time. ⑤There are also elves, tall beautiful creatures who have magical powers and never die. ⑥There are hobbits, who are like small humans and live in holes in hills. ⑦There are also dwarves, who are similar to small, ugly men and live deep in the mountains.

内容结构层面	第①②句引出主题，对这套书进行一个总体评价。从第③—⑦句介绍了书名、故事发生的地点以及相关人物。 接下来第2、3段引出故事的中心人物和中心事件
语言层面	短语： be made into be similar to 句式： One of the most famous ...is ... The story takes place in ... There are sb who...

In The Lord of the Rings, a wicked wizard called Sauron, who has great magical powers, has created nine rings. Any creature who possesses one of these rings has great power. But Sauron has created one ring—the Ring—that can control all of these rings. The person who has this ring controls the whole of Middle Earth.

Fortunately, this ring has been lost for hundreds of years. But then it is discovered by a hobbit.（此处has been lost与is discovered构成转折关系，所以使用连词but）

Sauron, realizing that the Ring has been found, sends his creatures to get it back. If he finds the Ring, Sauron will rule Middle Earth and it will become a place of darkness and fear. Gandalf, a good wizard, realises that in order to save Middle Earth, the Ring must be destroyed. To do this, someone must take the Ring into Sauron's kingdom. There, they must destroy the Ring in the fires that created it. The three books tell the story of the journey to destroy the Ring. In the last book of the trilogy there is a terrible war between Sauron and his creatures, and those who want to save Middle Earth.

内容结构层面	第2、3段引出故事的中心人物和中心事件。整个故事围绕the rings来展开。 这3段是学习如何介绍小说故事情节的一个很好的范例
语言层面	短语： have great power tell the story of 句式： The person who ...controls... Sb realise that in order to do..., ... To do this, ... Sb called..., who...has done sth... Any creature who...+v.... Sb, realizing that..., +v....

① Many people believe that The Lord of the Rings is the best twentieth century novel in English. ②Of course, there are always those who do not enjoy reading fantasy novels. ③But if you do, then this is one story you should definitely read.

内容结构层面	这一段是对这本书的评价，从第③句可以推断出作者高度评价这本书
语言层面	短语： enjoy doing 句式： Many people believe that... There are always those who... But if you do, then this is sth you should definitely do...

Book 6 Module 3 Reading 文本分析

Roy's Story

①I remember the first time I met Roy.② He was standing in the centre of a group of boys, and he was telling a joke. ③When he reached the final line, everyone burst out laughing. ④Roy laughed too, a loud happy laugh. ⑤ "Popular boy." I thought to myself. My name is Daniel. ⑥I was the new boy in the class. ⑦Our family was from the north of England, but my father had been offered a better job in London, and our whole family had moved there. ⑧I was twelve and, having lost all my old friends, I felt shy and lonely at my new school.

内容结构层面	第①句是中心句，后面几句话重点回忆他当时第一次见到Roy的情形。通过第②—⑤句可以看出Roy爱笑，深得同学的喜爱。第⑥—⑧句介绍他自己的情况，可以看出作者当时feeling shy and lonely at a new school
语言层面	短语： in the centre of tell a joke burst out laughing think to oneself feel shy and lonely 句式： I remember the first time ... Having lost..., I felt...

① There were 33 students in my new class, and most people weren't very interested in a shy new boy.② Roy was one of the few people who were kind to me.③ He often invited me to join his particular group, and as a result, I started getting to know people.④ Roy and I became good friends. ⑤We trusted each other and we could talk about personal matters, things that were important to us.

内容结构层面	这一段主要介绍作者和Roy 是怎样成为好朋友的。第②句是一个过渡句。第③④⑤句具体介绍Roy 怎样对他好。这一段要多关注动词，如：invite sb to do...， became good friends; trusted each other; talk about personal matters...
语言层面	短语： be interested in be kind to invite sb to do as a result get to know be important to sb 句式： Sb was one of the few people who... We could talk about personal matters, things that...

①Five years later, Roy and I are still in the same class.②But just under a year ago, Roy's father was knocked over by a car.③He died a few days later.④The family had to move to a much smaller house in order to manage financially.⑤Roy, who had always been very close to his father, changed completely, becoming silent and moody.⑥He had always been a clever, hard-working student but now he seemed to lose all interest in his work.⑦He started losing friends.⑧These days, Roy and I see each other from time to time, but we're no longer close.

内容结构层面	这一段主要介绍Roy遭遇家庭的变故对他带来的影响，同时也给他俩的友谊造成了影响。第⑤—⑧句详细地描述了Roy 的变化。如：changed completely; becoming silent and moody; seemed to lost all interest in his work; started losing friends; no longer close。第⑧句总结他们不再像以前那样亲近了
语言层面	短语： be knocked over by be close to lose all interest in from time to time 句式： Sb had to do ...in order to do... Sb, who... , changed completely, becoming... ..., but...

①About three months ago, a group of us were playing football together after school.② Having left something in the cloakroom, I went inside to get it, and found Roy going through the pockets of people's coats.③In his hand he had a wallet—and I knew it wasn't his! ④My mouth fell open and I just looked at him.⑤Roy went bright red.⑥ "I'll put it back right now." he said, and he did so.⑦I turned round and walked out without saying a word.

①I really hoped that Roy would explain why he had been stealing, but instead he started avoiding me.②At the same time, small amounts of money started disappearing from students' lockers.③I wonder if the thief was Roy but decided not to say anything to anyone. ④I hope it wasn't him.

内容结构层面	第1段，第②句为起因，第⑤句是经过+心理描写，第⑦句是结果。此两段，具体讲述了发生在3个月前的一个故事。故事情节非常清楚，有动作描写也有心理描写
语言层面	短语： fall open turn around at the same time 句式： Having left something, ... Sb turned round and walked out without saying a word I really hoped that... I wonder if...

①Last week our school had a big fair in order to raise money for a charity. ②It was very successful and by the end of the day, we had made about $500. ③Our class teacher, Mr White, came and chatted to a group of us that included Roy, and held up a box for us to see.④ "There's $500 in here." he said with a smile. ⑤But（转折词）to our surprise, the next morning, we were told that the money had been stolen. ⑥Mr White had left the box in a classroom for a few minutes, and when he came back it had disappeared. ⑦The head teacher asked anyone who thought they might know something about the theft to come to him.

内容结构层面	记叙文的几大要素： Time: Last week； Beginning（what happened）： made about $500； Development（what happened）： money had been stolen； Ending: investigate the theft；
语言层面	短语： raise money hold up with a smile to one's surprise 句式： ...in order to do... To one's surprise, we were told that... Sb asked anyone who ...to do...

①This weekend（时间）， having thought about the situation for a while, I decided to ask Roy about the theft（起因）, and this morning I went to see him. ②Roy was out, and I went upstairs to his bedroom to wait for him.③It was a cold day and his jacket was lying on the back of a chair. ④I put it on and put my hands in the pockets. ⑤I could feel a lot of paper notes and I pulled them out.

⑥It looked as if there was about $500 there. ⑦I was so surprised that I just stood there, holding the notes in my hands.（结果+心理描写）⑧At that moment, the door swung open, and Roy walked in.

内容结构层面	这一段是整个故事的尾声。故事的脉络：Went to see him—Roy was out—wait for him—put my hands in his pockets—feel a lot of paper notes—$500—Roy walked in
语言层面	短语： think about decide to do put on pull sth out at that moment 句式： Having thought about..., ... It looked as if... I was so surprised that...

Childhood Friends

The first time I lost my best friend, I thought it was the end of the world. I don't mean that he died, he just went away, but I still measure all pain by how hurt I was when Danny left.

I was blessed with a happy childhood, one that most people would want to have. We lived in a small bungalow in a tiny village in Scotland and we were a very close family. Our neighbours next door had a son named Danny, and we grew up together.

We spent long summer evenings in the pine forests, digging up worms for fishing, and collecting feathers left by the birds in the cages where they had been kept for the hunters. It was here that I discovered that I was allergic to the tiny flies which bit me and made my face swell. There were a few walnut trees above the village and we would chase the squirrels away and wait for them to ripen. Of course, it was too far north for a proper harvest. On windy days we'd slide down the stony slopes to the loch and feel the spray of the sea in our faces.

Danny was a good carpenter too, and we made brooms out of branches, and we tried to sell in the village shop. We built a tree house, where we smoked our first cigar, and I was sick! Once I slipped on some damp leaves, fell out, scratched my arms and cut the heel of my foot, so he washed my wounds in the stream. He was a very considerate boy for someone so young. My mother simply scolded me for tearing my underwear.

We were on good terms with everyone in the village, and we even gave a salute to the local policeman as he passed on his bicycle. But in our imagination, he was an enemy soldier, and we were two spies looking for secrets.

It was the finest friendship anyone could have, and life seemed perfect.

And then at the age of 14, his parents moved to London, over 400 kilometres away. The pain was acute and I couldn't forgive Danny for leaving me. I felt he had betrayed me. It was the worst loss I have ever experienced.

I'm now back in touch with Danny, and it's a privilege to call him my friend.

We're both much more mature now, and we're still very alike.

But while I'm nostalgic for the happy times we spent together many years ago, I'm ashamed of my feelings, and I don't want to rewind the recording of my life and remember my loss and my pain.

内容层面	第一段回顾作者的朋友对他的影响之深，下文以时间顺序来展开内容。 第二段从回顾童年开始。 第三段从 "long summer evenings" "on windy days" 介绍他们在一起干什么，本段要重点关注动词的使用，如dig up，collecting feathers，chase sth away，wait for，slide down。 第四段重点描写Danny,从字里行间看出Danny 的性格。 最后两段介绍作者和Danny的现状以及相互之间的影响
语言层面	短语： be blessed with grow up dig up scold sb for be on good terms with at the age of be in touch with be nostalgic for be ashamed of 句式： The first time..., ... I don't mean that... It was here that ... It was the finest friendship anyone could have It was the worst loss I have ever experienced. It's a privilege to do ...

Friends Reunited

①One of the biggest Internet successes is a website called Friends Reunited. ② Friends Reunited brings together—hat is, unites—old friends, people who used to be friends with each other, but have not seen each other for a long time.

内容结构层面	第①句是中心句，引出话题Friend Reunited. 第②句进一步介绍Friend Reunited 的特点
语言层面	短语： used to be 句式： One of the biggest...is...

The website was begun in 1999 by a London couple called Stephen and Julie Pankhurst. Julie wanted to know what her old school friends were doing. Did they all have families of their own? Did they still live in the same area? Were they married? Did they have children? She and her husband realised that the Internet was the perfect way to get in touch with old friends, and Steve and his business partner, Jason Porter, built the website. Slowly, people heard about the site and became interested. By the end of 2000 the site had 3000 members. Then the website was mentioned on a radio programme and suddenly the site became very popular.By the end of 2001 the website had 4 million members, and by the end of 2002 it had over 8 million!

内容结构层面	本段是按照时间顺序介绍website 发展的不同阶段。Begun in 1999—built the website—by the end of 2000—Then—by the end of 2001—by the end of 2002
语言层面	短语： get in touch with become interested by the end of become popular 句式： Sb wanted to know what ... Sb realised that ...be the perfect way to do...

①How do you find old friends using Friends Reunited? ②It's very easy. ③People join the website and give information about themselves—the name of their old school, the neighbourhood they lived in, the college they went to, the sports team they belonged to, etc. ④To find an old friend, you type in their name, school, etc. ⑤You may find that your friend is a member of the website, and you can then contact him or her through the website. ⑥Most people are very happy to reply, and people often become friends again as a result.

内容结构层面	本段采用总—分结构。第①句是中心句，是一个设问句。第②句自然过渡。第③—⑥句具体展开论述
语言层面	短语： belong to as a result 句式： To find..., ... You may find that...

①There are many wonderful stories about people who have found each other again through Friends Reunited. ②For example, there is the extraordinary story of a man who lost his memory as a result of a bad car accident.③He could not remember anything about his past. ④Through Friends Reunited he contacted old friends, and with their help, he was able to find out about his past and put his memory back together.⑤Another man writes： "Thanks to Friends Reunited, I have found my daughter, who I have not seen since she was 13. She is now 27 and I have discovered that I am a grandfather. It would have been impossible to find my daughter without the help of Friends Reunited. From the bottom of my heart, thank you."

内容结构层面	本段第①句是中心句. 由for example 引出下文，举例说明。第②—④句是其中一个例子。第⑤句由 "another man writes" 引出另外一个例子
语言层面	短语： as a result of with one's help find out thanks to from the bottom of one's heart 句式： There are many wonderful stories about people who... Through sth, sb be able to do... Thanks to ..., ... It would have been impossible to do ...without the help of ...

Book 6 Module 4 An interview with Liu Fang 文本分析

Part 1

①Liu Fang is an international music star, famous for her work with traditional Chinese instruments. ②She was born in 1974 and has played the pipa since the age of six. ③She has given concerts since she was eleven, including a performance for the Queen of England during her visit to China. ④She graduated from the Shanghai Conservatory of Music, where she also studied the guzheng in 1993.

内容结构层面	本段人物介绍。第①句是身份介绍；第②句介绍出生时间；第③④句介绍她的求学经历
语言层面	短语： be famous for since the age of graduate from 句式： Sb is ..., famous for... Sb was born in ... Sb graduated from..., where...

What is your musical training and background?

My mother is a Dianju actress. Dianju is a kind of Chinese opera, which includes singing, dancing and acting. When I was a child, she took me to performances. I listened to music before I could speak! When I was five years old, she taught me to play the yueqin.

In 1990, when I was 15 years old, I went to the Shanghai Conservatory of Music, where I studied the pipa and the guzheng. After I graduated, I went back to my hometown of Kunming and worked as a pipa soloist of the Kunming Music and Dance Troupe. In 1996, I moved to Canada with my husband and I have been living there since then.

内容结构层面	本段主要是按照时间顺序来介绍作者的学习经历。When I was a child—when I was five years old—when I was 15 years old—after I graduated—in 1996—since then 这是值得学习的一种写作手法
语言层面	短语： teach sb to do work as since then 句式： When I was a child, ... When I was five years old, ... I went to..., where... Since then, I have been doing...

What are the biggest challenges of playing the pipa and the guzheng?

If your technique is not good enough, it is impossible to play classical Chinese pipa music. Also, the repertoire for the pipa is large—some pieces written during the Tang Dynasty.

There are many different pipa schools, and each one has its special way of interpreting the classical pieces. The biggest challenge is to respect the traditions but to add my own style. The same is true of my second instrument, the guzheng.

内容结构层面	本段标题中的关键词"biggest challenge"，围绕这个关键词，文章从 technique, repertoire, different pipa schools, the biggest challenge这几个角度介绍不同的挑战
语言层面	短语： be true of 句式： It is impossible to do... The biggest challenge is to do... The same is true of ...

Part 2

Who or what are your musical influences?

The main influence is traditional singing. I listened to traditional opera singing and folk songs in my childhood. Now when I am playing a tune, I am singing in my heart. When I'm playing a sad tune, I am crying in my heart. Listeners often say that they can hear singing in my music.

内容结构层面	本段标题中的关键词是musical influences。围绕这个关键词，本段采用总—分论述的结构，运用了when I am playing a tune, ...和when I'm playing a sad tune两个排比句
语言层面	短语： listen to in one's childhood in one's heart 句式： The main influence is ... Listeners often say that...

What characteristics of Chinese classical music do you try to show in your playing?

Firstly, Chinese music is similar to the Chinese language. In Chinese, the same pronunciation with different tones has different meanings. The same is true for music. Secondly, classical Chinese music is closely connected to Chinese poetry, so it isn't surprising that most classical pieces have very poetictitles. Thirdly, classical Chinese music and traditional Chinese painting are like twinsisters. In Chinese art, there are some empty spaces, which are very important. They give life to the whole painting and they allow people to come into the picture, like a dialogue.

It's the same with classical Chinese music. There are empty spaces, and people say the silence is full of music. The pipa sounds and the pauses combine to make a poetry of sound. Listeners can experience the power and the beauty of the music, like enjoying a beautiful poem or painting.

内容结构层面	根据标题可以看出本段介绍的中国古典音乐的特点。使用了firstly, secondly, thirdly过渡衔接词进行分层论述。另外，It's the same with classical Chinese music是一个过渡句，由第一段介绍Chinese art过渡到第二段介绍Chinese music
语言层面	短语： be similar to be true for be closely connected to give life to allow sb to do the same with be full of 句式： It isn't surprising that... There are some..., which are very important

Part 3

What do you like best about performing live?

①I enjoy playing and I enjoy performing in public. ②I like the atmosphere in a concert hall and I always feel happy when I have a concert. ③I feel a little depressed or lonely when there is no concert for a long time. I also enjoy the time immediately after the concert to share the feelings and ideas with friends and music lovers, listening to their impressions and understanding about the music. I love my career. I also enjoy travelling: I enjoy sitting in a plane dreaming, or staying in a hotel.

内容结构层面	本段围绕"What do you like best..."这个问题运用了"I enjoy ..."和"I also enjoy..."展开论述，分成3个层次。其中①②③是一个层次，运用了总—分的写作手法，第②③句是对第①句的拓展
语言层面	短语： in public. feel a little depressed or lonely share...with... 句式： I enjoy doing sth I feel a little ...when... I also enjoy the time to do...

What are your goals as an artist?

I don't have a particular goal. But I hope to work with many composers, and I also wish to compose my own music. My background is traditional Chinese music. Since I moved to Canada, I have had opportunities to make contact with other musical traditions and play with master musicians. I wish to continue working with master musicians from other traditions and to be able to compose my own music, using elements from different cultures. I also wish to introduce classical Chinese pipa and guzheng music to every corner of the world.

内容结构层面	本段围绕"What are your goals..."这个问题运用了"I hope to do..." "I wish to do..." "I also wish to do..."展开论述
语言层面	短语： have opportunities to do make contact with wish to do 句式： Since I..., I have had opportunities to do... I wish to do...

Street Music 文本分析

①It is a warm Saturday afternoon in a busy side road in the old district of Barcelona. ②The pedestrians are standing in a semi-circle around someone or something in front of the cathedral. ③I push my way through the crowd and find a quarter of musicians playing a violin suite of classical music. ④The session lasts ten minutes. ⑤Then one of the musicians picks up a saucer on the ground, and asks for money. ⑥All contributions are voluntary, no one has to pay, but the crowd shrinks as some people slide away. ⑦But others happily throw in a few coins. ⑧They're grateful for this brief interval of music as they go shopping.

内容结构层面	本段是场景和人物动作描写。第①②句是背景介绍。 第③—⑧句详细描写了作者的所看所想，介绍了观看一群音乐家的表演以及表演结束后发生的事情。其中还重点对比了观众看完表演后的不同举动，使用了but转折连词。本段是学习场景描写的很好的范例
语言层面	短语： push one's way through the crowd pick up ask for money slide away be grateful for 句式： It is a warm ...afternoon. I push my way through...and find... ..., but... Sb be grateful for ...

①Below the window of my apartment in Paris, a music man takes a place made vacant by an earlier musician. ②He raises the lid of his barrel organ and turns the handle.③Then he sings the songs of old Paris, songs of the people and their love affairs. ④I remember some of the words even though I have never consciously learnt them.⑤ I tap my feet and sing along with him. ⑥Down there on the pavement, few passersby stop. ⑦Some smile, others walk past with their heads down.⑧ Cars pass, gangs of boys form and disappear, someone even puts a coin in the cup on the organ. ⑨But the music man ignores them all.⑩He's hot in the sun, so he mops his head with a spotted handkerchief. ⑪He just keeps singing and turning the handle.

内容结构层面	本段是另一处场景描写。关注的重点是人物和动作描写。所以要关注动词。第②③句是对表演者的动作描写。第⑤句是作者的反应。第⑥—⑧句是描写路人的反应。第⑨—⑪句是描写表演者
语言层面	短语： sing the songs with one's heads down keep doing 句式： I remember...even though... ..., so...

①In Harlem, New York, some locals place a sound system by an open window. ②They plug it into the electrical socket, and all of a sudden, there's dancing in the streets. ③In downtown Tokyo, young couples eat popcorn and dance to the music of a rockabilly band, which plays American music from the Fifties. ④In the London Underground a student plays classical guitar music, which echoes along the tunnels. ⑤It lifts the spirits of the passengers, who hurry past on their way to work. ⑥In a street in Vienna or Prague or Milan a group of pipe musicians from the far Andes fill the air with the sound of South America.

内容结构层面	本段按照4个不同的地点：in Harlem, New York; in downtown Tokyo; in the London Underground; in a street in Vienna or Prague or Milan来展开描述
语言层面	短语： all of a sudden dance to lift the spirits of on one's way to work; fill...with.... 句式： all of a sudden dance to 句子，which非限制性定语从句 句子，who非限制性定语从句

①The street musician is keeping alive a culture which has almost disappeared in our busy, organized, and regulated lives: the sound of music when you least expect it. ②In a recording studio, even when relayed by microphone, music loses some of its liveliness. ③But street music gives life to everyone who listens and offers relief from the cares of the day. ④It only exists in the present, it only has meaning in the context. ⑤It needs space.

内容结构层面	从本段的第③句可以推测作者是支持street music 的发展的
语言层面	句式： keep alive give life to offer relief When +非谓语动词，主句

Book 6 Module 5 Frankenstein's monster 文本分析

Part 1 The story of Frankenstein

①Frankenstein is the name of a young scientist from Geneva, in Switzerland. ②While studying at university, he discovers the secret of how to create life. ③Using bones from dead bodies, he creates a creature that resembles a human being and gives it life. ④The creature, which is very large and strong, and is also extremely ugly, terrifies anyone who sees it.⑤However, the monster, who has learnt to speak, is intelligent and has human emotions. ⑥He become lonely and unhappy when he cannot find any friends and soon he begins to hate his creator Frankenstein. ⑦When Frankenstein refuses to create a wife for him, the monster murders Frankenstein's brother, his best friend Clerval, and finally, Frankenstein's new wife Elizabeth. ⑧The scientist chases the creature to the Arctic in order to destroy him, but he dies there. ⑨At the end of the story, the monster disappears into the ice and snow to end his own life.

内容结构层面	本段中第①—③句描写了Frankenstein 创造了一个怪物。第④—⑨句描写了monster's story。从中可以了解到monster 的独特之处以及它的悲惨的下场
语言层面	短语： refuse to do at the end of end one's own life 句式： While doing sth，句子 Doing sth，句子 含who 、which引导的定语从句的句子 含不定式to do作目的状语的句子

Part 2 Extract from Frankenstein

①It was on a cold November night that I saw my creation for the first time. ②Feeling very anxious, I prepared the equipment that would give life to the thing that lay at my feet. ③It was already one in the morning and the rain fell against the window. ④My candle was almost burnt out when, by its tiny light, I saw the yellow eye of the creature open. ⑤It breathed hard, and moved its arms and legs.

内容结构层面	本段详细描写了作者创造的作品。里面包含天气描写、心理描写
语言层面	短语： for the first time give life to be burnt out 句式： It was ...that...强调句型 含现在分词作状语的句子

①How can I describe my emotions when I saw this happen? ② How can I describe the monster who I had worked so hard to create? ③I had tried to make him beautiful. ④Beautiful! ⑤He was the ugliest thing I had ever seen! ⑥ You could see the veins beneath his yellow skin. ⑦His hair was black and his teeth were white.⑧ But these things contrasted horribly with his yellow eyes, his wrinkled yellow skin and black lips.

内容结构层面	本段重点突出描写作者的作品的奇陋无比。先用两个排比句引出作者难以言表的心情。接着连续使用两个beautiful进行讽刺。最后两句详细地对这个怪物进行了外貌描写可见它的丑陋
语言层面	短语： contrast horribly with 句式： How can I describe my emotions when ...? He was the ugliest thing I had ever seen!

I had worked for nearly two years with one aim only, to give life to a lifeless body. For this I had not slept, I had destroyed my health. I had wanted it more than anything in the world.But now I had finished, the beauty of the dream vanished, and horror and disgust filled my heart. Now my only thoughts were, I wish I had not created this creature, I wish I was on the other side of the world, I wish I could disappear! When he turned to look at me, I felt unable to stay in the same room as him. I rushed out and for a long time I walked up and down my bedroom. At last I threw myself on the bed in my clothes, trying to find a few moments of sleep. But although I slept, I had terrible dreams. I dreamt I saw my fiancée walking in the streets of our town. She looked well and happy but as I kissed her lips, they became pale, as if she were dead. Her face changed and I thought I held the body of my dead mother in my arms. I woke, shaking with fear. At that same moment, I saw the creature that I had created. He was standing by my bed and watching me. His mouth opened and he made a sound, then seemed to smile. I think he wanted to speak, but I did not hear. He put out a hand, as if he wanted to keep me there, but I ran out of the room. I hid in the garden and stayed there till morning, terrified by what I had done.Again and again I thought， " I wish I had not done this terrible thing, I wish I was dead! "

You cannot imagine the horror of that face! I had seen him when he was unfinished—he was ugly then. But when he stood up and moved, he became a creature from my worst nightmares.

内容结构层面	本段以作者的心理感受描写为主，很多处细节描写都能看出作者对这个怪物的厌恶和后悔之情。文段中穿插了一处梦境描写也能从侧面反映出作者受到惊吓
语言层面	短语： destroy one's health fill one's heart turn to sb up and down shake with fear be terrified by 句式： I wish... ..., as if...

Book 6 Module 6 War and Peace文本分析

The D-Day Landings – Passage 1

In September 1939, Britain declared war on Germany after Germany invaded Poland. The war, which lasted until 1945, is known as the Second World War. During the war, Germany occupied many countries, including France. His most important battle of the war in Europe was Operation Overlord, the military operation in 1944 to invade France.

Operation Overlord started when boats full of soldiers landed on the beaches of Normandyin France, known as the D-Day landings. More than 5，000 ships crossed the English Channel, carrying 130，000 troops to the French coast.

Troops from the United States, Britain and Canada took part in the D-Day landings. The operation was extremely dangerous and many soldiers were killed before they even got off the boats. American soldiers attempted to land at the most dangerous place, known as Omaha Beach.

The situation at Omaha Beach was so bad that the US army commanders thought about abandoning the invasion. Eventually, the soldiers made a breakthrough and the D-Day landings were successful. It was the beginning of the end of the Second World War.

Operation Overlord started as a story of danger and confusion and ended as a story of bravery and acts of heroism.（对这场战争的总体性评价）

内容结构层面	本段从时间、地点和战争的序幕、战况和结果描写了诺曼底登陆
语言层面	短语： declare war on be known as take part in attempt to do make a breakthrough 句式： 含which引导的定语从句的句子 so...that...句型

四、基于文本分析的阅读教学设计

在文本解读模式思路下，设计出一套连贯的、循序渐进的有助于提升学生阅读文本分析能力的阅读课件、阅读学案集和文本分析案例集。阅读设计分别从Paraphrasing a text sentence by sentence、explicating the thesis of a text、explicating the logic of a text & evaluating the logic of a text四个方面进行文本分析，以培养学生的阅读策略进而提升写作能力。附上外研版Book 3& Book 4两本书的阅读学案设计。

Book 3 Module 1 Reading and Vocabulary

Learning goals：

1. Ss learn to know about the detailed information about great European cities.

2. Ss learn about how to introduce a city from the reading parts.

3. Ss learn to accumulate some languages and grammatical structures related to the writing topic.

Task 1: **Lead-in**

Show students some landmarks of European cities.

Task 2: **Reading for Content—Explicating the thesis of each paragraph**

Read the passage carefully and find out the following information from each passage to describe the main features of the cities.

Cities	Aspects	Related words & phrases& sentences to describe it
Paris	1. France 2. the River Seine 3. eight million _____ 4. _____ 5. _____ 6. _____	
Barcelona	1. Spain 2. Madrid 3. _____ 4. Antonio Gaudi	
Florence	1. an Italian city 2. The Renaissance 3. most beautiful _____ 4. the art galleries, _____ and _____ 5. The Uffizi Palace	
Athens	1. Greece 2. western civilization 3. Greece's _____ city 4. _____ such as the Parthenon 5. Greece's best _____	

Task 3: Reading for structures—Analyzing the Logic of the Declaration

Read again and summarize what aspects can be described when introducing a city.

Writing aspects {
_____
_____
_____
_____

...

Task 4: Evaluation of the Declaration Through Intellectual Standards

Discussions：

1. Is the author sufficiently precise in providing details and specifics?

2. Is the author true to their purpose ?

Task 5: Writing a passage to introduce a city

Book 3 Module 2 Reading and Vocabulary

Learning goals：

1. Ss learn to know about the detailed information about The Human Development Report.

2. Ss learn about how to introduce a report from the reading parts.

3. Ss learn to accumulate some languages and grammatical structures related to the writing topic.

Task 1: Reading for Content—Explicating the thesis of each paragraph

1. State the main point of the paragraph in one or two sentences.

Para 1：_____

Para 2：_____

Para 3：_____

Para 4：_____

Para 5：_____

2. Read each paragraph and answer the following questions.

Text	Monitoring
Paragraph 1	How did the Human Development Report come into being? What did world leaders agree to do in 2000?
Paragraph 2	What does the Human Development Index measure? What are some surprises in the Index?
Paragraph 3	Underline the topic sentence in this paragraph. What are the first two Development Goals?
Paragraph 4	Find out the two key words to describe the main idea of this paragraph.
Paragraph 5	What progress have we made towards these goals? What do developed countries need to do?

Task 2: Reading for structures—Analyzing the Logic of the Declaration

Take Para 2、4、5 as examples.

Paragraph 2

One of the most important sections of this report is the Human Development Index. This examines the achievement of 175 countries. The Index measures a country's achievements in three ways: life expectancy（how long people usually live）, education and income. The index has some surprises. Norway is at the top of the list, while the US is at number 7. The other top five countries are: Iceland（2）, Sweden（3）, Australia（4）, the Netherlands（5）. The UK is in the thirteenth position, while China is in the middle of the list. The bottom ten countries are all African countries, with Sierra Leone（in west Africa）at the bottom of the list.

Questions：

1. What is the function of the first sentence?

2. Underline other sentences that have the same function as the first sentence in this paragraph.

Paragraph 4

The 2003 Human Development Report gives examples of successful development. For example, in nine years（1953—1962）, China increased life expectancy by 13 years. In the last ten years in China, 150 million people moved out of poverty. However, the challenges are still great. Every day 799 million people in developing countries are hungry. Over half of these are in South Asia or Africa. Although more than 80% of children in developing countries go to primary school, about 115 million children are not being educated. More than 1 billion people in developing countries do not drink safe water. However, in other regions of the world, e.g. Eastern Europe, water is now mostly safe to drink.

Questions：

1. Analyze how is this paragraph organized?

2. How many parts can it be divided into? What are the transitional sentences?

Paragraph 5

The report shows that we are making some progress but that we need to make greater efforts. Although developed countries give some financial help, they need to give much more. Interestingly, the countries that give the most money are the Netherlands, Norway and Sweden. These are among the five richest countries in the world, so it is right that they should do so.

Questions：

Underline all the transitional sentences or words to see how this paragraph is well developed.

Task 3: Evaluation of the Declaration Through Intellectual Standards

Discussions：

1. Is the author sufficiently precise in providing details and specifics?

2. Is the author true to their purpose ?

Task 4: **Read aloud the passage and accumulate some languages and grammatical structures about describing the report**

Phrases	
Sentences	

Book 3 Module 3 Reading and Vocabulary

Learning goals：

1. Ss learn to know about the detailed information about some natural disasters.

2. Ss learn about how to introduce a natural disaster from the reading parts.

3. Ss learn to accumulate some languages and grammatical structures related to the writing topic.

Task 1: **Discussion—Leading-in the topic**

1. What does "violence of nature" refer to?

2. Can you tell me some other disasters?

Task 2: **Reading for Content—Explicating the thesis of each paragraph**

Read through each part and try to answer the following questions.

（1）How strong are tornado winds?

（2）What can happen to furniture when a house is destroyed by a tornado?

（3）How many tornadoes are there in the US every year?

（4）How many people died in the worst tornado of all time?

（5）What happens at sea during a hurricane?

（6）When was the worst hurricane of all time?

（7）Was the actor Charles Coghlan killed in it?

（8）What happened to him after the hurricane?

Task 3: **Reading for structures—Analyzing the Logic of the Declaration**

Read the passage again carefully and find out the following information from each passage.

Title	Writing content (from what aspects to describe)	Related words & phrases& sentences
What is a Tornado?		
What is a hurricane?		
An extraordinary event		

Task 4: **Evaluation of the Declaration Through Intellectual Standards**

Discussions：

1. From the title of paragraph 3 An extraordinary event, is the author sufficiently precise in providing details and specifics to prove the event is extraordinary? What are the clues?

2. Is the author true to their purpose ?

Task 5: **Writing practice**

Introduce one of the following disasters by imitating the text.

thunderstorm

volcanic eruption

earthquake

tsunami

flood

Book 3 Module 4 Reading and Vocabulary

Learning goals：

1. Ss learn to know about the detailed information about sandstorms in Asia.

2. Ss learn about how to design a poster that encourages people to look after the environment from the reading parts.

3. Ss learn to accumulate some languages and grammatical structures related to the writing topic.

Task 1: Work in pairs. Discuss these questions

1. What should you do in a sandstorm to protect yourself?

2. Which do you think is more dangerous, an earthquake or a sandstorm? Say why.

3. Where in China do sandstorms begin?

4. If you are in a desert, what is the first sign of a sandstorm?

5. Have you ever been in a sandstorm? If yes, describe it to your partner.

Task 2: Reading for Content—Explicating the thesis of each paragraph

1. Read through each part and try to get the main idea of each paragraph.

Para1: _____

Para2: _____

Para3: _____

Para4: _____

Para5: _____

Para6: _____

Then draw the structure map of this text.

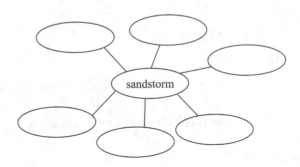

2. Read the passage again and try to answer the following questions.

(1) What did a mass campaign aim to do?

(2) What are the sandstorms?

(3) What is the cyclist wearing and why?

(4) What do you think happens to traffic in this situation? Why?

(5) What do you think experts advise people to do in this situation?

Task 3: Reading for structures—Analyzing the Logic of the Declaration

1. Read the text carefully and find out how each paragraph in the text is

connected.

2. Take paragraph 2&4&5 as examples to see how the paragraph is developed.

Paragraph 2：

Questions：

1. How many parts can be divided into and how each part is connected.

2. From what Ren Jianbo said, what can we infer?

Paragraph 4：

In this paragraph, what kinds of information are provided to prove *Sandstorms sometimes affect Beijing*?

Paragraph 5：

1. From the first sentence, what does the author intend to say?

2. From what Huang Xiaomei said, what can we know?

Task 4: **Evaluation of the Declaration Through Intellectual Standards**

Discussions：

1. Is the author sufficiently precise in providing details and specifics when introducing the sandstorms?

2. Is the author true to their purpose ?

Task 5: **Writing practice**

Design a poster that encourages people to look after the environment.

Book 3 Module 5 Reading and Vocabulary

Learning goals：

1. Ss learn to know about the detailed information about great people and great inventions of ancient China.

2. Ss learn about how to write about a famous person from ancient China from the reading parts.

3. Ss learn to accumulate some languages and grammatical structures related to the writing topic.

Task 1: **Read some ideas that Confucius taught and then express their ideas about whether they agree with them**

1. Man is born good.

2. All human beings are equal.

3. The family is important. We are members of a group.

4. Treat others in the way you want to be treated.

5. People are more important than rulers.

6. We should love all human beings.

Task 2: **Reading for Content—Explicating the thesis of each paragraph**

1. Read each paragraph and find out the idea each philosopher holds.

2. Read each paragraph and find out all the information introduced about each philosopher to develop the paragraph.

Philosopher	Writing content （from what aspects to describe）	Related words & phrases& sentences
Confucius		
Mencius		
Mozi		

Task 3: Evaluation of the Declaration Through Intellectual Standards

Discussions：

Does the author display fairness, or is the subject dealt with in an unfair manner?

Task 4: **Writing practice**

Write about a famous person from ancient China.

Book 3 Module 6 Reading and Vocabulary

Learning goals：

1. Ss learn to know about the detailed information about The Three Gorges Dam.

2. Ss learn about how to write about a news bulletin about changes that have taken place in your region.

3. Ss learn to accumulate some languages and grammatical structures related to the writing topic.

Task 1: Discussion

1. How much do you know about it?

2. What is the most famous place of interest that you have ever visited? Tell the rest of the class as much as you can.

Task 2: Reading for Content—Explicating the thesis of each paragraph

1. Read through each part and try to get the main idea of each paragraph.

Para1: _____

Para2: _____

Para3: _____

Para4: _____

Para5: _____

2. Read the passage again and answer the following questions.

（1）Why was the Three Gorges Dam built?

（2）How high is the dam?

（3）How wide is the dam?

（4）Who first suggested the idea?

（5）How much of China's energy is produced by burning coal?

（6）How many villages were flood when the dam was built?

3. Read the passage carefully and try to analyze the structures.

Paragraph	Questions
1	1. What is the function of Mao Zedong's poem? 2. What's the function of the last sentence?
2	1. Underline all the expressions and sentences to describe the Three Gorges Dam.
3—4	1. In what ways to prove the advantages of the Three Gorges Dam? 2. In what ways to prove the harmful effects of the dam?
5	1. What is the current situation of the Three Gorges Dam? 2. In what ways to introduce its current situation?

4. Discussion：

Do you think the advantages of the Three Gorges Dam are more important than the disadvantages?

Task 3: Reading for Writing materials

Read aloud the passage and try to find the expressions and sentences suitable for the writing.

Topic:

$$\text{Changes that have taken place in your region} \begin{cases} \text{old} \begin{cases} (\text{expressions \&sentences}) \\ \dots \end{cases} \\ \text{new} \begin{cases} (\text{expressions \&sentences}) \\ \dots \end{cases} \end{cases}$$

Task 4: Evaluation of the Declaration Through Intellectual Standards.

Discussions：

Is the author sufficiently precise in providing details and specifics when introducing the Three Gorges Dam?

Task 5: Writing practice

Write about a news bulletin about changes that have taken place in your region.

Book 4 Module 1 Reading and Vocabulary

Learning goals：

1. Ss learn to know about the detailed information about life in the future.

2. Ss learn about how to introduce the city of the future.

3. Ss learn to accumulate some languages and grammatical structures related to the writing topic.

Task 1: Oral discussion

Have a competition to say as many words as you can!

1. What materials do you think your house is made of in the future?

2. What will the city be like in the future? List your imagination.

Task 2: Prediction

What do you guess the passage will talk about? Tick the topics you think it will mention. Then, read the passage and check your ideas.

(   ) alternative energy

(   ) crime

(   ) schools

(   ) public services

(   ) shopping

(   ) environment

(   ) traffic

(   ) weather

(   ) entertainment

Task 3: Reading for Content—Explicating the thesis of each paragraph

1. Read the passage and answer the following questions.

（1）Where will garbage ships go?

（2）Who will batman nets catch?

（3）How will people go shopping?

（4）How will cars be different?

（5）What will doctors do from a distance?

（6）Where will old people go without moving?

2. Read each part and find out the following information from each passage.

Part	Writing content（from what aspects to describe）
Para1	In the future, ＿＿＿＿ will become very important as we will ＿＿＿ earth's natural resources. And we will use lots of ＿＿＿ and also have to rely on ＿＿＿.
Para 2—Para 12	How the students would run a city in the year 2025. 1. Garbage ships. The city will load huge＿＿＿with waste materials and send them towards ＿＿＿ 2. Batman Nets.Police will use them to ＿＿＿. 3. Forget smoking. If you want to smoke, you can go ＿＿＿, and ＿＿＿. 4. Forget the malls. All shopping will be done＿＿＿, and catalogues will have ＿＿＿ to place orders. 5. Telephones for life. Everyone will be given a telephone number at birth that will never change ＿＿＿they live. 6. Recreation. All forms of recreation will be provided ＿＿＿by the city. 7. Cars. All cars will use＿＿＿, and it will be possible to change the colour of cars. 8. Telesurgery. It will be common to perform ＿＿＿ surgery. 9. Holidays at home. People will be able to go anywhere in the world using ＿＿＿. 10. Space travel. It will be ＿＿＿ for ordinary people to travel in space.

Task 4: Reading for structures—Analyzing the Logic of the Declaration

1. Read the passage and think about how many parts can the passage be divided into?

2. Underline the topic sentences and draw the structure maps of the passage.

What will the city of the future look like? No one knows for sure, and making predictions is a risky business. But one thing is certain—they are going to get bigger before they get smaller. In the future, care for the environment will become very important as earth's natural resources run out. We will use lots of recycled materials, such as plastic, aluminum, steel, glass, wood and paper, and we will waste fewer natural resources. We will also have to rely more on alternative energy, such as solar and wind power. All this seems certain, but there are plenty of things about city life in the future which are not certain.

To find out what young people think about the future of urban life, a teacher at university in Texas in the United States asked his students to think how they would run a city of 50, 000 people in the year 2025. Here are some of the ideas they had:

Task 5: Evaluation of the Declaration Through Intellectual Standards

Discussions:

1. Is the author sufficiently precise in providing details and specifics when introducing the city of the future?

2. Is the author true to their purpose ?

Task 6: Read aloud the passage and accumulate some languages and grammatical structures about describing the report

Phrases	
Sentences	

Task 7: Writing practice

Imagine your city of the future and How will you run the city in the future if you have the chance to do so?

Book 4 Module 2 Reading and Vocabulary

Learning goals:

1. Ss learn to know about the detailed information about traffic jam in big cities.

2. Ss learn about how to design a poster giving advice to visitors to your city or hometown.

3. Ss learn to accumulate some languages and grammatical structures related to the writing topic.

Task 1: Oral practice

Discussion：

（1）Have you ever been stuck in a traffic jam?

（2）Where were you going?

（3）How long were you in the jam?

（4）What did you do then?

（5）If you haven't met a traffic jam, can you imagine what will happen in it?

Task 2: Reading for Content—Explicating the thesis of each paragraph

Read the passage quickly and answer the following questions.

（1）How easy is it to find a taxi in Beijing?

（2）What color are most taxis?

（3）What's the problem with buses?

（4）Which is the best bus for tourists?

（5）How many people can get in a minibus?

（6）What are the advantages of the underground?

（7）When does it close at night?

（8）What can you visit in a pedicab?

Task 3: Reading for structures—Analyzing the Logic of the Declaration

1. Read the passage again carefully and find out the following information from each passage.

means of Transportation	Writing content （from what aspects to describe）	Related words & phrases& sentences
Taxis		
Buses and trolleybuses		
Minibuses		
Underground		
Pedicabs		

2. Conclude the similarities and differences when describing the different means of transportation.

Task 4: **Evaluation of the Declaration Through Intellectual Standards**

Discussions：

1. Is the author sufficiently precise in providing details and specifics when introducing the different means of transportation?

2. Is the author true to their purpose ?

Task 5: **Writing practice**

Design a poster giving advice to visitors to your city or hometown.

Book 4 Module 3 Reading and Vocabulary

Learning goals：

1. Ss learn to know about the detailed information about body languages.

2. Ss learn about how to design a poster giving some social advice for visitors to China.

3. Ss learn to accumulate some languages and grammatical structures related to the writing topic.

Task 1: **Lead-in**

Discussion

Look at the pictures on the screen and discuss the meaning of them.

Task 2: Reading for Content—Explicating the thesis of each paragraph

1. Read the passage and choose the best title.

A. Saying it without words

B. When in Rome, Do as the Romans do.

C. Greetings around the world

D. Read my mind

2. Read through each part and try to get the main idea of each paragraph.

Para1: _____

Para2: _____

Para3: _____

Para4: _____

Para5: _____

Task 3: Reading for structures—Analyzing the Logic of the Declaration

1. Analyze each paragraph to see how this passage is well organized.

Paragraph	Questions
1	1. What is the topic sentence? 2. Underline the transitional words.
2	1. Underline the transitional words. 2. In what ways to prove the topic sentence? 3. Retell the given examples.
3	1. Underline the transitional words. 2. In what ways to prove the topic sentence? 3. Retell the given examples.
4	1. Underline the transitional words. 2. In what ways to prove the topic sentence? 3. Retell the given examples.
5	1. What is the topic sentence? 2. What does the author mean by saying "see if you are a mind reader"?

2. Draw the structure map of the passage.

Task 4: **Evaluation of the Declaration Through Intellectual Standards**

Discussions：

1. Is the author sufficiently precise in providing details and specifics?

2. Is the author true to their purpose ?

Task 5: **Writing a passage to introduce some body languages for visitors to China**

Book 4 Module 4 Reading and Vocabulary

Learning goals：

1. Ss learn to know about the detailed information about some great scientists.

2. Ss learn about how to write a biography about a famous scientist.

3. Ss learn to accumulate some languages and grammatical structures related to the writing topic.

Task 1: **Lead-in**

1. Introduction– Match the two parts

Qian Xuesen	Theory of Relativity
Marie Curie	Father of China's aerospace
Archimedes	discovered Radium
Stephen Hawking	Father of integral calculus
Albert Einstein	A Brief History of Time

2. Can you introduce some other famous scientists in China?

3. Look at the title and guess what it is about.

（1）Will the passage be about something or about someone?

（2）Do you think that the writer wrote about how the student studied in school?

（3）Did the writer write about what he did when he grew up? Why?

Task 2: **Reading for Content—Explicating the thesis of each paragraph**

1. Read through the passage and find the main idea of each paragraph

Para 1 _____

Para 2 _____

Para 3 _____

Para 4 _____

Para 5 _____

Para 6 _____

2. Read the passage carefully and answer the following questions.

（1）What was the key to feeding more people?

（2）When did Yuan Longping make a breakthrough in his research?

（3）What kind of student was Yuan?

（4）What way did he think to produce rice more quickly?

（5）What did he discover?

（6）How important was the discovery?

Task 3: Reading for structures—Analyzing the Logic of the Declaration

Analyze each paragraph to see how this passage is well organized and how the important ideas in the text are connected.

Questions：

（1）In paragraph 1, how does the author lead in Yuan Longping?

（2）In what ways to introduce Yuan Longping? Find out the related sentences to prove your ideas.

（3）Underline the phrases and sentence drills used to describe Yuan Longping.

phrases	
sentence drills	

Task 4: Evaluation of the Declaration Through Intellectual Standards

Discussions：

1. Is the author sufficiently precise in providing details and specifics?

2. Is the author true to their purpose ?

Task 5: **Writing a passage to introduce Yuan Longping and his achievements**

Book 4 Module 5 Reading and Vocabulary

Learning goals:

1. Ss learn to know about the detailed information about a trip along the Three Gorges.

2. Ss learn about how to introduce a trip.

3. Ss learn to accumulate some languages and grammatical structures related to the writing topic.

Task 1: Lead-in

Look at the following pictures and answer the questions.

1. Do you like traveling?

2. Have you traveled to the Three Gorges?

3. Imagining you're going on a trip through the Three Gorges, what topics will you talk about?

Task 2: Reading for Content—Explicating the thesis of each paragraph

1. Read the passage and answer the following questions.

（1）Who took a trip along the Three Gorges?

（2）Where were they from?

（3）Where did they start their trip?

（4）When did they start their trip?

（5）Why did Peter and his friend go downstream?

（6）Why did he choose the Jiangyou boat?

（7）What's the weather like when they started the trip?

（8）What did Peter and his friend do when the boat went through the first Gorge?

（9）When they reached the site of the dam, who came to look?

（10）What was Peter impressed by?

2. Read the passage again carefully and find out the following information from each passage.

A trip along the Three Gorges	
Writing content （from what aspects to describe）	Related words & phrases& sentences

3. Retell the trip logically.

Task 3: Evaluation of the Declaration Through Intellectual Standards

Discussions：

1. Is the author sufficiently precise in providing details and specifics?

2. From the passage, how can we see the writer enjoyed the trip? Give some ideas.

Task 4: Writing a passage to introduce one of your trips

Book 4 Module 6 Reading and Vocabulary

Learning goals：

1. Ss learn to know about the detailed information about one of the mysteries of the natural world.

2. Ss learn about how to introduce a mystery for visitors to China.

3. Ss learn to accumulate some languages and grammatical structures related to the writing topic.

Task 1: Lead-in

Discussion:

1. As we know, there are some unexplained mysteries in the natural world such as the Yeti, the Bigfoot, the Grey Man and the Loch Ness Monster. Have you ever heard of or read about any other monster? Tell us something you know.

2. How much do you know about Lake Tianchi? Where is it? How big/ deep is it?

Task 2: Reading for Content—Explicating the thesis of each paragraph

1. Read the beginning of the passage and decide where it comes from.

2. Read through the passage quickly and get the main idea of each paragraph.

Paragraph 1: _____

Paragraph 2: _____

Paragraph 3: _____

Paragraph 4: _____

Paragraph 5: _____

3. Read the passage carefully and answer the following questions.

（1）According to the text, what did the monster look like?

（2）How many people saw it?

（3）Who else saw the animal?

（4）What were they doing?

（5）What did it look like?

（6）What did Li Xiaohe see?

（7）Why could they see the animal clearly?

（8）How long was the history of reports of monsters in Lake Tianchi?

（9）What do many people think?

（10）What do the scientists think?

（11）How big is the Lake Tianchi?

（12）How high is it?

Task 3: **Reading for structures—Analyzing the Logic of the Declaration**

Read the passage and see how the passage is organized.

| The Monsters of Lake Tianchi | |
Writing content （from what aspects to describe）	Related words & phrases& sentences
Several recent sightings： _____ _____ _____ _____	

Task 4: **Evaluation of the Declaration Through Intellectual Standards**

Discussions：

1. Is the author sufficiently precise in providing details and specifics?

2. Is the author true to their purpose?

Task 5: **Writing a passage to introduce a mystery for visitors to China**

五、阅读教学中思维导图的运用

在实践教学中，高中英语的阅读难度一般是呈阶梯式增长，课文内容也是从简单到复杂，对课文的理解力也要求越来越高。为了让学生能够在短时间内了解课文的内容，课题组老师通过"思维导图"的方式来引导学生理解课文内容。运用点、线、面构成的图形模式不仅能够了解文章结构还能让学生的大脑被完全激活。比如在学习必修四Module 1 The City of the Future的时候，老师通过思维导图的方式，对"未来城市"的内容进行分类，从衣食住行这四大方面让学生根据课文的内容进行填充，让他们从宏观上对课文有一个具体的理解。厘清了课文的框架之后，对课文的学习就变得轻松了很多。同时，课题组老师还训练学生制作思维导图。比如，在讲授"Cloning: where is it leading us？"课文时，老师带领学生一起绘制段落的思维导图，有效地帮助学生梳理文章结构，理解文章意思。

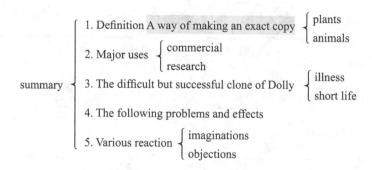

经过一段时间的训练和指导，部分学生已经养成了绘制思维导图的习惯并且能运用自如，效果较好。建议今后在阅读教学中我们要让学生多自己动手画出思维导图，培养他们的自主学习能力，增强他们的思维意识。下面以人教版必修一、二册以及外研版必修一、二、三册为例展示学生们绘制的思维导图。

【范例1】人教版Book 1 Module 1 My first day at Senior High思维结构图

Para 1 name—hometown
　　（I'm writing down my thoughts about it）——过渡句

Para 2 my new school is very good
- teachers（enthusiastic; friendly）
- Classrooms（amazing）

Para 3 the English class
- interesting
- Ms Shen's teaching method
- have fun

Para 4 what we did today
- introduce each other
- work by ourselves

Para 5 Ms Shen
- help us improve spelling and handwriting
- in a fun way
- her attitude

Para 6 my class
- the number
- hard-working
- my homework tonight

【范例2】人教版Book1 Module 2 My new teachers 思维结构图

Characters	Personalities	Feeling
Mrs Li	nervous; shy; kind; patient; good at teaching	appreciate her
Mrs Chen	strict; serious; well-organised; clear; good at teaching	appreciate her
Mr wu	popular; enjoy teaching; energetic; good-looking; talk loudly and fast; amusing; telling jokes	respect him

【范例3】人教版Book1 Module 3 My first ride on a train 思维结构图

Para 1　the author's first ride on a long-distance train

　　　　1. name
　　　　2. hometown
　　　　3. age
　　　　4. descriptions of the train and the journey
　　　　5. time

Para 2　food on the train and the scenery outside the train

　　　　1. Train: wonderful
　　　　2. Food: great
　　　　3. Scenery: colorful; fields; dark red soil; desert; abandoned farms

Para 3　what the author did on the train verbs

　　　　1. sat; looked out of; talked to; read; listened to
　　　　2. watched the sky

Para 4　the reason why the train is called the Ghan

　　　　1. a long way to travel
　　　　2. didn't like the hot weather and sand

Para 5　the use of camels in the past

　　　　much better; trained; carry food and other supplies

Para 6　how the Afghans dealt with the camels

　　　　didn't need camels any more; be shot

【范例4】人教版Book1 Module 4 A lively city 思维结构图

Para（1—7）Greetings and feelings or impressions

　　1. six years
　　2. the first time
　　3. one of the most attractive places
　　4. lively
　　5. friendly
　　6. one of the most interesting cities
　　7. feel fortunate living here

Para（8—22）Introductions of this city

1. Climate
- pretty hot and wet in the summer
- quite cold in the winter

2. Two districts
- the business district—high-rise buildings
　　　　　　　　　　　—shopping malls
- the western district—the most interesting

3. Gulangyu Island
- gorgeous island with interesting architecture
- a nice little fish restaurant

【范例5】人教版Book1 Module 5 A simple scientific experiment思维结构图

Topic

Below is a description of a simple scientific experiment.

It shows us how iron reacts with air and with water.

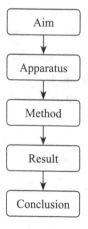

Aim

Apparatus

Method

Result

Conclusion

【范例6】人教版Book1 Module 6 The Internet and telecommunications思维结构图

Para 1 General description of the Internet
- 1. biggest source of information
- 2. accessible
- 3. millions of pages of data

Para 2 How the Internet starts
- In 1969 → a network called DARPANET
- In 1984 → NSFNET known as the Internet

Para 3 What is the WWW?
- 1. computer network
- 2. access information via the Internet
- 3. in English
- 4. in Chinese

Para 4—6 Who invented it?
- 1. in 1991
- 2. an English scientist, Tim Berners-Lee
- 3. the idea of the World Wide Web in 1989
- 4. the first "web browser"
- 5. the number of Internet users rose
- 6. work as a lecturer

【范例7】人教版Book 2 Module 1 Our body and healthy habits 思维结构图

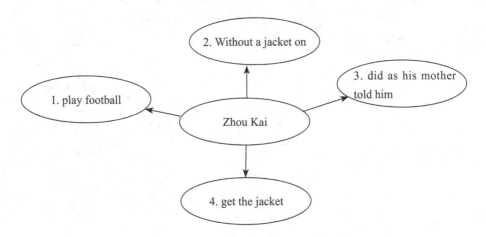

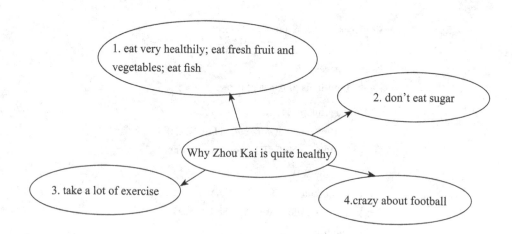

【范例8】人教版Book 2 Module 3 Music 思维结构图

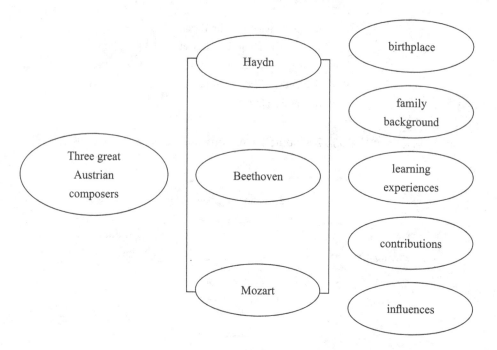

【范例9】Book 2 Module 4 Fine arts-Western, Chinese and Pop arts思维结构图

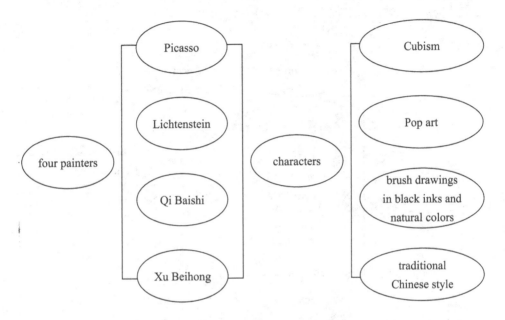

【范例10】人教版Book 2 Module 5 Chinese Taikonaut back on Earth思维结构图

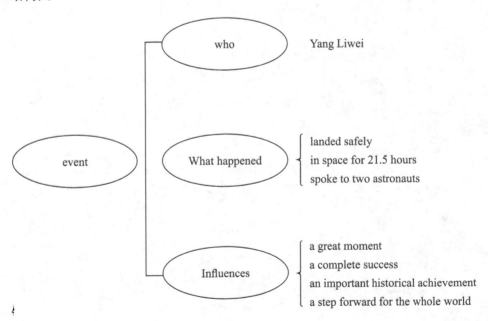

【范例11】人教版Book 2 Module 6 Film review: crouching tiger, hidden dragon
思维结构图

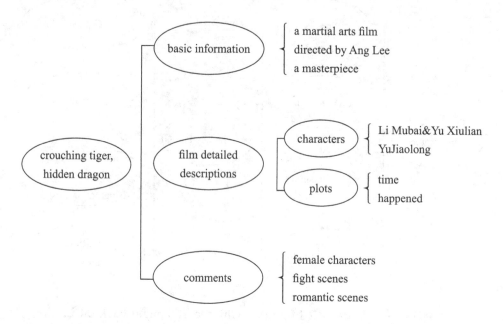

【范例12】外研版Book1 Unit 1 A new start 思维结构图

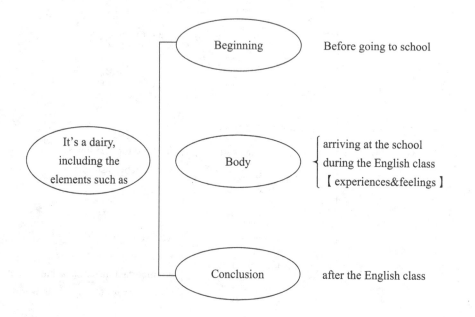

【范例13】外研版Book1 Unit 2 Neither Pie Nor Apple in Pineapple 思维结构图

Paragraph 1　Introduce the topic

English can be a crazy language to learn.

Paragraph 2-6　List some examples

sculpt a sculpture/paint a painting VS take a photo

In the car or taxi VS on the tram or bus

seasick / airsick / carsick VS homesick

hard/ soft VS hardly/ softly

shameless VS shameful

It's raining /snowing VS It's sunshining

WHO VS who

IT VS it; US VS

Paragraph 7　Draw a conclusion: the author's opinion

English reflects the creativity of the human race.

【范例14】外研版Book1 Unit 3 Family matters 思维结构图

I can describe the characters, setting and events in the story

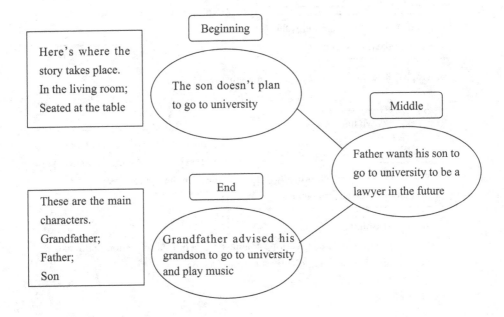

Here's where the story takes place.
In the living room;
Seated at the table

Beginning

The son doesn't plan to go to university

Middle

Father wants his son to go to university to be a lawyer in the future

End

These are the main characters.
Grandfather;
Father;
Son

Grandfather advised his grandson to go to university and play music

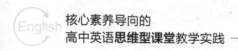
【范例15】外研版Book1 Unit 4 Click for a friend 思维结构图

Paragraph 1—3　Different ways of making friends
　　　　　　　　{ In the past
　　　　　　　　{ At present

Paragraph 4—7　Different arguments
　　　　　　　　{ Author's opinion
　　　　　　　　{ Arguments about whether online friendship is real or not

Paragraph 8　Different arguments
　　　　　　　the meaning of friendship and our longing for friends
　　　　　　　remain the same

【范例16】外研版Book1 Unit 5 Click for a friend 思维结构图

Paragraph 1—2　The introduction of the background to the monarch's migration

Paragraph 3　The mystery of the monarch's migration

Cause Effect

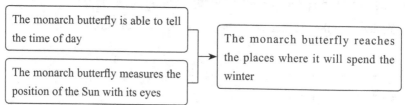

The monarch butterfly is able to tell the time of day

The monarch butterfly measures the position of the Sun with its eyes

The monarch butterfly reaches the places where it will spend the winter

Paragraph 4　The influences of human's activities

Cause Effect

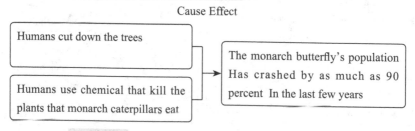

Humans cut down the trees

Humans use chemical that kill the plants that monarch caterpillars eat

The monarch butterfly's population Has crashed by as much as 90 percent In the last few years

Paragraph 5　Its solution
　　　　　　People have been working together to record its migration and make
　　　　　　sure there are enough plants for it to feed on.

【范例17】外研版Book1 Unit 6 At one with nature 思维结构图

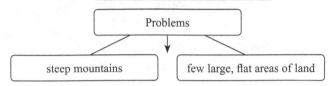

Paragraph 1 The vivid description of the terraces

Paragraph 2 The history of the terraces

Paragraph 3 The reasons for building the terraces

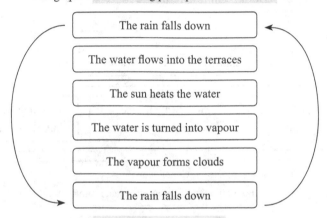

Problems

steep mountains | few large, flat areas of land

Paragraph 4 The working principles of the terraces

The rain falls down

The water flows into the terraces

The sun heats the water

The water is turned into vapour

The vapour forms clouds

The rain falls down

Paragraph 5 Its meaning to local people

【范例18】外研版Book2 Unit 1 Food for thoughts 思维结构图

Topic： How the family combines food from two cultures.

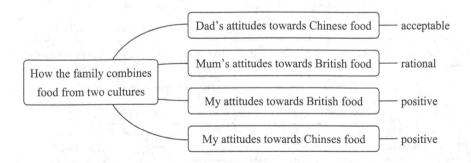

How the family combines food from two cultures

Dad's attitudes towards Chinese food — acceptable

Mum's attitudes towards British food — rational

My attitudes towards British food — positive

My attitudes towards Chinses food — positive

【范例19】外研版Book2 Unit2 Let's celebrate 思维结构图

Paragraph 1—2 Introduction

- The name of the book
- Its author

Paragraph 2—4 Background information

The contents of the book

Paragraph 5 Summary

The writer's evaluation

【范例20】外研版Book2 Unit3 On the move 思维结构图

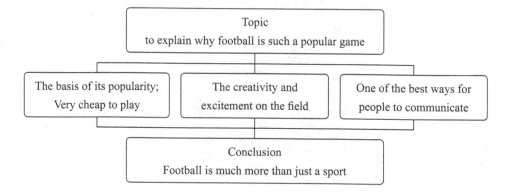

Topic
to explain why football is such a popular game

The basis of its popularity; Very cheap to play

The creativity and excitement on the field

One of the best ways for people to communicate

Conclusion
Football is much more than just a sport

【范例21】外研版Book2 Unit4 Stage and screen 思维结构图

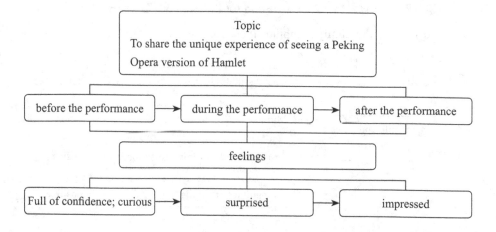

Topic
To share the unique experience of seeing a Peking Opera version of Hamlet

before the performance → during the performance → after the performance

feelings

Full of confidence; curious → surprised → impressed

【范例22】外研版Book2 Unit5 On the road 思维结构图

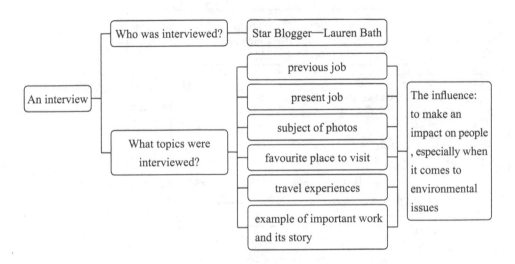

【范例23】外研版Book2 Unit6 Earth first 思维结构图

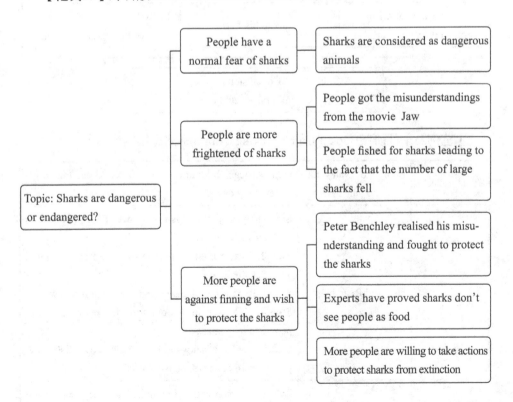

【范例24】外研版Book 3 Unit 1 Knowing me， knowing you 思维结构图

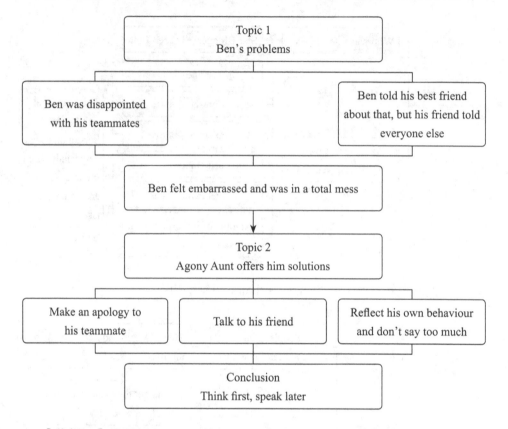

Topic 1
Ben's problems

Ben was disappointed
with his teammates

Ben told his best friend
about that, but his friend told
everyone else

Ben felt embarrassed and was in a total mess

Topic 2
Agony Aunt offers him solutions

Make an apology to
his teammate

Talk to his friend

Reflect his own behaviour
and don't say too much

Conclusion
Think first, speak later

【范例25】外研版Book 3 Unit 2 Making a difference 思维结构图

Paragraph 1	Why did Ryan want to help?	some African children had to walk ten kilometres to get water every day
Paragraph 2—5	How did Ryan help?	Step 1: Ryan reached his first target of $70, but he was told it wasn't enough. Step 2: Ryan called on people to donate money and a well was finally built. Step 3: Ryan visited Uganda and saw the finished well. Step 4: Ryan set up a foundation to encourage more people to help later. Step 5: Finally, clean water has benefited over 800， 000 people in 16 countries across Africa
Paragraph 6	conclusion	Ryan is a person with a determined attitude, courage and perseverance

【范例26】外研版Book 3 Unit 3 The world of science 思维结构图

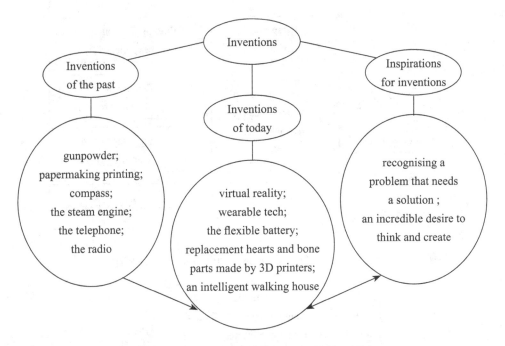

【范例27】外研版 Book 3 Unit4 Amazing art 思维结构图

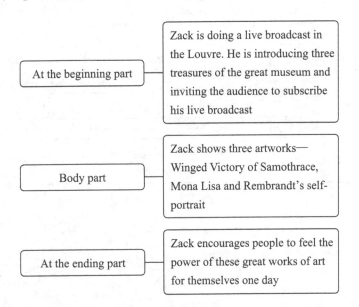

【范例28】外研版 Book 3 Unit 5 What an adventure 思维结构图

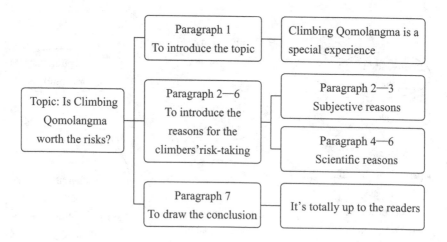

【范例29】外研版 Book 3 Unit 6 Disaster and hope 思维结构图

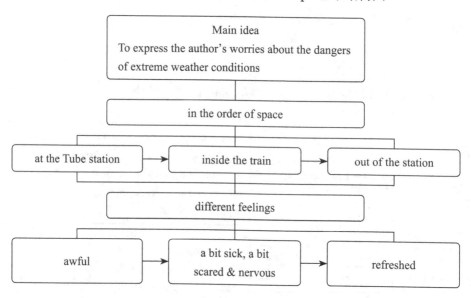

第二章　写作能力的培养策略

一、英语写作教学的重要性

在中国，对于英语学习者而言，作为基本语言技能中的一项基础而重要的技能，写作是一种很重要的沟通与交流的渠道，更是衡量学生英语学习综合能力的重要指标。它能全面地反映一个人语言学习的能力。正如Nunan（2001）所说，流畅地写出一篇连贯的文章或许是语言学习过程中最难的一件事。

在中国，2003年颁布的新课程标准对写作提出了更高的要求。《普通高中英语新课标》指出，中国高中英语课程的总目标是在义务教育的基础上"进一步发展学生综合语言运用能力，着重提高学生用英语获取信息、处理信息、分析问题和解决问题的能力，特别注重提高学生用英语进行思维和表达的能力"。

所以，英语写作能力的培养与训练是高中英语教学中的重要内容，也是培养学生进行英语思维的有效手段之一。一方面，英语写作训练能够促进学生更好地掌握英语语言知识；另一方面，英语写作要求学生以严密的思维对主题选择、逻辑表达、语义表述等做出分析，是一个积极发挥主体创作性的过程。换句话说，英语写作能力的培养是发展学生思维能力和表达能力的有效途径。

二、英语写作教学问题剖析

1. 学生层面

长期以来，高中生对写作文没有很大的兴趣，感觉作文很难写。一方面，学生写作基础薄弱，没有素材，缺乏足够的写作词汇和多样的句式表达，有些甚至写不出正确的英语句子；另一方面，他们常以母语的思维定势展开思维，缺乏篇章思维的能力，不具备较为严密的逻辑思维能力和较为宽广的写作内容。

2. 教师层面

在中国，高中英语教学受传统写作教学观念以及英语教材的影响，情况不容乐观。很多老师忽视了写作的交际功能，甚至错误地认为只要学生写出正确的句子就行了，所以他们特别重视语言能力的培养，侧重文章句子层面的表达，注重机械性的句型操练，而忽视写作的篇章整体意识，忽视了思维能力在语言学习中的核心地位，因而弱化了英语思维能力在写作中的培养与训练。

同时，老师缺乏对学生写作的整体性指导。很多一线老师重结果，轻过程，认为写作不需要教，平时按部就班地布置写作任务，一味要求学生多背多写。学生写完后，较少指导学生进行自我批改、同伴互评，也很少引导学生关注作文体裁、内容的构思、语言表达的修订完善。长此以往，这种无指导、无评价、无激励的"放任式"写作教学模式脱离了发展学生英语写作技能的宗旨，很难有效提高学生的写作水平。因为，我们知道写作是一种思维过程。教师在外语教学过程中应重点关注如何在训练学生听说读写技能的同时训练学生分析与综合、抽象与概括、多角度分析问题等多种思维能力以及发现问题、解决问题等创新能力。换句话说，如何在教学中正确处理语言技能训练和思维能力、创新能力培养的关系应成为教师关注的热点问题。

三、核心概念界定

（一）写作

写作是写作主体运用"语言符号"这个工具，通过取材、构思、分析、综合和加工等"制作"活动，进行精神产品的生产过程。它是以语言文字为工具，通过大脑的积极活动，以文章的方式呈现写作主体对生命、对社会、对环境的认识成果及其主体在认识过程中的情感变化的一种"精神劳动"。因而，写作，究其实质是一种逻辑表达。写作和思维密不可分。Kellogg（1994）认为写作是思维的一种形式，写作和思维是智能生活的双生子。同时，写作也是学生认识水平和语言文字表达能力的体现。写作能力的提高必须依赖于学生的"认识能力"和"语言文字表达能力"两个方面的因素。语言材料、写作素材、人的精神劳动，是写作成功的要素，它们对文章的形成起着重要作用。

（二）写作思维

写作是英语学习综合素养的表现，它涉及学生语言的运用、语感的灵敏度、对生活的感悟以及语言天赋等，而这几种素养又都受思维的调控。就像叶圣陶所言：作文是思维的演练。有道是"心无外物"，任何事物的存在都不是简单的物理状态，都会被欣赏者烙上不同的主观色彩，写作也是如此。

思辨能力由两个维度组成，在情感态度层面包括勤学好问、相信理性、尊重事实、谨慎判断、公正评价、敏于探究、持之以恒地追求真理等一系列思维品质或心理倾向； 在认知层面包括对证据、概念、方法、标准、背景等要素进行阐述、分析、评价、推理与解释的一系列技能。思辨能力的重要性不言而喻。

对于学习者而言，他应该要掌握如下具体的思辨方法：如何阐释和理解文本信息与观点？如何解析文本结构？如何评价论述的有效性？如何把已有理论和方法运用于新的场景？ 如何收集和鉴别信息和证据？如何论证说理？如何识别逻辑谬误？如何提问？如何对自己的思维进行反思和矫正？等等。

写作思维能力的提高必须经过系统的训练。思维能力的发展是一个从低级思维向高级思维发展的过程，必须经过思辨的标准一以贯之地训练思维的各要素，在英语学习过程中练习思维，在实际语言环境下使用思辨，最终使良好的思维习惯成为第二本能。

（三）抽象思维

写作中常用的思维方法包括抽象思维与形象思维两大类。抽象思维是一种思维方式，以反映现实的概念、判断和推理的认知过程。这种思维活动旨在揭示事物的本质及其关系，以抽象为一个内在特性和撇开具体的形象。

抽象思维包括逻辑思维方法与辩证思维方法，逻辑思维方法主要有分析、综合、概括、演绎、归类、类比等。抽象思维的形式可分为逻辑思维和辩证逻辑思维。分析和综合、比较和分类、抽象和概括、演绎和归纳都属于抽象思维。概念化和解决问题需要抽象思维。具有良好的抽象思维可以更好地把握主题，准确地使用概念、判断以及在理性和辩证分析、状态和合成的过程中去思考问题，做到思维清晰、独立又连贯。

四、理论依据

（一）过程写作理论

过程写作理论可追溯到20世纪80年代早期。它强调写作是一个复杂的认知过程，不是一蹴而就的事，有一系列相互关联的活动，包括发明、组织起草和修订。Hayes-Flower（1980），Bereiter and Scardamalia（1987）研究了写作过程的认知模型，发现写作过程是一个复杂的和循环的过程，涉及规划的阶段、句子生成和审查。每个阶段包括额外的递归子过程，如编辑和组织。另外Bereiter and Scardamalia（1987）通过研究发现了不同水平的二语写作者其写作过程的差异。写作水平高的在写作过程中会通过问题分析、目标设定和翻译问题等一系列过程，试图找到解决问题的内容或话语。写作过程就是一个思维的过程。

"过程写作教学法"强调写作过程的重要性，而不仅仅看重写作成果。注重写作过程是"过程写作法"的核心，它认为写作是一种发现意义的循环式过程。在"过程写作法"的视域中，写作是学习者由产生想法至收集材料到完成文本的一个过程，它主要与思维和写作技巧相连，而写作能力的发展是在写作技巧的训练过程中不知不觉完成的。过程写作教学法的理论基础是交际理论，写作的过程实质上是一种群体间的交际活动，而不是写作者的单独行为。在这一过程中，教师负责组织、协调和指导学生将写作过程变成一种协作性的学习过程，使其理解和内化写作的每个步骤，从而掌握有效的写作技能，而不再以学生是否能交上一篇按规定写好的作文为教学目的。其教学原理符合写作教学的本质规律。

（二）范例式教学理论

心理学家M.瓦根舍因首创了"范例教学理论"，他认为，范例教学法的基本思想在于，反对庞杂臃肿的传统课程内容和注入式的死记硬背教学方法。所谓范例，就是那些在日常生活素材中隐含着本质因素、根本因素、基础因素的典型事例。范例教学主张，通过个别的范例即关键性问题，来掌握一般的科学原理和方法。它旨在使学生从个别到一般，掌握教材结构，理解带有普遍性的规律性知识，以此培养学生具有独立的判断能力和创造能力。

范例式教学其主要理论特点可概括为"三个性""四个统一"和"五个分析"。"三个性"指：①基本性，应教给学生基本概念、基本科学规律或知识结构；②基础性，教学内容应适合学生的智力水平、基本经验和生活实际；③范例性，教给学生精选的知识，从而让学生进行学习迁移和实际应用。"四个统一"指：①教学与教育的统一；②问题解决与系统学习的统一；③掌握知识与培养能力的统一；④主体与客体的统一。"五个分析"指教师备课要对教学内容进行五大方面的分析，每个方面又有许多细目，总称"教学论分析"，它们是：①基本原理；②智力作用；③未来意义；④内容结构；⑤内容特点。范例教学的一般程序包括四个阶段：①范例地阐明"个"的阶段；②范例地阐明类型和"类"的阶段；③范例地掌握法则性、范畴性关系的阶段；④范例地获得关于世界以及生活关系的经验。即"个"的认识→"类"的认识→规律性的认识→通过自己的体验提高对客观世界行动的自觉性。

（三）文秋芳相关理论

1. 文秋芳测量抽象思维能力的4个维度

thinking process	parameters
understanding the composition topic	relevance
developing a thesis statement and supporting arguments	explicitness
organizing a coherent discourse	coherence
putting ideas into writing	sufficiency

2. 文秋芳思辨能力层级理论模型

元思辨能力（自我调控能力）第一层次	
（思辨能力）第二层次	
认知	
技能	标准
分析（归类、识别、比较、澄清、区分、阐释等） 推理（质疑、假设、推论、阐述、论证等） 评价（评判预设、假定、论点、论据、结论等）	清晰性（清晰、精确） 相关性（切题、详略得当、主次分明） 逻辑性（条理清楚、说理有根据） 深刻性（有广度与深度） 灵活性（快速变化角度、娴熟自如地交替使用不同思辨技能）

五、英语写作教学改进行动——思维训练与提升

（一）写作过程性指导的基本模式——读写实践

在所有的语言技能中，写作是高中生非常重要的语言技能。通过对学生作

文进行文本分析，教师发现学生的分析综合能力差以及思维缺乏深度。篇章连贯性维度表明学生的逻辑思维能力差直接影响文章的连贯和逻辑。大多数学生写作缺乏技巧，写作内容空洞，语言表达不规范。同时，通过问卷及访谈，我们发现坪山高级中学高一大部分学生对英语作文不感兴趣，对提高写作能力也信心不足。"写作"成了学生最薄弱的英语技能。他们普遍感觉没什么可写，不知从何写起，同时语言贫乏，表达不好。这些都源自他们平时没有有意识地背诵识记写作范文或模版；平时没有摘抄好词好句、积累写作素材的习惯。另一方面，问卷从侧面反映出老师对学生作文缺乏针对性的指导。写作课取得的效果最不理想。所以，教师要改变观念，改变那种传统的"以教师为中心"的写作教学模式，切实采取一些有效措施和策略来培养学生的写作兴趣和提高其写作能力。

阅读和写作是一对孪生兄弟。它们之间是相互依存、相辅相成的。所以，阅读与写作教学应该结合在一起，这样才能顺应这两种技能内在本质关系的规律。语言学家研究表明阅读与写作教学同时进行能够促进学生学习效率的最大化。所以教师要有读写结合的教学意识，有意识地在阅读教学中融入写作活动，并在写作活动中融入阅读活动。对于写作而言，阅读材料就是一个写作范例。阅读文本的特点是读写整合的起点。在对阅读材料进行文本解读之后，充分利用文本特点探索"读写结合，读中有写，以读促写"的写作教学新思路，引导学生重点学习和鉴赏某种写作手法或写作思路，在原文的基础上设计合理的续写、扩写或仿写练习。在平时的阅读教学中，老师们引导学生去把握文本的语言特征，寻找一些美句，尤其是寻找细节描写的语言，让学生们去模仿和背诵，积累大量的语言素材，以备实现语用知识的迁移。另外，在课外阅读中严格挑选结构严谨的阅读材料，使涵盖中国文化、体美劳教育、环保、和谐人际关系、科技发展前沿等话题的文章尽可能丰富多样。在阅读中让学生积累，这样学生在写作时就会有创意。

同时，教师要重视赏析范文，让学生从内容、语言（短语和句型）以及过渡衔接几个方面深入地学习范文。实践证明，正确分析学习范文是提高学生写作水平的有效途径。教师们可以运用范文进行层层分析，关注语篇的结构、连贯性。随后提供量身定制的模仿练习，让学生进行语言模仿和实践，写出自己的作品。但是，在这个过程中的范文学习，必须关注思维。只有从思维出发，才能改变目前仿写实践效率不高的问题。新课程标准对思维培养极其重视，文章语言又与思维密切相关，仿写的技巧方法又依靠思维，思维是仿写的重点。所以，老师们要注重写作的程序性、策略性知识，强化学生不同文体的作文图式，为学生创新写作打下基础。这样，学生们自然会将这些领悟到的语篇知识内化为自身的知识结构，提高学生的谋篇布局的能力。

（二）教学设计案例展示

Analysis of Discourse Organization
——一堂高中英语读写课的教学设计

Lesson type	Reading and writing	
Learning objectives	I. Knowledge objectives Students will learn about the new discovery about William Shakespeare's portraits. II. Ability objectives Students will learn about the skills on how to analyze the discourse organization and select the key words. Student will be able to practice writing the topic sentences and transitional sentences based on the discourse organization. Students will be able to develop their critical thinking ability by reading the passage as a model. III. Emotion and attitude objectives Students will learn to cooperate with others and build their self-confidence by successfully finishing the task	
Learning methods	Task-based approach, cooperative learning model	
Teaching aids	Multi-media	
Teaching procedure		
Step	Teaching/Learning activity	Purpose
Pre-reading	Students read aloud the passage correctly. Teacher helps them to understand their unknown words and expressions	Warm up Ss and help students to learn about the main idea of the passage
While-reading	Task 1: Discovering the discourse organization by finding the following tips: topic sentence key words transitional words or sentences	Help students figure out the features of how the passage is organized and how the paragraph is developed

Teaching procedure		
Step	Teaching/Learning activity	Purpose
While-reading	Task 2: Group discussion 1. Fill in the blanks to complete the passage, using one sentence for each blank chosen from the discourse. 2. Show students the answers and ask them to read aloud the passage	1. Help Students to raise their awareness of the importance of the topic sentence and transitional words. 2. Develop students' skills on how to write appropriate topic sentences for the discourse
Post reading	Teacher makes a summary on how to read and write a passage	To emphasis the importance of the analysis of the discourse organization
Homework	Writing task： Students write a passage to introduce one of their special birthdays based on the given beginning. Given beginning： Birthdays often involve surprise. But the surprise on my 16th birthday is surely one of the most dramatic	To Consolidate what they have learnt in this class and train their writing skills
Blackboard design	Skills to identify how the passage is well organized and how each paragraph is developed： （1）topic sentence （2）key words （3）transitional words	

点评：教学设计应以教学目标为起点，以学生的学习效果为中心去预设教学过程。一个好的教学设计是保证课堂教学质量的关键所在。黄焱老师在本节课中预设了SMART的教学目标，即Specific, Measurable, Achievable, Relevant and Time-framed，教学过程紧扣读写技能整合课的读取语篇信息、感知篇章结构、以读促写等要点。正因为如此，她的课立足于学生的学习需求，循序渐进，学生最终获得"输出"的技能是自然而然的结果。

Coast to coast教学设计

授课教师姓名	黄焱	名称	Book 2 Unit 5 Developing ideas —Coast to coast
设计思路			本堂课通过图片引出话题，通过scanning and detailed reading训练学生的阅读技巧。借助mindmap帮助学生梳理文章结构，建立写作框架。有意识地分析长难句，培养学生仿写的意识

内容

教学目的	通过本节课学习，学生能够： 1. 知识层面：了解相关描述旅行话题所需的词汇和句式。 2. 能力层面：训练阅读微技能，培养学生构架写作框架以及仿写的能力
教学重点难点	引导学生掌握阅读和写作微技能

教学过程

步骤	教学问题	教学任务
Step 1: Lead-in	What do you think of this saying "Travel broadens the mind"？ Show some information about Canada	结合图片表达对这句谚语的看法。通过一些信息引出Canada
Step 2: Scanning	Scan the passage and write the places on the map	快速锁定旅行的路线
Step 3: Reading aloud	Listen to the passage and practise reading aloud again and again	通过示范朗读，训练学生连读、语调和意群停顿微技能
Step 4: Careful reading	Read the passage carefully to fill in the blanks	训练学生查找细节的阅读微技能
Step 5: Thinking	Think about how the passage is well developed and conclude the mindmap	通过文本分析帮助学生构架写作框架
Step 6: Understanding of the complex sentences	Try to analyse the sentence structure of the complex sentences	训练学生分析长难句，为仿写奠定基础
Step 7: Homework	Have you ever travelled with your family? Write down your experience	完成一篇游记，训练学生写作能力

Review of attributive clauses

Teaching aims:

1. Students will be guided to know the differences among the relative words and how to choose the relative words in the real context.

2. Students will practice using the attributive clauses in provided situations.

Teaching important and difficult points:

1. How to choose the relative words correctly in the real context.

2. How to identify the differences between attributive clause and other clauses in provided situations.

Teaching procedures:

Step I Observe and discover

Task1 Read through the following passage and find out the attributive clauses.

Science and technology have been bringing human beings benefits. For example, online shopping is coming into fashion in most cities, where people are able to make full use of the rapidly-developed Internet technology. Nowadays, can we find a person who has not experienced online shopping? Definitely not. Online shopping is welcomed by most people for various reasons. From the perspective of consumers, it can save time for people who don't have much spare time. Just click the mouse, and they can get whatever they want while staying at home. For the retailers, it can cut some costs for those who don't have much circulating funds because they don't have to spend money in renting a house. However, there are still some disadvantages in online shopping. First, a face-to-face deal makes online shopping less reliable and trustworthy. Second, people will lose the fun of bargain.

It is undeniable that shopping on the Internet has become an irresistible trend in modern society and dramatically changed the way that people live. It's of great urgency that we need to make the relative laws. Only in this way can we enjoy the pleasure and convenience of online shopping without the concern of being cheated.

Step II Discuss and make a summary

From the above selected attributive clauses and discuss about the features of the attributive clauses.

1. What is the attributive clause?

2. What's the relationship between the relative word and the modified noun?

3. What are the relative words leading the attributive clause?

引导词	先行词	在从句中充当

Task 2 Try to complete the sentences using the attributive clause.

1. She couldn't forget the day when_____.

2. You must find out the reason why _____.

3. Many children, whose _____, are taken good care of in the village.

4. This is a factory which _____.

5. The man whom _____is my father.

Step III Practice

Fill in the blanks in discourse using the correct words.

It was the summer of 2012, _____I came to Guangning No.1 Senior High School. Our school is a wonderful place, _____I can see a lot of beautiful buildings and a large square. Our classroom, the roof of _____looks like a rocket in the distance, is located in the center of our school. The main reason _____I like our school is that I can make many friends. I can get along with my classmates here, two of _____are my best friends. Jack, _____comes from Tanbu Junior High School, is very active. He likes various sports, among _____he likes running very much. He will run 5 kilometres every day, _____makes him look strong. Nick, _____father is a teacher in Lianhe Junior High School, studies very hard. We often talk about the people and the things _____we see in our school. Nick prefers the food _____ is made in our canteen. The teacher _____ he likes is Mr Zhang, our math teacher, while my beloved teacher is my English teacher, Miss Chen. To be honest, I gradually fall in love with our school.

Step Ⅵ Application

Fill in the blanks and identify different kinds of clauses.

Influenza, or flu, is a common infection of the nose and throat, and sometimes the lungs. The cause is a virus _____ passes from one person to another. The virus spreads through the air _____ an infected person expels air suddenly.

Medical experts have identified three major kinds of influenza. They call them type A, B and C. Type C is the least serious. People may not even know they have it. _____ researchers study the other kinds very closely. Viruses change to survive. This can make it difficult for the body to recognize _____ fight an infection.

A person _____ has suffered one kind of flu can't develop that same kind again. The body's defense system produces antibodies. These substances stay in the blood and destroy the virus _____ it appears again. _____ the body may not recognize a flu virus _____ has even a small change.

Each year, researchers develop vaccines to prevent the spread of the flu virus. The World Health Organization holds meetings in _____ experts discuss _____ kinds of flu viruses to include on the next vaccine.

学习自评表：

项目	优	良	中	差
语言知识：掌握关系词的用法				
语言技能：在语境中学会辨析并熟练运用定语从句				
情感态度：小组合作学习的参与情况				
学习策略：总结关系词的规律				

课后反思：

经过专家的指导，现将本堂课的亮点和需要改进的地方做个总结：

老师领悟能力较强，有语篇意识。落实了在语篇中教语法，在语篇中体验语法的理念。这点是非常值得肯定的。

　　但是，这堂课最大的问题是老师没有给学生足够的时间去讨论交流和消化。课堂活动形式单一，学生之间缺少互动。回答问题的学生数量太少。

　　所以通过本堂课的反思，我最大的收获就是在教学上，首先老师的教学理念要转变。要做到心中有学生，多从学生角度去考虑。任何活动都要围绕学生开展。同时，理念转变后，在课堂实际操作上一定要与理念相吻合。课堂上给足时间让学生先尝试，多思考，然后组织讨论。通过讨论，学生就能思考更多，明确自己的问题。最后有针对性地帮助学生解决疑难问题。这样的课堂才更有效。

（三）语料库的储备

　　创新型单元学案集——写作思维培养的基石。

　　要在英语考试作文中拿高分，背诵和学习一些范文是很重要的，但是会背更应该会仿写。作文中真正的模仿重点永远都是放在一定的句式结构上的。所以经过实践，本人探索出了范例式作文的作法，从句子到篇章的模仿，精选材料，让学生在做中学。通过研读教材，对整个单元进行合理整合和取舍，最终形成了词汇、语篇填空、句子学习三个课时学案。词汇学案侧重学习单元重点考纲词汇的词性转化和重点词组。这些词汇的学习和积累是写作的基础。在平时的学习中就要强化记忆。语篇填空是将课文改编成高考题型中的语法填空题，训练学生在具体语境中学习语法和运用语法知识的能力。一方面，培养学生的语篇整体意识；另一方面，夯实写作基础，熟练掌握语法知识，扫清写作障碍。句子学习学案是梳理各类句型，通过大量例句的呈现帮助学生掌握句子结构并学会仿写。句型的模仿是学英文必要的途径之一。练就了一身模仿本事，英文造句能力必然会精进，英文写作能力才会提高。学生要仿写成功首先必须对句子结构有个基本的认识，掌握句子结构是仿写的基础，在掌握句子结构之后再进行模仿创作。而这所有的环节都离不开思维。没有思维的参与，学生寸步难行，不可能写出正确的句子。

　　这套单元学案集为学生下一阶段的写作训练奠定了坚实的基础，深受老师和学生们的好评，并且在坪山新区第三届教育教学科研成果评审中获教育技术类三等奖。下面展示一套完整的单元学案集作为参考。

Book 3 Module 1 Vocabulary learning

目标：熟记单词和短语，掌握相关词汇的用法。

一、根据要求写出下列单词的不同形式

1. _____（n. 大陆）——_____（adj. 大陆的）

2. _____（v. 面向）——_____（n. 脸）——_____（adj. 脸部的）

3. _____（adj. 坐落的）——_____（n. 形势；. 状况）_____（v. 使位于，使处于）

4. _____（n. 建筑师）——_____（n. 建筑）

5. _____（v. 同意）——_____（n. 协议）——_____（v. 不同意）——_____（n. 分歧）——_____（adj. 令人愉快的；适合的）

6. _____（v. 统治）——_____（n. 统治者）——_____（n. 政府）

7. _____（n. 地区）——_____（adj. 区域的）

8. _____（n. 地理）——_____（adj. 地理的）

9. _____（n. 产品；. 结果）——_____（v. 制造；生产）——_____（n. 成果；产品；生产；作品）

二、课文单词默写

1. One of Barcelona's most famous _____（标志性建筑）is the Church of the Sagrada Familia, which was designed by an _____（建筑师）called Antonia Gaudi.

2. One of the world's largest art _____（美术馆；画廊）, the Louvre, is also _____（位于）in Paris.

3. Paris is the capital and largest city of France, _____（位于）on the River Seine.

4. The most popular place for tourists is the Eiffel Tower, the famous _____（象征；符号）of Paris.

5. Gaudi worked on the _____（项目；工程）from 1882 until his death in 1926.

6. Many of Florence's most beautiful paintings and _____（雕刻；泥塑）were produced by great artists such as Leonardo da Vinci and Michelangelo.

7. The Uffizi Palace is the most famous art _____（美术馆；画廊）in the city.

8. Barcelona is the second largest city of Spain and _____（位于）on the northeast coast, about five hundred kilometers east of the Spanish capital, Madrid.

9. Athen，the capital of Greece, is known as the _____（发源地）of western _____（文明）.

10. Greece's best writers lived in _____（古代的）Athens.

三、写出下列短语的意思

1. be off the coast

2. be covered by

3. be famous for

4. work on

5. because of

6. last for

7. of all time

8. be known as

9. such as

10. ever since

11. be easy to do

12. on the coast

13. be situated/ located in/on /at

14. at the moment

15. in terms of

16. in the long / short term

17. compared with

18. in different ways

19. on the other hand

20. on one hand

21. have some control over

22. in the 1950s

23. little by little

24. increase to

25. have a population of

26. look like

27. be faced with

28. face to face

29. in the face of

30. range from A to B

31. refer to

32. belong to

33. be opposite to

34. sign up

35. come to an agreement

四、短语填空

1. Florence is an Italian city which became famous _____ （因为）the Renaissance, a great artistic movement which began in the 1300s and lasted for three hundred years.

2. Athens, the capital of Greece, _____ （作为而出名）the birthplace of western civilization.

3. Their work has influenced other writers _____. （自从……一直）

4. _____ （就……而言）size and population, how big is the European Union compared with China?

5. _____ （另一方面）, the head of state is a president.

6. _____ （逐渐地；一点点地）, the number increased during the second half of the twentieth century.

7. The city _____ （因……而出名）its restaurants, cafes and theatres.

8. Gaudi _____ （从事于）the project from 1882 until his death in 1926.

9. During the Renaissance, some of the greatest painters _____ （一直）lived and worked in Florence.

10. Many of Florence's most beautiful paintings and sculptures were produced by

great artists _____（例如）Leonardo da Vinci and Michelangelo.

Book 3 Module1 Sentence learning

目标：

1. 熟读句子。

2. 学会分析句子结构。

3. 学会造句或仿写。

一、熟读例句，分析句子

（一）简单句

1. Between France and Spain is another mountain range—the Pyrenees.

2. Paris is the capital and largest city of France, situated on the River Seine.

3. The artistic movement called the Renaissance began in Florence.

4.（1）The most popular place for tourists is the Eiffel Tower, the famous symbol of Paris.

（2）One of the world's largest art galleries, the Loure, is also located in Paris.

（3）Barcelona is the second largest city of Spain and is situated on the northeast coast, about five hundred kilometers east of the Spanish capital, Madrid.

（4）Athens, the capital of Greece, is known as the birthplace of western civilization.

（二）复合句

1. One of Barcelona's most famous landmark is the Church of the Sagrada Familia, which was designed by an architect called Antonio Gaudi.

2. Florence is an Italian city which became famous because of the Renaissance, a great artistic movement which began in the 1300s and lasted for three hundred years.

3. Florence is visited each year by about a million tourists who come to see the art galleries, churches and museums.

4. But each of them sends representatives to the European parliament, which has some control over what happens in each of the member countries.

5. The expanded European Union has a population of more than half a billion people, twice as big as the population of the United States.

二、从下列个体B句画线的A、B、C、D 四个选项中，选出与A 句的画线部分成分相当的最佳选项

1. A: A gallery is a large building <u>where people can see famous pieces of art</u>.

   B: The <u>injured</u> <u>people</u> <u>are being taken good care of</u> <u>in the hospital</u>.

           A   B   C   D

2. A: A long time ago, Athens was the <u>world's</u> <u>most powerful</u> <u>city</u>.

   B: <u>Between France and Spain</u> <u>is</u> <u>another</u> mountain range—<u>the Pyrenees</u>.

                 A   B   C   D

3. A: What did you know about these cities <u>before you read the text</u>?

   B: Florence is <u>an Italian city</u> <u>which became famous</u> <u>because of the Renaissance</u>,

             A   B   C

   <u>a great artistic movement</u> which began in the 1300s.

          D

4. A: The <u>expanded</u> European Union has a population of more than half a billion people, twice as big as the population of the United States.

   B: Florence <u>is visited</u> <u>each year</u> by <u>about a million tourists</u> <u>who come to see the</u>

           A   B   C   D

   <u>art galleries, churches and museums</u>.

           D

5. A: Their work has influenced <u>other writers</u> ever since.

   B: But <u>each of them</u> sends representatives to <u>the European Parliament</u>, which

           A   B

   has some control over <u>what happens</u> in each of the member countries.

               C   D

三、翻译

1. 该房子坐落在郊区（suburb），它有着悠久的历史。（一句多译）

_____

_____

_____

2. 史密斯先生，我们学校的教授，很受学生欢迎。（一句多译）

_____

_____

_____

3. 这本小说很感人，我已经读了三遍。（一句多译）

_____

_____

_____

4. 这里有人想和你说话。（一句多译）

_____

_____

_____

5. 这个餐厅能容纳很多人，比汤姆的餐厅大一倍。（一句多译）

_____

_____

_____

Book 3 Module 1课文语篇填空

目标：

1. 熟读背诵课文，掌握文章中重要知识点。

2. 提高语法填空题解题能力。

Paris

Paris is _____ capital and largest city of France, _____ (situate)
on the River Seine. It is one of the most beautiful _____ (city) in the world
and _____ (visit) by more than eight million tourists every year. The most
popular place for tourists is the Eiffel Tower, the famous symbol of Paris. One of the
world's _____ (large) art galleries, the Loure, is also located in Paris. The city is
also famous _____ its restaurants, cafes and theatres. About two-thirds of France's
artists and writers live in Paris.

Barcelona

Barcelona is the _____ (two) largest city of Spain and _____ (situate) on the northeast coast, about five hundred kilometers east of the Spanish capital, Madrid. One of Barcelona's most famous landmark is the Church of the Sagrada Familia, which _____ (design) by an architect _____ (call) Antonio Gaudi. Gaudi worked on the project from 1882 _____ his death in 1926. The church hasn't been finished yet!

Florence

Florence is _____ Italian city _____ became famous because of the Renaissance, _____ great artistic movement which _____ (begin) in the 1300s and lasted for three hundred years. During the Renaissance, some of the greatest painters of all time lived and worked in Florence. Many of Florence's most beautiful paintings and sculptures _____ (produce) by great artists such as Leonardo da Vinci and Michelangelo. Florence _____ (visit) each year by about a million tourists _____ come _____ (see) the art galleries, churches and museums. The Uffizi Palace is the most famous art gallery in the city.

Athens

Athens, _____ capital of Greece, is known _____ the birthplace of western civilization. Two thousand four hundred years ago, it was the world's most _____ (power) city. Buildings such as the Parthenon on the Acropolis Hill _____ (build) during this period. Greece's best writers lived in ancient Athens. Their work _____ (influence) other writers ever since.

（四）语境记忆单词文本资料——写作思维培养的基石

1. 特色学案展示

本人还利用考纲词汇3500语境记忆文本资料编制了一套学案，让学生通过在具体的语篇环境下记忆单词并学习语法。创造性思维是一种连续的而不是全有全无的思维品质。每个人其思维品质中都具有潜在的创造性。不仅阅读教学可以培养学生思维的独创性，写作教学也是如此。本学案中的故事创写就是这样一种具体而有效的教学方法，能达到培养学生语言综合运用能力的目的。一方面，故事创写有利于克服遗忘；另一方面，也有利于抽象思维及创造性思维的培养、健康人格的培养。

实践证明，学生们非常喜欢这套材料，肯定了它的价值。本套学案集已经作为学校的校本课程在学校内推广使用，具体范例如下。

A Hard Trip 一次辛苦的旅行

一、语篇学习

思考：考什么？解题依据在哪呢？

My sister was fond _____ traveling. Ever since graduating, she had been determined _____ (organize) a trip to _____ old temple. Since transporting fare was expensive, she decided _____ (use) a bicycle to cycle there not _____ (care) about the _____ (disadvantage).
_____ (she) stubborn attitude was always her shortcoming. Once she made up her mind _____ (do) something, no one could persuade her _____ (change) her mind. _____ (final), we gave in _____ usual _____ we preferred _____ (take) a train. After we prepared everything, _____ (include) the schedule, _____ (rely) weather forecast and the insurance, we _____ (begin) our trip.

Our journey was along a river _____ (flow) from a high altitude. Our pace was slow _____ the river frequently had many sharp _____ (bend) through deep valleys, _____ the water seemed to boil. Just _____ I recorded in my journal, it was really _____ hard journey. _____ we also enjoyed great views. One night, I put my head on my pillow——a parcel of wool coats, and _____ (lie) beneath the stars. When the flame in front of our cave _____ (go) out _____ midnight, I found the sky so _____ (beauty)！

二、大声朗读故事，画思维导图，复述这个故事

Part 1　听和读

Part 2　画思维导图

Part 3　复述或背诵

三、句子仿写

1. Since transporting fare was expensive, she decided to use a bicycle to cycle

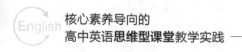
there not caring about the disadvantages.

句式分析：

仿写：

2. Once she made up her mind to do something, no one could persuade her to change her mind.

句式分析：

仿写：

3. Our pace was slow because the river frequently had many sharp bends through deep valleys, where the water seemed to boil.

句式分析：

仿写：

4. Just as I recorded in my journal, it was really a hard journey.

句式分析：

仿写：

四、语段创写

Choose some above phrases and sentence drills to make up a short passage and then read it aloud.

2. 学生故事创写习作展示

（1）

Mary was a doctor and she couldn't give birth, so she adopted a boy from hospital.She took good care of him and brought him up.She named him after a famous athlete, Tom. As a child, his intelligence surprised everyone around him.The teacher told students to do things.Tom always could do it best. As he grew up, he became much smarter than before. Mary wanted her son to be like the famous athlete, so she trained Tom strictly.A year later, he attended a competition and competed with the best athlete in his country. Finally, he won the championship, which made his mother happy and proud. At the age of 18, he was the best-known athlete all over the world. He turned more professional after training and set a record.

He was so famous that almost everyone, including woman and child knew him.

Although he retired from his team when he was 60 years old, he still held the record, even until today.

（2）

Tom worked in an international company. He got good grades on his business and his buss was pleased with him.Last month, he was allowed to take a long vacation for a rest.So he decided to go on a trip to Malaysia with his wife.They went there by plane, which was very fast and comfortable.At the start of their trip, they went to swimming and enjoyed the wonderful sunshine on the beach.The second day, they went camping with their friends in Malaysia and had a good time.All of them fell asleep except for Tom, who had a sense of joy and happiness, which he didn't feel for a long time.

In fact, everyone will be needed to do something or some tasks, which may make us feel bored and tired.The best idea to settle these problems is to take a action and relax yourself completely.

（3）

Tom is a twenty-eight years old businessman, known for his special trading methods. Therefore, he always gives speeches in many famous universities offering support and guidance to those who have ideas on business.

As a matter of fact, Tom was so clever when he was a child that he was thought to be the most successful person in the town. He was encouraged to earn money by himself if he wanted to buy something. Fortunately, Tom nearly became a successful businessman when he grew older. Last year, he went back to his hometown but was astonished by the appearance. The environment was badly affected by human activities. For example, cutting down trees, burning the fuel, which caused serious damage. So he decided to take actions to prevent the environment from being destroyed. He signed the agreement with the local company, hiring people to plant trees. Finally, the environment was recovered after being rebuilt. The town was listed as one of the most beautiful attractions in China.

（4）

Tom was born in Africa. No sooner did he arrive at the world than his mother died. He didn't have any relatives except for his. father, a man who liked drinking. Every time his father got drunk, he would got angry easily. So Tom always suffered from starvation from his early age. His father was put in prison because he killed a person after drinking. Then Tom had to work in a factory to make his living. He was the youngest one. However, to his great astonishment, the workers there were all kind to him. For this reason, he began to work hard and gradually got used to it. As he grew older, a business man picked Tom out and let him manage his company. Tom was fond of his job and later made a lot of money. His boss died because of the heart attack, so Tom had to continue managing the company. In Tom's thirties, he was known as a successful businessman over the world.

（5）

Mary, a beautiful girl, was born in a rich family. At the age of eight, her parents found that their daughter was strongly influenced by them. Why? Because they are both dancers when they were young. Although they retired from the company a few years ago, they often kept dancing at the spare time. Their behaviour had an effect on Mary, which made her develop a good habit. So they decided to send her to a dancing school. Fortunately, Mary made an impression on teachers. At the time, her parents took advantage of their experiences, trying to teach Mary to become a good dancer. They often made comparisons between Mary and other dancers because they wished her to be better. Finally, Mary managed to perform on the international stage. After becoming famous, a book written by herself came out.

（6）

Vivian is a manager in a big company. She is famous for her outstanding abilities in the city. Although she had learned so much about her work, she felt a bit tired and wanted to travel around China to relax herself. Last week, she put off her schedules and made her decision finally. The next day, she got on the plane with pleasure. She went to Xi Shuang banna, a city with beautiful scenery in Yunnan Province. The people there had the custom of pulling the water towards others on Water Festival. At first, Vivian was completely uninterested in it. However, she came across her old friend in a pub one night. They talked happily, and her friend offered to take her to the places of interest. Gradually, she adjusted to having fun with the local people and spend time learning the history of Yunnan. Yesterday Vivian came back full of energy.

（7）

Tom is known as a famous writer, who always wrote his articles in the form of his life experiences.He went on a trip to America last month, aiming to learn about the culture and experience the life there.When he set foot on land, he knew that it would take him a few days to adapt to the life.

On his first day, he went diving and reached a depth of 50 meters, seeing many wonderful scenes under the sea. After a series of relaxing activities, he went to some famous universities to experience the classes. He found that American students replied to the teachers' questions actively. What's more, some topics were open to discussion, which were not allowed in China. Teachers helped students overcome difficulties and gave students a right to express their opinions.

Tom came up with an idea after returning to China. He wanted more people to know the differences between Chinese education and American. So he wrote down his experience in a book in great detail.

（8）

Tom was the best-known athlete. He also was named the most valued player. He holds a record now. He was born in a countryside. At the age of 15, he won the championship in the running race. His grade surprised all the people. Then he began to practise. As he grew up, he turned professional. He was known as a runner. However, he retired from the competition at the age of 25. Although he had retired, he deserved the title because he was the best all the time.

（9）

Tom was a student. He got good grades on his study. His parents were pleased about it. So they decided to take a long vacation. Tom was looking forward to going camping so they decided to go to the beach at first. They had a good time on the beach. Then they went backpacking. But Tom was tired. He was encouraged to keep walking. At the moment, he wanted to give up. But at last, he succeeded. He knew that his parents were good to him and how to get on with them. The vacation plays an important part in his life.

（10）

Tom inherited from the company which his father set up. But he was completely uninterested in the business. So he offered to leave the company. Then he got his money with pleasure. Having enough money, he made his decision to travel. So he spent time travelling around. One day, he set off to a forest. When he walked up to it, he was astonished by the nature. It was covered with trees. He kept walking. A moment later, he found that he got lost. He was very afraid. He tried to make a call. But there was no sign. Fortunately, he came across a river, which run through the forest. So he walked along the river. At last, he saw the town in the distance.

（11）

Tom is a policeman. One day, he was asked to save people from a dangerous situation. After being told the situation in great detail, he set foot on the mountain and looked for the people. He overcame difficulty. At last, he found the people. But it was difficult for him to save them. Then he came up with an idea and saved them successfully. He kept his promise that he will save the people. Although he got badly sunburnt, he still didn't regret to do it. As a result, he is known as a kind policeman.

（12）

William was born in a happy family. He is a selfless and kind person. He has been brought up in this way. It <u>is not rude to</u> everyone. <u>As a child</u>, he had a dream to be the best-known athlete, <u>which surprised someone</u>. His mother believed him and <u>encouraged him to</u> make it <u>come true</u>. William wanted to be the Jordan. He learned to be more hard-working. <u>At the age of</u> 20, he <u>competed with</u> a player and finally William <u>won the championship</u>. He <u>turned professional</u>. <u>In the history of</u> NBA, he <u>holds a record</u> all the time and he <u>is named</u> the most valued player. William <u>draws attention to</u> basketball.

（13）

Jack's experience <u>spread to</u> all schools. The school <u>gave Jack the chance to</u> give a speech about what he had experienced.

Jack went to a forest to explore. Suddenly, a heavy rain <u>took place</u> which <u>caused serious damage</u>. Jack was <u>in danger</u>. A local person went through and helped Jack.

Then he took Jack to his village. The village was poor and many children didn't go to school. When Jack went back home, he <u>raised money</u> and <u>encouraged people to</u> go with him. He went to the village and <u>offered support and guidance to</u> local person <u>in return</u>. Jack <u>was honored for</u> it. Jack undertook to change the village. <u>Apart from</u> that, he made an advertisement to <u>raise public awareness</u> about village.

（14）

At meal times, Joe was eating food and watching TV. Suddenly, the door was open. Joe looked out and saw her son coming back. <u>To her astonishment</u>, her son seemed very weak. Her son said he was hungry <u>in a weak voice</u>. Joe stared at his son and let him go into the room to eat food. Joe really wanted to know what happened today and what made her son <u>become quite wild with hunger</u>. So he <u>whispered to</u> her son what happened. Her son told her that he <u>was fond of</u> basketball and <u>intended to</u> join in school team. For this reason, he practised a lot. Joe heard it but <u>disagreed with</u> her son's decision.

（五）高考真题的二次开发

毫不夸张地说，历年的高考真题涉及的话题广泛，是帮助学生提高语言能力最宝贵的资源。高考原题可以反复做，也可以反复改编。一方面，教师通过反复改编，提升了自身的教研水平；另一方面学生们反复接触、反复记忆、反复训练，日积月累最终就能达到提高语言和思维能力的目标。本人对2017—2021年高考真题进行了二次开发，包含了核心词汇、语篇填空和仿写三个方面。实践证明，把同一份高考真题反复做几遍比做几十篇新题更有价值。学生普遍反映这种做法利于夯实基础，提分效果明显。现选取2019年高考部分原题为模板，供大家参考。

高考原题专项训练之2019年全国卷1

【范例1】阅读B篇

For Canaan Elementary's second grade in Patchogue, N.Y., today is speech day, and right now it's Chris Palaez's turn. The 8-year-old is the joker of the class. With shining dark eyes, he seems like the kind of kid who would enjoy public speaking.

But he's nervous. "I'm here to tell you today why you should...should..." Chris trips on the "-ld", a pronunciation difficulty for many non-native English speakers. His teacher, Thomas Whaley, is next to him, whispering support. "...Vote for...me..." Except for some stumbles, Chris is doing amazingly well. When he brings his speech to a nice conclusion, Whaley invites the rest of the class to praise him.

A son of immigrants, Chris started learning English a little over three years ago. Whaley recalls（回想起）how at the beginning of the year, when called upon to read, Chris would excuse himself to go to the bathroom.

Learning English as a second language can be a painful experience. What you need is a great teacher who lets you make mistakes. "It takes a lot for any student，" Whaley explains， "especially for a student who is learning English as their new language, to feel confident enough to say, 'I don't know, but I want to know.'"

Whaley got the idea of this second-grade presidential campaign project when he asked the children one day to raise their hands if they thought they could never be a president. The answer broke his heart. Whaley says the project is about more than just learning to read and speak in public. He wants these kids to learn to boast（夸耀）about themselves.

"Boasting about yourself, and your best qualities," Whaley says, "is very difficult for a child who came into the classroom not feeling confident."

任务1：词汇学习

1. speech day

2. It's one's turn

3. joker

4. shine（v.）——_____（过去式）——_____（过去分词）

5. seem like

6. kid

7. public speaking

8. nervous

9. pronounce（v.）——_____（n.）

10. difficult（adj.）——_____（n.）

11. whisper

12. support

13. vote

14. except for

15. amaze（v.）——_____（adj.）——_____（adj.）——_____（n.）

16. conclude（v.）——_____（n.）

17. praise

18. immigrant

19. recall

20. a painful experience

21. make mistakes

22. explain（v.）——_____（n.）

23. feel confident

24. presidential campaign project

25. raise one's hands

26. break one's heart break（v.）——_____（过去式）——_____（过去分词）

27. in public

28. boast about

29. quality（n.）——_____（名词复数）

任务2：如何找出下列问题的答案？

24. What made Chris nervous?

    A. Telling a story.   B. Making a speech.

    C. Taking a test.   D. Answering a question.

25. What does the underlined word "stumbles" in Paragraph 2 refer to?

    A. Improper pauses.   B. Bad manners.

    C. Spelling mistakes.   D. Silly jokes.

26. We can infer that the purpose of Whaley's project is to_____.

    A. help students see their own strengths

    B. assess students' public speaking skills

    C. prepare students for their future jobs

    D. inspire students' love for politics

27. Which of the following best describes Whaley as a teacher?

    A. Humorous.   B. Ambitious.

    C. Caring.   D. Demanding.

任务3：画出文章的结构图

任务4：语篇填空

For Canaan Elementary's second grade in Patchogue, N.Y., today is speech day, and right now it's Chris Palaez's turn. The 8-year-old is the joker of the class. 1. _____ shining dark eyes, he seems like the kind of kid 2. _____ would enjoy public speaking.

But he's nervous. "I'm here 3. _____（tell）you today why you should...should..." Chris trips on the "-ld", a pronunciation 4. _____（difficult）for many non-native English speakers. His teacher, Thomas Whaley, is next to him, 5. _____（whisper）support. "...Vote for...me..." Except for some stumbles, Chris is doing 6. _____（amazing）well. When he brings his speech to a nice 7. _____（conclude）, Whaley invites the rest of the class

8. _____（praise）him.

A son of immigrants, Chris 9. _____（start）learning English a little over three years ago. Whaley recalls（回想起）how at the beginning of the year, when 10. _____（call）upon to read, Chris would excuse himself to go to the bathroom.

11. _____（learn）English as a second language can be a 12. _____（pain）experience. 13. _____ you need is a great teacher who 14. _____（let）you make mistakes. "It takes a lot for any student," Whaley explains, "especially for a student 15. _____ is learning English 16. _____their new language, to feel confident enough 17. _____（say）,'I don't know, but I want to know.'"

Whaley got the idea of this second-grade presidential campaign project when he asked the children one day 18. _____（raise）their hands if they thought they could never be 19. _____ president. The answer broke his heart. Whaley says the project is about more than just learning to read and speak in public. He wants these kids 20. _____（learn）to boast（夸耀）about themselves.

"Boasting about yourself, and your best qualities," Whaley says, "is very difficult for a child 21. _____ came into the classroom not 22. _____（feel）confident."

任务5：仿写

1. With shining dark eyes, he seems like the kind of kid who would enjoy public speaking.

句式分析：

仿写：

2. I'm here to tell you today why you should...should...

句式分析：

仿写：

3. Learning English as a second language can be a painful experience.

句式分析：

仿写：

4. What you need is a great teacher who lets you make mistakes.

句式分析：

仿写：

5. He wants these kids to learn to boast（夸耀）about themselves.

句式分析：

仿写：

6. "Boasting about yourself, and your best qualities," Whaley says, "is very difficult for a child who came into the classroom not feeling confident."

句式分析：

仿写：

【范例2】完形填空

阅读下面短文，从短文后各题所给的A、B、C和D四个选项中，选出可以填入空白处的最佳选项。

Every year about 40,000 people attempt to climb Kilimanjaro, the highest mountain in Africa. They __41__ with them lots of waste. The __42__ might damage the beauty of the place. The glaciers（冰川）are disappearing, changing the __43__ of Kilimanjaro.

Hearing these stories, I'm __44__ about the place—other destinations are described as "purer" natural experiences.

However, I soon __45__ that much has changed since the days of disturbing reports of __46__ among tons of rubbish. I find a __47__ mountain, with toilets at camps and along the paths. The environmental challenges are __48__ but the efforts made by the Tanzania National Park Authority seem to be __49__.

The best of a Kilimanjaro __50__, in my opinion, isn't reaching the top. Mountains are __51__ as spiritual places by many cultures. This __52__ is especially evident on Kilimanjaro as __53__ go through five ecosystems（生态系统）in the space of a few kilometres. At the base is a rainforest. It ends abruptly at 3,000 metres, __54__ lands of low growing plants. Further up, the weather __55__ —low clouds envelop the mountainsides, which are covered with thick grass. I __56__ twelve shades of green from where I stand. Above 4,000 metres is the highland __57__: gravel（砾石）, stones and rocks. __58__ you climb into an arctic-like zone with __59__ snow and the glaciers that may soon disappear.

Does Kilimanjaro __60__ its reputation as a crowded mountain with lines of tourists ruining the atmosphere of peace? I found the opposite to be true.

41. A. keep   B. mix

    C. connect   D. bring

42. A. stories   B. buildings

    C. crowds   D. reporters

43. A. position   B. age

    C. face   D. name

44. A. silent   B. sceptical

    C. serious   D. crazy

45. A. discover   B. argue

    C. decide   D. advocate

46. A. equipment   B. grass

    C. camps   D. stones

47. A. remote   B. quiet

    C. tall   D. clean

48. A. new   B. special

    C. significant   D. necessary

49. A. paying off   B.spreading out

    C. blowing up   D. fading away

50. A. atmosphere   B. experience

    C. experiment   D. sight

51. A. studied   B. observed

    C. explored   D. regarded

52. A. view   B. quality

    C. reason   D. purpose

53. A. scientists   B. climbers

    C. locals   D. officials

54. A. holding on to   B.going back to

C. living up to   D. giving way to

55. A. changes   B. clears

    C. improves   D. permits

56. A. match   B. imagine

    C. count   D. add

57. A. village   B. desert

    C. road   D. lake

58. A. Obviously   B. Easily

    C. Consequently   D. Finally

59. A. permanent   B. little

    C. fresh   D. artificial

60. A. enjoy   B. deserve

    C. save   D. acquire

任务1：词汇学习

1. attempt to do

2. mountain

3. waste

4. damage（v.）——_____（adj.）

5. beautiful（adj.）——_____（n.）

6. disappear（v.）——_____（n.）

7. destination

8. be described as

9. pure（adj.）——_____（比较级）

10. nature（n.）——_____（adj.）

11. experience（v./n.）——_____（adj.）

12. disturb

13. toilet

14. camp

15. path

16. environment（n.）——_____（adj.）

17. challenge

18. make effort to do

19. in one's opinion

20. spirit（n.）——_____（adj.）

21. evident（adj.）——_____（n.）

22. abruptly

23. be covered with

24. thick

25. shade

26. zone

27. reputation

28. crowd（n.）——_____（adj.）

29. tour（n.）——_____（n.）——_____（n.）

30. ruin

31. atmosphere

32. peace（n.）——_____（adj.）

33. opposite

任务2：语篇填空

Every year about 40, 000 people attempt to climb Kilimanjaro, the 1. _____（high）mountain in Africa. They bring with them lots of waste. The crowds might damage the 2. _____（beautiful）of the place. The glaciers（冰川）are disappearing, 3. _____（change）the face of Kilimanjaro.

4. _____（hear）these stories, I'm skeptical 5. _____ the place—other destinations are described 6. _____ "purer" natural experiences.

7. _____, I soon discover that much has 8. _____（change）since the days of disturbing reports of camps among tons of rubbish. I find a clean mountain, with toilets at camps and along the paths. The 9. _____（environment）challenges are significant but the efforts 10. _____（make）by the Tanzania National Park Authority seem to be paying off.

The best of a Kilimanjaro experience, in my opinion, isn't reaching the top.

Mountains 11. _____ (regard) as spiritual places by many cultures. This view is 12. _____ (especial) evident on Kilimanjaro as climbers go through five ecosystems（生态系统）in the space of a few kilometres. At the base is a rainforest. It ends abruptly at 3, 000 metres, 13. _____ (give) way to lands of low growing plants. Further up, the weather changes—low clouds envelop the mountainsides, which 14. _____ (cover) with thick grass. I count twelve shades of green from 15. _____ I stand. Above 4, 000 metres is the highland desert：gravel（砾石）, stones and rocks. Finally you climb into 16. _____ arctic-like zone with permanent snow and the glaciers 17. _____ may soon disappear.

Does Kilimanjaro deserve its reputation as a 18. _____ (crowd) mountain with lines of tourists 19. _____ (ruin) the atmosphere of peace? I found the opposite to be true.

任务3：仿写

1. Every year about 40, 000 people attempt to climb Kilimanjaro, the highest mountain in Africa.

句式分析：

仿写：

2. The glaciers are disappearing, changing the face of Kilimanjaro.

句式分析：

仿写：

3. Finally you climb into an arctic-like zone with permanent snow and the glaciers that may soon disappear.

句式分析：

仿写：

（六）语篇写作教学实践

学生们有了一定的语言积累之后，进行写作专项指导也是很重要的。在以往传统写作教学中，教师指导写作学习通常只是泛泛要求学生读一读、背一背，模仿"范文"进行写作。学生自己摸索、自己体悟，老师对于范文并没有进行深入的指导。这种模式效果并不显著，其效果仅仅比教师不做指导让学生"自由写作"略好。

作文是一个由若干个单句组成的有逻辑有条理的语篇，所以在单句训练之后，自然就要关注语篇的写作。我在处理应用文写作教学时，确定了篇章写作的"四部曲"基本模式：Brainstorming—Sample analysis—Imitation writing—Evaluation。其中Brainstorming侧重关注话题相关的词汇、短语和句型；Sample analysis侧重学习文章的结构和好词好句，组织编写学生个人专用范文集。格式如下：

［学习收获］

1. 内容

_____

_____

2. 语言

（1）短语

_____

_____

（2）句型

_____

_____

3. 过渡衔接

_____

_____

_____

通过呈现范文，让学生从内容、语言（短语和句型）以及过渡衔接几个方面深入地学习范文，以达到知识的积累和思维的提升。

Imitation writing环节注重写作的程序性、策略性知识，强化学生不同文体的作文图式，令分散的知识点形成网状结构，培养写作思维，促进写作能力的提高。最后的Evaluation环节也很重要。通过班级生生和师生之间的交流和讨论让学生积极思考，学会品鉴自己的文章，对提升学生的写作思维和写作水平作用很大。

我们知道，新高考题型中增加了读后续写。这道新题型以读为辅，以写为主，其目标是考查学生的综合语言运用能力。最重要的是要求续写内容的语言表达需延续原材料的语言风格，体现协同性。所以对原文材料的语言风格进行分析并模仿显得尤为重要。在平时的课堂教学中，除了带着学生们阅读获取故事情节和分析人物之外，我还重点分析原文材料的语言风格，潜移默化地去培养学生关注原文语言特色，学会模仿。如下图：

［原文句式分析］

1. One day, Ben was playing basketball in the living room after school, when he accidentally threw the ball at a vase sitting on the shelf.［句型 sb was doing sth when .... ］

2. The vase dropped to the floor and a large piece broke off.［并列句］

3. What made Ben more upset was that the vase was not a common decoration but an antique, which was handed down through generations from the 18th century.［What made sb +adj + was th... ; which 引导的非限制定语从句］

4. To cover his tenible action, the tenified boy glued the pieces together hastily（匆忙地）and put the vase back to its place.［To do sth, 主句，其中不定式表目的］

5. As the mother herself dusted the vase every day, she naturally noticed the cracks（裂纹）that evening.［as 引导状语从句］

6. At dinner time, she asked her boy if he broke the vase.［if 引导宾语从句，表示"是否"］

7.（1）Fearing punishment, the suddenly inspired boy said that a neighbour's cat jumped in from the window and he couldn't drive it away no matter how hard he tried.［现在分词 fearing 作状语的句式；no matter how 引导的状语从句］

（2）The boy thought he would now be punished, but as he had already lied, he was detemined to deny everything to the end, no matter how angry his mum became.［but 并列句；as 引导状语从句；no matter how 引导状语从句］

（3）Before going to bed, the boy found a note from his mother in his room, asking him to go to the study at once.［现在分词 asking 作状语的句式；］

8. His mother was quite clear that her son was lying, for all the windows were closed before she 1eft for work each moming and opened after she retumed.［sb was quite clear th... before 引导的从句和 after 引导的从句］

9.（1）She realised she shouldn't just simply blame and punish her son for lying.［and 连接并列谓语动词］

（2）On seeing her son push open the door and cautiously enter, she took a chocolate box out of a drawer and gave him one.［句型：on doing sth, 主句；and 连接并列谓语动词］

实践证明，词汇、句法和语法是写作的基础，没有这些语言知识的积累就不用谈写作。而通过阅读文本获取大量的语言知识的积累恰恰能让学生的写作游刃有余。这也进一步说明阅读与写作相辅相成。写作能力的培养不是一蹴而就的，它是一个系统性工程。下面展示学生的部分作文。虽然学生的作文中或多或少还是有一些语言表达等方面的问题，但客观来讲通过循序渐进的训练，学生的写作水平得到了很大的提高。

（1）

As the twins looked around them in disappointment, their father appeared. "Oh, my God! What happened？" He said with a surprised face. After knowing the plan of the twins for the Mother's day, he got a great shock and said "How hard you are! Let me give you a hand." Then the twins followed the instructions of their father and tried their best to do them perfectly. When it is really too difficult or dangerous for them to do, their father gave them some helps. After the hard work and with the help of their father, they finally prepared the breakfast and added a card they had made. Then they stepped out of the kitchen.

The twins carried the breakfast upstairs and woke their mother up. Although their mum woke up tiredly, she soon felt very happy and surprised after she saw the delicate breakfast. She hugged them tightly and said "Thank you for your surprise! I am really proud of you！" Then they had the breakfast together. The whole family was bathed in deep happiness.

（2）

Finally John started his long walk. Listening to the water rolling down the river, he moved towards the light of city. In the dim light, he held the bat and kitchen knife tightly. He quickened up, which made him arrive at blocks of the city rapidly.With the heart beating quickly, he ran as fast as his legs could carry him. Meanwhile, a light of car shined his eyes.

At that time, a car was drawing closer.What caught his eyes most is that the stranger shook the window. "Hi! The handsome fellow, can I help you？" he uttered mildly. And then, John explained why he had a walk at the midnight breathlessly. With the assistance of the warm-hearted man, he reached the company in time. Thanks to the stranger's nice behaviour, everything went well on his first day.

（3）

As if by miracle, that middle-aged turned out to be the answer to my prayer. "Don't worry. I'll save her." he said as jumping into the sea without hesitation. Others on the beach stared at the man in shock. No sooner had he jumped into the sea than he was swallowed by the water. Gathering up his strength, the man swam to the boat. My daughter was so nervous that she shook all over and burst into tears. Just at that time, seeing the boat moving towards the bank, I felt a little relieved.

I reached out my hands as my daughter got out of the boat. The man breathed a sign of relief as others cast admiring glance at him. I held my daughter tight in my arms, deeply moved by him. Then I patted the man on the back saying "thank you very much". Looking back, I felt blessed someone had wanted to help a stranger.

（4）

Berlin thought it was a good idea. Then the brothers came into the forest and found a young tree. After coming back, Jack got some tools from the old box and they started their secret plan. After two days sculpting, the work finished. But Berlin thought there must be a bird on the cane, so a bird was added on it. After sculpting and polishing, the cane became more beautiful. The brothers came into the Grandpa's room, carrying cane behind, "We have a gift for you?" Jack and Berlin said.

Jack and Berlin handed the cane to Grandpa. Grandpa got the cane in surprise. "For me?" said Grandpa. "Yeah, we made it for you, we want you to cheer up!" They nodded. Grandpa gave them a big hug and kissed on their faces. "It's the best gift I've ever had." His eyes was filled with tears. At that time, Grandma, mum and dad came in. They smiled to each other happily. It's the love and care that makes the family members being closer and closer.

（5）

As if by miracle, that middle-aged man turned out to be the answer to my prayer. He jumped into the sea without hesitation and swam towards to my oldest daughter. Everyone stared at him in shock. My older girl was nearly swallowed by the boat. She was struggling painfully as well as I felt so nervous that I shook all over. Fortunately, the middle-aged man gathered up his strength and dragged my girl out of the sea.

I reached out my hands as my girl got out of the boat. Slowly and gently, he took her back to the beach. Then he patted her on the back professionally for some times. Several minutes later, my older girl gradually recovered. I holding her tight in my arms, we burst into tears. He could hardly conceal his excitement too. Finally, we conveyed our sincere gratitude to him. The others cast admiring glances at him. He gave us a smile again. This smile was so sweet that I haven't seem . Blanketing us, the sunlight witnessed the middle-aged man's kindness and selflessness.

（6）

Berlin thought it was a good idea. Thus, they began to make a cane. Excited and joyful, they were looking for a proper tree. Several minutes later, they found out a strong and tall tree.That is! They yelled happily.Then, they couldn't wait to cut down its branch by using tools. Eventually, getting a long branch, they were so tired that their clothes were sweaty.Nevertheless, perseverance is the success! Jack said. Blanketing them, the sun lit their strong will and great determination. After an hour of hard work, a steely and perfect cane came out.

Jack and Berlin the to Grandpa.Superb! Grandpa shouted wildly and hugged two boys in his Chest.Filled with tears in his eyes, he was deeply moved and surprised."I'll always take it! grandpa stated.The colors of the sunset was diffused across the sky. Only a sincere and heartfelt gift can not only make grandpa happy, but also make their love stronger.A pleasant breeze blew, making the tree leaves swinging, as if to be cheering for them.What the two boys did would serve as a reminder of love to grandpa.

六、写作思维培养过程化的实践意义

作文教学系列化、阶段化有效地引导学生写作从随意胡乱到自主有序，进而达到自我升华的境界，使学生的写作水平和学习成绩有了较大的提高。写作思维培养过程化指导丰富了写作教学的理论和实践。

我国高中英语课程的总目标中特别提到要注重提高学生用英语进行思维和表达的能力。探索能保证这一理念贯穿于教与学全过程的教学模式已成了当前教学研究的首要课题。《普通高中英语课程标准（2017年版）》（以下简称《课标》）界定思维品质时指出，思维品质的发展有助于学生分析和解决问题的能力。也就是说，发展思维品质的目的也是提高学生分析和解决问题的能力。同时，《课标》描述课程内容时指出，语言学习活动都应该在一定的主题语境下进行，即学生围绕某一具体的主题语境，基于不同类型的语篇，在解决问题的过程中，运用语言技能获取、梳理、整合语言知识和文化知识。写作思维培养过程化正是以《课标》为指导，以有效的探索应答了写作教学如何使教与学始终走在素质教育轨道上这一重要问题，并且以富有成效的探索建构了一系列写作思维培养过程化指导体系——文本阅读、范例仿写、创写以及特色学案使学生的作文写作面貌为之一新。学生的写作潜能逐步得到演进、升华，学生在写作能力、读写水平和高考成绩等方面都有了显著的提高，取得了良好的教学效益。

实践证明，阅读和写作是互逆的过程。阅读是理解吸收，写作是理解表达，充分吸收有助于有力表达。阅读是写作的基础。所以，回归课本，以关注不同题材和体裁的文本阅读为抓手进行范例式教学，通过阅读文本获取写作的源泉——内容、结构、语言。首先，以读带写，以写促读，引导学生把学到的语言知识、悟得的谋篇布局、激发的情感思维自觉地应用到写作中去，能够达到学以致用、提升学生的思维能力的目的。大量的语言积累是思维的源泉，没有一定的语言积累无法促使思维的运作和提升。读写结合这种模式适用于议论文、记叙文和说明文等各种文体，它对写作能力的提高以及写作抽象思维的发展有显著的促进作用。经过长时间的训练后，学生的作文结构清晰，能熟练运用中心句、过渡句以及过渡词；文章内容充实，言之有物、言之有序、言之有理。这些都是学生思维能力特别是抽象思维能力得到提升的表现。其次，充分利用文本，多样化阅读有针对性地设计仿写、创写等形式进行多层次的写作训练也是有效提高学生的写作能力和培养写作思维的重要手段。

　　总之，仅仅通过带领学生训练写作技能迅速有效提升学生的写作能力是远远不够的。想要发展学生的写作水平和能力，教师必须首先培养学生成为更好的阅读者。读写结合的过程是一个发现意义和创造意义的过程，读写结合的过程也是一个感知和模仿语言的过程。模仿是十分有效的语言学习路径，模仿也是培养学生写作思维品质的重要途径。

第三章 校本课程建设

一、背景介绍

1. 素质教育要求

2001年6月8日，教育部印发《基础教育课程改革纲要（试行）》标志着我国基础教育课程改革的基本方向的确立。根据指导纲要，要把转变教育观念，把握指导思想放在首位，并贯穿在整个过程中。坚持教师参与，使教师成为课程的执行者、设计者和创造者。教材不再是教学的唯一依据，教师要在全面透彻地领会课程标准的内容和体系的前提下，根据教学目标的需要、学生和学校的实际，对课程资源，特别是教材进行开发，以更有效地实现教学目标。

校本课程的开发是实施素质教育对学校提出的必然要求，是学校充分发展办学优势和特色，积极参与国家创新工程，贯彻落实国家教育方针，促进学生和谐发展继而推动社会的发展，培养和造就"创造新世纪的人"的一项基本建设。

素质教育要求培养全面发展的人才，要求突出学生的个性发展需求，这就要求传统的以应试教育为指导思想的教育目的、课程内容、教学方法等进行改革。而基础教育课程的改革只是这个变革的一个环节，也是最为重要和基础的一个环节。

2. 教师校本课程开发现状

在我国，传统课程一般难繁偏旧，结构单一。课程教学一般都是教师、课堂、书本三中心。而且长期以来课程开发主要由国家教育部门召集专家来进行，都是实行"研制—开发—推广"的国家课程开发模式，而教师则被排斥在课程开发之外，致使教师欠缺课程开发能力。同时，在中小学教师的继续教育工作中，培训一般多是针对教师的专业知识和教育教学技能进行的，而针对课程理论及课程开发能力的培训甚少。中小学教师普遍缺乏课程开发意识。不同层次、不同学历水平的教师对在学科教学中实施课程开发也缺少实践经验。

所以，转变广大教师的观念，提高他们的课程开发能力和教学效果已是刻不容缓要解决的问题。这对推动教育行政部门课程改革的实施有很大的借鉴作用，也能够在一定程度上促进课程理论的发展。

3. 坪山高级中学学生学情

大多数学生英语基础薄弱，英语学习兴趣不浓厚，国家课程相对较难，学生学习起来比较吃力，所以开发出一套适合学生实际水平又能提升学生学习本课程的兴趣和综合能力的校本课程尤为重要。

二、理论基础

（一）学习风格和学习策略

语言学习中，语言作为学习的对象，其本身特质是不变的。学习者在学习过程中之所以会产生各种差异，并且在学习成效上出现千差万别的特点，主要是由于学习者在生理和心理方面的差异，不同的个体在接受信息时所依赖的感官是不同的，每个个体针对不同的情况都有自己偏好的接受外部信息的感官（Ronald R. Schmeck）。

从二语习得的相关理论来看，当学生按照自己的学习风格（learning styles）来学习时，他们将学得更加有效；当学生的学习风格和教师的教学方式相匹配的时候，他们学习的动力、表现和成绩将得到大幅度的提升和加强。

学习者的学习风格与学习策略（learning strategies）中的认知策略、元认知策略、情感策略、社会策略等方面可以通过一定的学习活动联系在一起，两者是相互影响的。并且它们可通过一定的语言学习活动（activities）相互促进，学习风格、学习策略和学习活动之间的交叉联系如下表：

Learning styles	Strategies needed	Possible activities （some examples）
Auditory	Cognitive	Watch English language TV programs or movies spoken in English; Listen to English radio programs
Extroverted	Cognitive&Social/ Affective	To relax oneself when he feels afraid of using English; more pair work and group work
Reflective	Metacognitive	Consider and reflect on the process of self-English learning; Make schedules for studying English

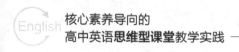

（Learning Strategies and Learning Styles by Ronald R. Schmeck）

学习风格、学习策略和学习活动将教师和学生这对教与学的主体有机地联系了起来。既关注了学生的心理特点，又关注了语言本身的特性，此外还将教师的教学活动与学生的学习活动有机地融合了起来。

（二）布鲁纳的结构主义课程论

布鲁纳主张，不论我们教什么学科，务必使学生理解学科的基本结构。所谓学科的基本结构，就是学科的基本的原理、基础的公理和普遍性的主题。学科结构不是只有单一的模式，故可重组为各种特殊的结构。课程设计应依据学科知识的基本结构。他提出了以螺旋课程来组织和实施学科的课程结构，要求：

第一，课程内容的编排要系列化。

第二，使学科的知识结构与儿童的认知结构相统一。

第三，重视知识的形成过程。

布鲁纳结构主义课程论对我国当今课程改革有着重要启示。树立主体性教育的思想和意识是我国课程改革成功的根本前提。进行教材改革和课程开发是我国教改，实施素质教育的必要辅助。

（三）泰勒原理

泰勒在《课程与教学的基本原理》一书中开宗明义地指出，开发任何课程和教学计划都必须回答四个基本问题：

（1）学校应该试图达到什么教育目标？

（2）提供什么教育经验最有可能达到这些目标？

（3）怎样有效地组织这些教育经验？

（4）我们如何确定这些目标正在得以实现？

这四个基本问题可进一步归纳为"确定教育目标""选择教育经验""组织教育经验""评价教育计划"，这就是"泰勒原理"的基本内容。现代课程开发的理论研究和实践探索可谓蔚为壮观，但都是围绕这四个基本问题建构起来的。这四个问题因而被称为课程开发的"永恒的分析范畴"。"泰勒原理"被称为课程领域中"主导的课程范式"。

（四）扎根过程原理

英国课程专家斯滕豪斯在《课程研究与研制导论》一书中首倡课程开发

的过程模式。过程模式重视基于"教育宗旨"的课程活动过程，强调通过对知识形式和活动价值的分析来确定内容，主张通过加强教师的发展来激活学校课程，要求教师在课程开发过程中，通过反思澄清隐含在课程实践过程中的价值要素，提升课程实践过程的价值理解力和判断力。美国课程学者施瓦布认为：课程是一个相互作用的"生态系统"，它是建立在对课程意义的"一致性解释"基础上，通过这个"生态系统"要素间的相互理解、相互作用，实现学生学习需求的满足和德行的生长。

（五）吴刚平课程开发类型三维图

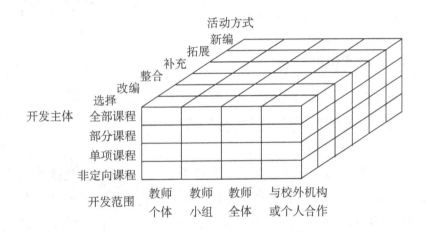

如图所示，校本课程的开发方式主要有六种：

1. 课程选择

它是指在众多可能的课程中由学生自主选择，由学生及教师付诸实施的课程开发方式。

2. 课程改编

这是针对原有课程，根据不同的教学对象进行一些课程上的修改，主要是指教师对正式课程的目标和内容进行某些具体的改动，以适应具体的教学对象与教学环境。

3. 课程整合

这是指超越不同知识体系，以关注共同要素的方式来安排学习的课程开发活动。课程整合的方式一般有关联课程与跨学科课程两类。

4. 课程补充

这是指为提高国家、地方课程的教学成效而进行的课程材料开发活动。课程补充可以是矫正性和补救性练习、报纸杂志、声像材料、图画、模型的摘选等。

5. 课程拓展

课程拓展的目标是拓宽正规课程，为学生提供获取知识、内化价值观和掌握技能的更多机会。

6. 课程新编

校本课程开发也可以开发全新的课程板块和课程单元。例如，特色课程、乡土课程、时事专题课程等。

三、校本课程的开发

（一）合美英语校本课程的提出及教材编写

1. 对现有英语校本课程与教学问题的分析

（1）调查问卷的设计

目的：本次问卷调查一方面旨在获得关于高中英语教学现状及英语校本教材开发情况的数据，了解高中阶段学生学习英语的困难和心理压力存在的程度，为思考开发何种适合学生的教材提供依据。另一方面，调研教师课程开发的现状及能力，了解英语教师在校本课程开发过程中遇到的问题。通过收集师生意见与期望，更好地开发高中英语校本教材。

时间：2020年11月—12月。

对象：坪山高级中学高一高二部分学生及所有英语教师。

样本组成概况：发放数据550份，其中有效问卷542份。

（2）调查结果的分析

① 对英语教学中存在问题的分析

学生：82%的学生喜欢英语，但是超过半数的学生对目前学校英语教学现状表示不满，其中对课堂教师教学内容不感兴趣和认为授课方式过于传统的分别占统计总数的37.47%和26.98%。其中，68%的学生明确希望老师上课的内容能丰富有趣一点，能多增加一些视听活动，不要整天讲语法做习题。43%的学生认同有亲和力、幽默感的英语老师能带动他们的学习热情。

教师：90%的教师承认平时课堂教学中教学内容都是围绕高考考纲，大都进行纯应试化教学，缺乏对学生兴趣和综合语言素质能力培养的关注。

通过调查与分析，我们发现受访学生中有36.1%的同学存在心理压力，经常会因为课堂上听不懂老师的讲课、课后不能完成作业、英语成绩差而对英语学习产生排斥心理，进而引发和老师的一系列矛盾冲突。还有21%的学生认为自己记忆力差、学习能力存在问题，认为自己无论怎样努力都不可能学好英语，缺乏学习英语的自信心。

② 对学校校本课程中存在问题的分析

学生：63%的学生表示对校本课程的内容不感兴趣，他们认为目前学校的校本课程的内容大部分都是根据学校的需要或教师的专业特长来开发，很少关注学生的需要。有45%的学生对能有机会参与校本课程的开发表现出很大的好奇和兴趣，希望能参与到校本课程的开发中，选择自己感兴趣的学习内容，并且希望尝试自主上课的课堂形式。

教师：98%的教师认同校本课程在目前课程改革体系中的重要作用。80%的教师有强烈的课程开发意识，但因为平时学校各项教学任务繁多而没有时间去关注课程的设计、实施和评价，使校本课程的开发只流于形式。部分教师表示对课程开发的流程不熟悉，缺乏相应的实践经验，希望今后能参加专业培训或得到专家指导参与课程开发。

（3）对师生问卷调查结果的小结

教师和学生都非常认同校本课程的开设。转变广大教师的观念，提高他们的课程开发能力和教学效果刻不容缓。

2. 合美英语校本课程开发的思路

（1）合美英语校本课程开发的关注点

① 课程开发要基于学生学情

作为教师，我们都知道课程的授课对象是学生，他们是一个个具有鲜明个性特色的独立生命体，所以，从课程内容的选择设计到课程的开发实施都应该充分考虑"学生的主体性"。我们要充分考虑学生的需求，"以人为本"，让学生成为学习的主体，营造轻松的学习氛围，精心设计平等交流的教学活动，引导学生积极参与课堂活动，激发学生学习英语的积极情感。俗话说，兴趣是最好的老师。

②课程开发要聚焦英语学科核心素养

课程建设是实现教育目标和教育理想的必要抓手，是促进教师专业发展的重要手段，更是培养学生核心素养的重要载体。英语学科核心素养包括语言能力、学习能力、思维品质和文化意识。核心素养的英语课程理念，就是从英语的工具性和英语学科的人文性这两个角度达成英语教学的目标。学科拓展型校本课程的研发也要聚焦学科核心素养，培养学生用英语做事的能力，在活动中发展学生的语言能力、思维能力以及交流合作的能力，突出对学生综合语言运用能力、创新精神和实践能力的培养。

（2）英语教师进行课程开发及教学的改进点

①转变教学观念

在英语教学中渗透人文关怀，落实核心素养理念，一线教师的教学观念至关重要。作为教师我们应认识到每一位学生都是处于不断发展中的、具有无限潜能的独立个体，所以不能因为学业成绩不理想而放弃帮助他们提升。每个老师都有职责和义务去帮助学生发现他们身上的闪光点，通过综合性活动激发学生的英语学习潜能，让每个学生都能不同程度地提升英语核心素养。所以，我们首先要改变思想观念，设身处地，以人为本地去设计开展我们的教育互动，通过多元化的拓展性学科活动涵养学生的身心，提升他们的综合素质。

②提升学科素养

校本课程的开发与实施关键在于教师，教师的职业道德修养、人文素养和课程开发能力迫切需要提高。只有加强教师的"育人"责任感，只有教师的业务水平提高了才能真正理解课程建设的重要意义，从而设计开发出适合本校学情的课程内容。

③多实践反思

通过问卷调查反馈，我们发现很多教师缺乏课程开发的实践经验，这对教师的专业发展是不利的。教师的确有很多机会参加各类专家学者的培训讲座。在培训时，教师可能理解了新理论，但一段时间过后，如果没有大量的实际工作情境来历练，那些新听来的教育理念就被抛到九霄云外，根本无法理解理论的全貌了。那么，课程开发也是如此。没有亲自实践的话，课程开发的能力永远也无法得到提高。所以，要培养教师课程开发的能力，学习、实践和反思是主要途径。不管结果如何，一线教师要勇敢地迈出第一步，做到"行思并进"。

3. 合美英语校本课程的教材编写

拓展型英语课程内容的重要载体就是校本课程。在课程教材的编写过程中，既要体现新课标精神，也要努力构建科学的、开放的教材框架体系，使教材融入文性、基础性、趣味性于一体。我希望通过校本课程的研发提高学生的英语学习积极性，让学生在教师的指导下成为学习真正的主人，学生审美品位、创新能力和个性品质得到发展，为此，开发了《合美英语》这套校本教材。这套教材不再是简单的知识体系的浓缩与再现，而是成了引导学生认知发展、学会学习、人格构建的最佳载体，同时也成了师生对话、沟通的桥梁。

（1）编写理念

高中阶段教育是学生个性形成、自主发展的关键时期，对提高国民素质和培养创新人才具有特殊意义。《普通高中英语课程标准（2017年版）》中提道："普通高中英语课程强调对学生语言能力、文化意识、思维品质和学习能力的综合培养，具有工具性和人文性融合统一的特点。"实施普通高中英语课程应以德育为魂、能力为重、基础为先、创新为上，注重在发展学生英语语言运用能力的过程中，帮助他们学习、理解和鉴赏中外优秀文化，培育家国情怀，坚定文化自信，拓宽国际视野，增进国际理解，逐步提升跨文化沟通能力、思辨能力、学习能力和创新能力，形成正确的世界观、人生观和价值观。这些学科核心价值的提出让我们真正关注英语学科人文性在日常教学中的体现。笔者任教的学校的办学理念之一就是"尚美"。在此办学理念的引导下我们培养的是追求心灵、语言、行为之美，具有创新精神和国际视野的现代高中生。拓展型学科校本课程的开发是学校课程体系建设的重要组成部分。课题组开发的校本课程是学校英语学科课程的重要补充，具有自身的突出特点。课程建设凸显人文关怀，课程的根本任务是全面提升学生的英语学科核心素养，培养学生英语学习的兴趣，促进其身心健康成长，并为其终身发展奠定扎实的基础。

（2）课程教材的编写原则

① 教材编写符合新课标要求

教材的设计和编写要依据《普通高中英语课程标准（2017年版）》的要求，以高中阶段学生身心发展水平为参考，确保教材设计的总体思路与《普通高中英语课程标准（2017年版）》的要求相吻合，合美英语校本课程的设计强调的就是凸显"人文关怀"的特质，正是顺应了《普通高中英语课程标准

（2017年版）》的要求。我们在此前提下统摄合美英语校本课程内容、教材编写、教学模式、教学策略、课程评价等课程要素，帮助学生通过感知、体验、探究、创造和评价等具有英语学科特点的学习活动，在英语文本欣赏及实践活动中形成英语核心素养、发展综合学习能力，促进学生全面而有个性地发展。

②教材编写突出学生主体

教材编写力求突出"以学生发展为本"的理念，从学生的兴趣、能力和实际需要着手，将学生已有的知识经验作为基点，尽力调动各种课程资源，适当增加课程内容与其他学科及学生实际生活的联系，尽量使课程内容多样化、丰富化，为学生营造一个自主学习的环境，培养学生主动探索、合作学习、自主研究的学习能力，满足学生全面而有个性的发展需求。课题组成员将通过课程内容的组织筛选、资料整理、研究讨论等方式，完成教材的编写。对于课程中不断出现的新问题、新情况，课题组成员合力、共同思考，并随时根据具体情境和出现的问题，反思调整、完善课程内容。由此课程开发、教材编写都成为全体课题组成员共同探索、解决问题、感受惊喜和共同成长的过程。

③教材内容体现人文价值

课程教材内容的组织要充分考虑语言学习的特点，凸显学科的人文价值，让学生通过英语教学感受语言之美。我们精选能充分发挥学科育人功能的相关内容，尽力挖掘各种资源，使课程内容既丰富多样化又能贴近学生生活，同时兼具时代特征。依据教材内容我们设计了相关的主题性研究型教学活动，将课程学习内容有机而巧妙地融入每个主题下的学习单元中，我们为学生营造自主选择的学习环境、积极创设富有意义的学习情境。

（3）编写思路

①课程总目标与架构

通过参与合美英语校本课程四大主题的英语学习活动，在学习英语基础知识技能的同时运用感受体验、创意想象、创造表现等形式和方法，学会英文表达，培养英语学习自信心，提升综合素养。

校本课程由"英语趣配音""英文歌曲大比拼""走进英语诗歌"以及"英语故事大王"4大模块组成，各模块包含若干个单元，涵盖了合美英语课程比较重要的几个方面。

② 课程教材的内容

英语趣配音系列属于高中英语拓展课程。英语语言的学习是"听说读写"各方面共同发展的学习，听说能力在语言学习和语言实际使用中占有很大的比重。同时，广东省高中设有听说考试，测验学生模仿朗读、听力获取信息和复述文本的能力。本系列选取适合学生学情且有趣的英文素材，运用通过准备、欣赏、模仿、展示、评价五个教学步骤，在课堂上开展教学活动，促进学生的语言学习、文化习得和价值观培养，从而提高学生的英语综合运用能力（特别是听说能力）和综合素质的一门课程。课程以学生为中心，以文化为依托，以语音为基础，以艺术为升华，通过真实的语境，培养学生具有国际视野和人文素养。

歌曲是一种富有表现力的艺术形式，英文歌曲也不例外。通过欣赏英文歌曲，学习英语已成为学生英语学习过程中不可或缺的一部分。本课题组正是基于上述考虑，开设了英文歌曲赏析选修课程系列，以介绍英文歌曲的基本知识并通过学唱与赏析学习英语，让学生在学习歌曲的过程中感知美、欣赏美、传递美和表达美，提高学生的人文素养，促进学生全面发展。英文歌曲赏析选修课程的设置旨在全面贯彻"关注学生情感和提高学生人文素养"的基本理念，这种选修课通过合理规划，进一步优化课堂结构，让学生亲身感受英文歌曲的无穷魅力，在鉴赏与学唱歌曲的同时，不断激发兴趣，得到跨文化意识教育，提高综合语言运用能力，促进身心健康发展。

为进一步培养高中学生的英语学习兴趣，激发他们的学习潜能，实现全面而有个性的发展，本人编写了英语诗歌鉴赏选修课程系列，精选具有不同风格的代表性的中外诗歌让学生去感悟体验诗歌的韵律之美、形式之美、内容之美。

故事教学是各学段英语教师都十分关注的话题，也是英语教学十分重要的研究领域，值得我们深入探讨。英语课程应当在提高公民素养、培育健康人格、深化生活教育、树立人生信念、发展创新思维、增强审美体验等几方面发挥更大的作用，而故事教学可以有力地推动上述改革任务的实施进展，这也正是研究和开发合美英语校本课程系列之"英语故事大王"的初衷。中学生的求知欲强，颇具好奇心。他们爱听爱看有趣的故事，教师应抓住学生的这个特点，激发学生的兴趣，提高其学习的积极性。恰当地运用故事学习新课，不仅能激起学生学习的欲望，而且能使教材深入浅出，加强学生的理解。本系列分为三个部分：读故事，讲故事、续写故事。精心挑选短小有趣的故事，通过复述、辩论、自由发言、表演、续写等不同的互动性教学活动，让学生爱上英文故事，学会英文表达，学会创作。

（二）合美英语校本课程设计与实施

1. 合美英语校本课程的教学模式

众所周知，教学模式是教学活动的一种表现形式，是在一定的教学思想或理论指导下并在教学实践中形成的，是用以规范教师组织教学过程的模型，具有指导师生进行教学活动的功能。

后现代教育的重要观点就是主张建构学习。建构主义的教学模式一般是以学生为中心，教师成为教学过程中的组织引导者，教师往往通过利用情境、协作、会话等要素组织开展教学活动，充分调动学生的学习积极性，帮助促进学生意义建构过程的开展，并最终使学生有效地实现对当前所学知识的主动建构。坪山高级中学合美英语校本课程的教学模式就是借鉴和运用了建构主义的教学模式，强调"情境""协作""会话"和"意义建构"这四要素在教学中的重要作用。在教学设计中，我们不仅考虑教学目标分析，还考虑有利于学生知识建构的情境来创设问题。协作应该发生在学习过程的始终。整个课程教学中通过师生间、生生间的协作分别完成对课程学习资料的分析、学习问题的提出与验证、学习成果的展示与评价等直至最终达成学生对学习知识的意义建构。会话是协作过程中不可或缺的环节，通过学习小组成员之间的不断会话来商讨如何完成规定的学习任务。在此过程中，每个学生的思维成果都为大家更好地学习所服务，成为集体学习的共享资源。意义建构是整个学习过程的最终目标，帮助学生对当前学习内容所反映的学科本质达到较深刻的理解。

2. 合美英语校本课程的实施策略

校本课程的实施策略主要侧重解决教学活动行为中所产生的问题，它包括教学方式选择的策略和激发学生学习兴趣的策略。

（1）重视课堂的生生对话，组织开展合作学习

合美英语校本课程的课堂注重学生的学习需求和情感体验，一切以学生的发展为本，教师不再是主宰，课堂完全通过小组合作的方式完成教学活动。课堂生生之间的平等对话使课程的实施过程成为学生学习经验的形成和成长过程，学生合作学习的过程也使课程内容具有多元性和开放性的特性。

（2）激发兴趣的策略

兴趣是学生获取知识、拓宽视野、充实内心的重要动力。在课程实施过程中尽量鼓励学生的全员参与，通过各种多元化的呈现方式来诠释学生们对歌曲、诗歌或故事的理解。如角色扮演、情景剧演出、即兴问答、模拟创作、诗歌朗诵等，学生们自编、自导、自演，在轻松愉快的氛围中完成学习。

3. 合美英语校本课程的教学评价

教学评价是以一定的客观标准对教学计划、教学目标、教学过程和结果的价值或特点做出判断，教学评价对教学的各个环节起着导向与质量监控的作用，是决定教学成败的关键之一。合美英语校本课程的教学评价是对课程教学进行质量评估和监控反馈的过程，能及时发现、总结课程教学过程中的经验和问题，不断调整，完善校本课程，使之更利于学生的发展。它的目的是促进学生的全面发展，改进教师的教学，是课程不断发展的重要环节。

合美英语校本课程的教学评价，弱化对学生的鉴定和甄别功能，贯彻素质教育的精神和"以学生发展为本"的指导思想，旨在促进学生的学习。课程评价的核心是促进学生英语素养的发展，通过突出学生评价的过程性和个体差异性等，建立发展性的、开放性的评价体系。

学生评价应是对学生学习过程和各方面的综合评价，而不是一个与固定标准符合的终结性判断。我们的英语学习不是为了培养语言学家，而是重在培养学生去感受英语的语言美，用英语去创造美的能力，所以课程评价应当具有多元化的评价标准和方法，用相对的量化分析和定性描述相结合的评价方法来达成"促进学生发展"的根本目标。合美英语校本课程倡导"学习共同体"的实现，顺应这一要求学生学习评价的主体应当从教师扩大为同学、自己，是一个围绕共同学习目标的共同体。教师在帮助学生学会自评互评、学会学习和自我教育的同时也应通过其他评价主体的评价反馈及时反思教学，调整策略，成为"可持续发展"的学习者。也就是说，有效的学生评价体系应当是一个相互制约、相互促进，不断提高完善的组织系统。

四、《走进英语诗歌》校本课程设计与实施案例

诗歌是用一种高度凝练的语言，形象表达作者丰富的内在情感并具有一定节奏和韵律的文学体裁。本课程系列以欣赏为主，引领学生走进诗歌的境界。

教师通过导—学—评这三个教学环节有效地渗透每一项核心素养。学生通过读、悟、述、品、评、诵和仿去感悟体验诗歌的韵律之美、形式之美、内容之美。在诵读的基础上，反复琢磨品味，激发学生自己去想象，走进诗歌的情境去体验，提高学生的感悟能力。同时，引导学生去品味诗歌的语言，为后续模仿创作诗歌奠定基础。模仿创作是本系列课程的点睛之笔。老师鼓励学生大胆进行创作，让学生在做中学以提高他们的创造性思维品质。

（一）Seasons of the year 教学案例

Task 1 静默阅读

Read the poem silently. When you read this poem, please find out the poet's feelings of different reasons.

Task 2 反复诵读

Read the poems repeatedly and try to answer the following questions：

（1）What are described in the first part of the poem? What kind of feelings can these things bring us?

（2）Why does the writer describe a kite and bees and butterflies in the second part of the poem?

（3）How does the writer describe summer in the third part of the poem?

（4）What is the function of mentioning snowy season in Autumn?

Task 3 深情朗读，感悟诗歌艺术

Read aloud the poem with great emotion. You will find in the first part of the poem, snow rhymes grows. They share the same vowel. Can you find out all the other rhymes in this poem?

Task 4 聚集点读，分析诗歌意象

When the poem says "trees and flowers forget to grow", do you really think that plants can forget some-thing? Can you find some other similar uses in this poem?

Task 5 学以致用，实现诗歌的创新

（1）Please fill in the blanks with proper words, making them rhyme certain words in the poem.

（2）Work with your group members and write a little poem with the topics of spring, summer, autumn, winter.

（二）《走进英语诗歌》学生创作作品展示

作品一：

> Thanksgiving Day
>
> Over the river, and through the Wood,
> oh, how the horse does neigh!
> The day is fantastic like flying the sky.
> The meal is delicious like broadering the sight.
> Hurra for Thanksgiving Day!

作品二：

> 登幽州台歌
>
> 陈子昂
>
> 前不见古人，后不见来者。
> 念天地之悠悠，独怆然而涕下！
>
> Before seeing the ancients, after seeing the comer.
> I think of heaven and earth, without limit, without limits.
> without end, yet I'm all alone and my tears fall down.

作品三：

> Mirror
>
> Aiqing
>
> Just a surface, which is unpriedicated
> It's the best of reality, and never hides any fault.
> It always be faithful to its owner
> People can find themselves from it
> Some likes it
> Because they are petty
> Some hates it
> Because its honesty
> Even others wants to break it fiercely
>
> 高二（21）
> 黄诗纬

作品四：

> 雨
>
> Rain is falling everywhere 雨儿正到处洒落
> It falls on field and till 它落在田野和山间
> It rains on the umbrella 它落在这把雨伞上
> And on the ships at sea 大海上航行的船队.

作品五：

相思
王维
红豆生南国，春来发几枝。
愿君多采撷，此物最相思。

YEARNING
By Wang Wei
Red beans grow in sunny South.
How many branches sprouted in spring.
I wish you pick more, dear friend I miss
The closest yearning they will bring.

作品六：

Unfortunately, there will never be "if only"
If only I had a wonderful journey.
If only my mother hadn't made such a bad cookie.
If only bees could send me some honey.
If only the honey thief were not a bunny.
If only the barber's name were Tony.
If only the boy's name were not Annie.
If only the child's house were made of candy.
If only the beggar's clothes were not made of gunny.
If only Mr. clown could still be funny.
If only he didn't have to worry about money.
If only the guy were not crappy.
If only everybody would be sunny.
Unfortunately, there will not be "if only"

高二(9) 石雨梦

总评：虽然学生的作品很稚嫩，不完美，但是能让学生们感受到创作的乐趣，增强学习英语的信心这就是最大的成就。

（三）《走进英语诗歌》学习心得

学习心得一：

> 这个学期我报了《走进英语诗歌》这个课程，在这个课程里有学到一些东西。在这个课程中，我们的授课老师让我们以小组的形式分享一个类型的英文诗歌，分享完后也会让我们创作一些简单的诗歌，一学期下来让我们受到诗歌的美好熏陶，获益匪浅。
>
> 世界上诗歌种类繁多，语言的差异也造成了诗歌的差异。不同时代也产生了不同风格的诗。它们给我带来不一样的感受，也能让我们感受到诗歌本身所具有的独特的文化和魅力。

学习心得二：

> Time flies like an arrow, time flies like a shuttle. 光阴似箭，岁月如梭。一学期也将迎来ending，英文诗歌鉴赏课也已完美落幕！
>
> 回想那些与同学们一起上鉴赏课的美好时光，让我难以忘怀！英文诗歌鉴赏课使我了解到许许多多的诗歌类型，也感谢黄老师给我们提供了这么多不同类型、不同时代的诗歌。课堂上黄老师娓娓道来，给我们设计了各类活动让我们参与其中。我最喜欢的就是诗歌创作这个环节。小组成员一起开动脑筋，乐趣颇多。虽然我们的作品质量不行，但是我们很喜欢这个思考的过程。
>
> In general, 我非常感谢黄老师能给我们拓展课外知识，提升我们的文学素养。Finally，也希望黄老师后面能开发新的课程，让更多同学爱上英语！

学习心得三：

> 校园中五彩缤纷的校本课程丰富了我们的课余生活，也为我们提供了展示自我能力与发挥创造力的平台。不知不觉一学期的校本课程就结束了，而这学期的校本课程让我感受颇多。
>
> 黄焱老师在第一节课时，就给我们每一小组布置了任务，让每一组的同学都做关于英文诗歌鉴赏的PPT，并让每一组上台展示。经过这一学期的学习，同学们在老师的指导下，每一个人都有了不错的成就，各小组都发挥了团队精神并且积极配合老师的要求。当每一组同学讲述自己喜欢的诗歌风格和类型时，不仅能锻炼同学们上台展示的能力，提高了他们的自信心，还能让我们在台下听的同学了解到更多的知识。同时，听英文诗歌配乐朗诵，还起到了放松心情、舒缓压力的作用。

五、校本课程开发的实际意义

新的历史时期对课程的思索成为摆在每个教师面前的新课题。后现代课程观主张构建动态的开放式的课程框架，无论是培养目标、课程内容还是师生关系都发生了改变，变得更为重视人的价值。本课题通过系列语言学习和创作活动涵养学生的身心，帮助学生形成英语的核心素养，塑造学生健康的人格。合美英语校本课程的开发实践是基于四大主题下的课程活动，通过具体的课程实施策略在我们的英语教学中渗透核心素养的培养。本课程真正从学生的发展需要出发，对学生未来的英语能力的提升产生深远影响。

当下，校本课程的开发已经成为一种必然趋势。校本课程的开发与实施有利于推动学校教学特色与品牌的形成。在目前国家的三级课程管理体制中校本课程有着它不可替代的独特之处，所以校本课程的开发应当结合地方特色、学校特色。本课程虽然只实施了一年半，但已取得初步成效。

1. 有助于坪山高级中学办学特色的形成

坪山高级中学合美英语校本课程的开发充分考虑学校、课程教师和坪山高级中学学生的学习水平和个性特色，在此基础上形成完备的课程框架体系。校本课程的开发是学校特色构建的一部分，本课程顺应学校"尚美"的办学理念以及"乐学、善学、活学"的学风，为学校的课程建设拓宽了道路，为构建高中生学科素养系列课程和创设多元化人才培养模式奠定了扎实的基础，有助于学校办学特色的形成。

2. 促进了教师的专业成长

合美英语校本课程的开发使教师的角色发生了根本性的转变。在校本课程的开发和实施过程中，教师从原先的课程执行者渐渐转变为课程的开发者、实施者和评价者，教学活动的促进者，而课程开发中解决问题的整个过程也将促进教师自身专业水平的提升，做到教学相长。

在校本课程的开发实践过程中，教师需要热情饱满地投入教学之中，不仅需要精心策划教学主题、创造性地设计各个教学环节，充分激发、调动学生的学习热情，更需要与学生建立融洽的、亦师亦友的新型师生关系。教学是一门艺术，课程开发的过程切实帮助教师锻炼了自身的能力，提高了教学领导力，使教学进入师生相互促进、共同学习、共同进步、共同探索研究的良性循环中,成为学生学习的促进者、教育教学的研究者、课程的建设者和开发者。

通过这次的课程开发我逐渐认识到研究并不神秘,从某种意义上而言我们每天都在进行研究,只要我们在日常教学中善于发现问题、懂得及时反思和积累,那就能在纷繁复杂的教育实践中发现有价值的问题,加以思考,并采取一些有效措施加以改进。

3. 学生的英语核心素养、综合能力得到提高

首先,学生通过系列校本教材的赏析学习、自主课堂活动的积极参与和一些创作实践活动,提升了学生的综合素质,英语学科成绩有了很大的进步。

其次,校本课程也激发了学生的英语学习兴趣。在整个课程教学中通过多样化的教学策略帮助学生融入不同的教学情境中,学生们在与小组成员的交流合作中,共享学习成果,分享学习喜悦。同时,我们通过对学生的整个学习过程的关注,及时发现问题,调整完善学习进程,大家群策群力,优化学习成果,客观公正的评价体系也帮助了学生更好地发现自身问题并及时加以改正。

再次,生生、师生情感的交流更为融洽。在整个校本课程的开发实施中,师生成为一个学习的共同体,通过一系列教学活动的开展,学生在教师的组织引领下共同学习、合作探究。在合作性学习活动中,学生以合作小组的形式参与各类教学活动,在小组学习的方式中学会了分享与交流,学会了分工与合作。

最后,校本课程锤炼了学生的心理素质。合美英语校本课程通过三大系列的课程学习,帮助学生获取解决现实问题的能力、锤炼学生独特的心理品质。在学习过程中教师鼓励学生大量运用了自主、探究的合作学习的方式,充分发挥每一位组员的特长和优势,在学习的过程中大家从陌生到熟悉,从一开始小组合作中的不知所措到之后的各尽其职,大家都因为有着相同的兴趣爱好和对英语学习的执着,为了达成既定的学习目标齐心协力共同完成学习任务。学生们在合作学习中逐渐形成了彼此间的信任尊重、体谅互助、自律反省等良好的品质,这也大大促进了同学间的人际交流,对于一些平时性格内向、羞于交流的学生而言,一起构思探讨的过程就是帮助其锻炼表达能力、提高自信的契机。

当然,在开发英语校本课程取得初步成效的同时,我们也清楚地意识到目前在英语校本课程开发过程中存在的一些问题。尽管以技术和知识的传授为价

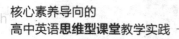
值坐标的教育方式正在慢慢转变，但纵观我们的英语课堂仍延续以学科知识技能为主导的教学模式。因此，一线教师必须着眼于每个学生的发展，推进素质教育，深刻认识到校本课程开发对学生未来发展的重要性和迫切性，并内化为英语教师的具体行为。虽然坪山高级中学的英语校本课程开发做了一定的尝试，但课程开发是一个长远的过程，针对课程开发中出现的问题和局限，仍需不断改进努力。

下 篇

课例研究与反思

第四章 教学论文

优化英语阅读教学，培养学生思维品质

一、思维能力的解读

思维品质作为英语学科核心素养的构成要素之一，对高中英语教学提出了新的要求。所谓思维就是通过分析、综合、概括、抽象、比较、具体化和系统化等一系列过程，对感性材料进行加工并转化为理性认识及解决问题的能力。我们常说的概念、判断和推理是思维的基本形式。无论是学生的学习活动，还是人类的一切发明创造活动，都离不开思维，思维能力是学习能力的核心。

阅读思维是指学生在感知阅读材料的基础上，运用自己原有的知识，去理解读物内容的一种心理活动。它能使阅读由现象进入本质，从而达到一定的深度。学生的阅读效果在很大程度上取决于学生思维能力的发展情况。

高中生的思维特点是从形象思维逐渐向抽象思维过渡，辩证逻辑思维日趋发展。这一时期是他们思维发展的"黄金时期"，而这一时期如果思维没有得到有效的启发，思辨能力的发展会受到制约，进而影响其创造性思维能力的发展，甚至影响其终身全面发展。因此在教学中培养学生的思辨能力，尤为重要。

二、课堂实录

下面以外研社Book 5 Module 2阅读课为例，介绍如何在阅读教学中贯穿思维能力的培养。

Lesson type	Reading		
Learning objectives	I. Knowledge objectives Students will master the key words, phrases and sentence patterns and make a good knowledge reserve for reading and writing. II. Ability objectives （1）Students will be trained to get the main idea of the passage and will learn how to get the detailed information. （2）Students' English critical thinking ability will be cultivated by group discussion. III. Emotion and attitude objectives Students' team cooperation consciousness is cultivated through the group activities and students will learn to judge others correctly and know themselves correctly through mutual evaluation		
Learning methods	Task-based approach, cooperative learning model		
Teaching aids	Multi-media		
Teaching procedure			
Step	Teaching/Learning activity		Purpose
Pre-reading	Look at the picture on page 12 and answer the questions. Where is the man standing? What is he holding? Can the bus driver see the lorry? Can the lorry driver see the bus? Predict what the title The Human Traffic Signal refers to		Warm up Ss and help students to guess what the human traffic signal refers to. Then try to predict the main idea of the passage
While-reading	1. Skimming for general idea	（1）Read the passage and find out the main idea of the passage. （2）Read the passage again and match the headings with the paragraphs	To train students' ability to obtain main information
	2. Scanning for details	Read the text carefully and do the following . Paragraph 1 The Road Find out the words and sentences to describe the road. Paragraph 2 The man Who is Timoteo? What is Timoteo's job?	

续 表

Teaching procedure		
Step	Teaching/Learning activity	Purpose
While-reading	3. Scanning for details	What does Timoteo get for directing the traffic? Paragraph 3 The reason why he does it What made him start this job? Describe the accident he experienced in detail. Why does Timoteo continue to do the job?	To guide students to grasp the main line of the article, clarify the structure of the article and mobilize the enthusiasm of students to explore
	4. Checking information from memory	Fill in the blanks with the words or phrases from the text	Train students' memory ability. Effectively output their knowledge
Post reading	Appreciate the passage	Work in teams and pick out the well-chosen words and well-organized sentences used by the writer and give reasons why they think they are good	Constantly update the language, improve English literacy and English expression level
	Reading for fluency	Follow the tape to practice the pronunciation and get enough fluency	To improve the fluency of the language, but also to deepen the understanding of the article
	Thinking critically	Group discussion and share your ideas with your group members. Is the job Timoteo performed worth doing? Why? If you were Timoteo, are you willing to do it?	To cultivate students' English critical thinking and knowledge transfer ability
	Writing	Topic: Timoteo and his job Introduce Timoteo and his job Comment on his job What can you learn from him?	To improve students' writing ability
Homework	1. Better your composition according to your teacher's and partner's corrections 2. Surf the internet to find more heroes who do the ordinary job and give a report to the class		To Consolidate what they have learnt in this class and train their writing skills

三、阅读思维能力培养的策略

以上教学实例说明阅读过程实际上是读者尝试与作者产生共识的活动。整个的教学活动清楚地划分成读前、读中、读后三个阶段。每个阶段的设计思路明确，读前活动体现背景知识的激活和语言准备，读中活动突出阅读技能、阅读策略的训练，读后活动指向语言的应用、话题的拓展和思维的培养。整个环节的设计由表及里，层层深入，步步为营，使阅读活动从整体到部分最后回到整体，理解的层次也由读懂到读深最终到读透。另外，在学生对文章理解之后，借助语境更深入地理解语言现象，同时，也培养了学生的自主学习、自我探究能力，赏析好词好句还可以引导学生感受英语语言之美，提升英语学习的兴趣。下面我将具体谈谈如何在阅读中将阅读技能和思维能力培养有机结合。

（一）读前：发散性思维能力的培养——头脑风暴法

读前活动是一项服务于课堂阅读教学的准备活动，它是阅读的起点，其成功与否直接影响学生后面活动的参与度。读前活动做得充分有利于阅读的顺利进行，因此需要具备一定的针对性。活动目的必须明确。课前活动要以学生为活动主体，紧紧围绕学生学什么和怎样学而设计活动内容与形式。读前活动的形式可以多样，如分组式讨论，熟悉话题，还可直接讨论文章题目或师生相互问答，也可采用预测法激发学生兴趣，为阅读做好铺垫。其中，预测法最有助于引发学生思考。教师可以利用课文插图、标题、相关词汇和信息提示预测课文内容，让学生说出或用笔写下预测情况。文章的标题就是文章的灵魂和中心。通过解读标题，采用头脑风暴法激活学生已有知识，并预测文章内容，以小组合作的模式，让每个小组成员说出一两个句子，连接成文，以此来促使学生提升发散性思维能力。在阅读中，通过比较，学生可以验证自己的想法或者纠正原有思路，使得思维更加深刻。

（二）读中：抽象思维能力的培养——整体阅读训练法与结构思维导图法的完美结合

第一步：整体阅读训练

"整体阅读"英语课堂教学模式是指在英语阅读课堂教学过程中对课文侧重整体把握、整体理解的一种教学模式，这种教学模式着眼于文章的整体，注重厘清内部的相互关系，从宏观上居高临下驾驭文章，领会文章的主旨内涵，吸收文章的精髓。

在整体阅读教学实践中，最关键的环节之一就是精读文本，寻找中心句，厘清段落逻辑关系。我们知道，在英语文章中，每段都有一个中心意思，有时候用一句话来总结，我们称之为中心句。中心句有助于把握文章的总体逻辑。阅读时应培养学生画出中心句的习惯。但当有些段落没有中心句的时候，则需要我们稍做总结。寻找概括中心句的过程正是培养学生抽象思维能力的有效策略之一。学生在归纳总结段落大意之后接下来就是对段落内部层次进行分析。即把握段落之间的相互联系以及把握文段内部结构层次，梳理段落中的各个句子的关系。我们要明白，在理解全文大意的基础上加深对语言形式和部分内容的理解，从写词句入手，经过判断和推理、分析与综合、抽象与概括的思维活动，达到对课文中心思想的理解，这才算读懂了一篇课文。

第二步：结构思维导图法

在实践教学中，高中英语的阅读难度一般是呈阶梯式增长，课文内容也是从简单到复杂，对课文理解力的要求也越来越高。在训练完查找中心句以及分析段落内部层次之后，老师通过"思维导图"的方式来引导学生巩固所学内容。实践证明，利用"思维导图"的方式引导学生运用点、线、面构成的图形模式来理解课文内容并让学生自己动手画出思维导图，有助于开动学生的左右脑，调动学生的学习兴趣，提高学习效率，增强了学生们的思维意识。思维导图是一种非常有用的图形技术。它能使学生知识的获取、储存和提取更加高效。

以上环节环环相扣，能帮助学生有效疏通文章大意，获取有效信息。从标题到文本体裁分析到中心句归纳，进而到分析段落内部层次，每个环节无不需要学生的抽象思维能力的参与。阅读能力的核心是思维能力，语言是思想物质外壳，作品语言信息的传递实质上是思维活动。因此，在阅读过程中要引导学生了解作品表现的一般思维规律，遵循认识思维规律，学会抓住词句以至段章的内在联系，从模糊含混中体会丰富的意蕴。这一做法长期坚持下去将有助于学生抽象思维的培养。

（三）读后：创造性与批判性思维能力的培养

读后活动是帮助学生围绕阅读材料巩固知识的环节，是让学生通过活动进行知识的内化、迁移，从而掌握英语知识的技能，陶冶情操，拓宽视野，发展思维能力。读后活动的开展可以检测前两个阶段的教学效果，了解学生对文章的理解程度。为提高读后活动的有效性，针对学生的思维训练可以尝试以下教学活动。

1. 概要写作

应新课程高考综合改革的需要，高考英语写作出现了概要写作这种新题型。它属于综合性语言测试，是将阅读与写作紧密结合的考查形式。概要写作把语言输入与输出整合在同一语境下，主要考查学生对文本的解读能力，对文本主旨大意和篇章结构的把控能力，准确获取关键信息和归纳概括能力以及独立表达要点的语言运用能力。这些能力的培养必须立足课堂实践，从多维度、深层次、全方位来开发学生思维能力。基于此，在阅读训练的读后环节，老师们在读中环节的文本分析的基础上指导学生利用思维导图，通过提取主题句技能，提取关键词和次要点技能，衔接与连贯技能，转换表达方式等概要微技能完成相关的概要写作任务。

2. 仿写

阅读是一种很好的语言输入。阅读之后的读后活动可以设置范文仿写的练习。通过阅读文本获取写作源泉，以读带写，以写促读，引导学生把学到的语言知识、悟得的谋篇布局、激发的情感思维自觉地应用到写作中去，能够达到学以致用，提升学生的思维能力的目的。

3. 问题讨论

读后讨论是运用已学知识参与课堂教学的有效形式之一。设计学生分组讨论可以深化学生对阅读内容的理解，进行情感升华，可以有效地提高学生的口语表达能力，又可以培养学生的批判性思维能力。以外研版Book 5 Module 2 A job worth doing为例，学生们学习完课文后，抛出问题"Is the job Timoteo performed worth doing? Why？"Imagine: If you were Timoteo, are you willing to do it？……让学生分组讨论。在学生讨论的同时教师加强组织调控，恰当地反馈评价。这一环节问题的设置非常重要。问题要具有深度和广度才对学生的批判性思维培养有帮助。通过激烈的辩论，学生之间进行思维的碰撞，有助于培养学生质疑辨析的思维习惯，养成富于机智灵气，清晰敏捷的日常思维能力，有助于提升学生的人文精神气质。

综上所述，阅读的过程就是发展思维能力的过程。阅读能引领学生的人生，实现其和作者思维的共鸣。所以，在实际的教学过程中，老师们要转变观念，优化英语阅读教学，注重培养学生思维品质，那么学生阅读能力的进一步提升也将指日可待。

参考文献

［1］曹刚阳.谈中学英语课堂教学的有效导入［J］.中小学外语教学（中学篇），2007（9）.

［2］黄远振.新课程英语教与学［M］.福州：福建教育出版社，2003.

［3］中华人民共和国教育部.全日制义务教育普通高中英语课程标准［S］.北京：北京师范大学出版社，2007.

［4］McDonough，Jo & Shaw，Christopher.英语教学中的教材和方法：教师手册［M］.北京：北京大学出版社，2004.

［5］王玉艳.新高考英语概要写作实践指南（基础版）［M］.广州：世界图书出版公司，2018.

［6］王笃勤.英语阅读教学［M］.北京：外语教学与研究出版社，2012.

语感阅读法与学生学习策略发展的研究

英语语言教育是对学生知识、技能、心智、个性、人文素养等多方面的培养。所以，基础教育阶段英语教育的本质是文化教育和人文教育，不只是单纯的语言技能训练；英语教育的目标是用英语学习文化，认识世界，培养心智，不只是单纯掌握一种交际工具。正如母语教育是对本民族文化传承的教育，那么外语教育也应该是对另一种文化理解、吸收和消化的过程。因此，外语教育的内容不应局限于知识的传授和技能的培养，应以人文素养的培养和学生心智发展为本。

但长期以来，我们面临的客观事实就是在倡导素质教育的背景下实际上是在搞应试教育。老师们为了片面追求升学率和考试分数，外语教育一直以学科课程为主，注重书本知识的学习，夸大语法学习的重要性，搞题海战术，侧重语言技能的培养。而在学生知识结构的完善、能力的训练、兴趣爱好的发展及个体特长的培养等方面就有所欠缺，妨碍了学生的全面发展。换句话说，当今的外语教育培养了一大批只会考试的工具。学生学习语言失去了原汁原味。那么，长此下去，学生自然就会对英语学习越来越没有兴趣，老师们教得辛苦但成效甚微，怨声载道。

为解决这一难题，转变一线教师教学理念、改变教学方法和内容成为关键。近年来，部分中小学校以"实施英语素质教育"为目标，实施"语感阅读法"，极大地促进了英语教学质量的提高。鉴于此，笔者展开了"语感阅读法对高中学生英语学习的影响"这一课题，探索能否通过语感阅读法培养学生英语学习策略的能力，提升他们的英语综合运用能力，进而提高成绩。

一、理论依据

在语言学习中，培养语感十分重要。语感是指透过语言形式对语义的直觉性理解；按乔姆斯基学说，则是语言习得装置对语音、语义、语言的系统感受能力（张正东，1999）。在语言学习的基础阶段，语言积累的重要方法就是"语感阅读法"。

第二语言习得过程是指"在自然和指导的情况下通过有意识学习或无意识吸收掌握母语以外的一门语言的过程"（Ellis，1985）。在二语习得的过程中，输入、吸收与输出是三个最为关键的环节。"输入"是指在语言学习中，学习者能接收到的并能作为学习对象的语言，输入的形式包括听和读；"吸收"是指被内化并纳入中介语系统的输入部分，从根本上讲，只有被吸收的输入才会对二语习得起作用；"输出"是指学习者在经过输入吸收后产出的语言与信息，输出的形式包括说和写。根据美国南加州大学克拉申（Krashen）教授提出的第二语言习得"输入假说模式"，如果学习者接触到的语言输入具备以下四个特点：可理解性、既有趣又有关、非语法程序安排、足够的输入量，那么学习者就能自然获得必要的语法知识，自然习得语言。

在二语习得理论的指导下，英语"语感阅读法"就是通过大量阅读（尤其是文学读本的阅读）来获得语言感受能力的方法。它强调学英语要"以读为本，拼读领先，听读结合，形成语感，分级加量，促说带写"；要"整进整出"，而且要大量地整体输入，整体输出，从中自然吸收语言。（韩宝成、霍庆文，2008）。"语感阅读法"所选的文学读本集知识性、趣味性、可读性于一体，并且语言纯正地道，因此非常适合作为语言输入材料。在这样的大量阅读之后，学生获取足够的可理解性语言输入，最终才能实现有效的输出。

二、已有研究成果

"语感阅读法"已经在国内100多所学校进行了实验研究。几年来的课题实验证明，英语语感阅读法不仅培养了学生的语感，还增强了他们学习英语的兴趣，提升了他们自主学习英语的能力，开拓了他们的国际视野，很多学校最终突破了英语教学的瓶颈，步入了良性发展、迅速提高的阶段。

综上所述，本文基于语感阅读法的实际可操作性，将对语感阅读法对学生学习策略能力的发展有何影响以及能否提高学生的整体成绩进行研究。

三、研究的设计

（一）研究对象

笔者选取了深圳市坪山高级中学高一年级的两个班级作为研究对象，其中，高一（20）班作为对照班，该班共54名学生；高一（19）班作为实验班，该班共54名学生。这两个班级的基本情况比较接近：两个班级都是理科重点班，两个班级男女生比例相似，两个班级的起点成绩比较接近，两个班级的英语任课教师教学水平基本相当。

（二）实施过程

根据坪山高级中学学生的实际情况，结合"语感阅读法"的特点，笔者使用《典范英语8》这本教材，每两周完成一个故事。要求学生利用周末（周六、周日）在家集中阅读，预习文本，做好读书笔记，摘抄译记书中优美的句子。每天课下念书20分钟，通过出声读给自己听，将"听"和"读"结合起来，增强记忆，培养语感。同时，每周抽出一课时，专门围绕所读作品开展各种教学活动，其中最重要的两项活动就是聆听和朗读活动，用它来促动学生听力和阅读能力的提高，其目标就是让英语听读成为真正的快乐体验。具体步骤如下。

1. 聆听

聆听先行，不阅读文字文本直接聆听素材3遍以上。在聆听的过程中，要求学生去欣赏朗读者纯正的发音、优美的朗读、张弛自如的节奏和抑扬顿挫的语调，尽量辨别出并逐渐熟悉英语发音中一些独特的音素、连读和音素组合分布模式。

为什么聆听是第一步呢？这是有一定理论基础的。原典英语学习法创始人徐火辉老师在《英语学习的革命——论中国人学英语》这部中英文专著中，强调任何自然的正确的恰当的语言学习法，必须坚持聆听先行、聆听为纲，而不是听说读写并行，也不是听说先行，或口语先行，更不是阅读为纲。这恰好说明了聆听在外语学习中具有本原的重要性。通过常识和心理语言学的大量研究告诉人们，聆听在语言交流中占据45%的比重，远高于口语或阅读。通过聆听获得语言信息，并以此在大脑中建立目标语言的正确的语音流表达模式，是阅读的基础。做一个并不完全恰当的类比：聆听与阅读，可以看作古代海上船舰的两大"动力"，前者是风帆，后者是划桨。如果只有划桨而不利用风帆，那么，任何船长水手都无法远航。

2. 朗读

首先，教师声情并茂地做示范性朗读供学生模仿，简单提示朗读方法。接着让学生自由模仿朗读，老师巡回检查，随时解答学生问题，如单词发音、词义及难句等，此时只给答案，不做解析。最后，朗读检查。让学生朗读任意一段，并用一两句话概括其主要内容，以检查学生的发音和理解。

3. 聆听

在基本理解文章大意后，要求学生不阅读文本，再次聆听英语素材2—3遍，仔细欣赏经典朗诵的传意、传情和传神，体会听懂比例大幅提升的快乐。

4. 拓展活动

在学习完整个阅读材料之后，教师让学生进行一些故事接龙、热点讨论、角色扮演、表演等拓展性活动，以帮助学生更进一步地理解阅读的文章，同时更进一步地提高语言的综合运用能力，从而达到学以致用的目的。

四、数据的收集与分析

本研究主要通过问卷调查、访谈和收集3次考试成绩作为研究数据。

（一）问卷调查

此次问卷调查采用了Oxford 1990年关于英语语言学习策略问卷。问卷共分记忆、认知、元认知、补偿、情感和社会策略六个部分，共50项。采用李克特1—5级量表计分进行答题。在发放问卷之前向学生做了详细的培训，并向学生说明，如实反映个人英语学习的客观情况，有助于确保研究结果的科学性。调查采取随机无记名抽样调查的方法，共发放108份问卷，问卷填写大概用时30分钟，答卷完毕后立即全部收回，回收率为100%，其中有效问卷为108份，有效率为100%。数据分析采用SPSS19.0进行统计分析。结果如下。

实验组英语语言学习策略平均分：

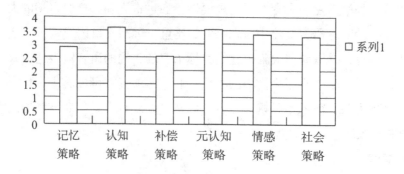

控制组英语语言学习策略平均分：

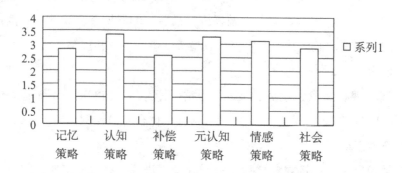

通过对比上面两个图可以看出，两个组的学生在某种程度上都有使用学习策略的习惯。但控制组的学生学习策略的使用频率均要低于实验组的学生。同时，在实验组中学生最常使用的学习策略有：

（1）认知策略

10.我练习英语发音。11.我模仿以英语为母语者的说话方式。12.我反复说写新学的英语生词。14.我主动用英语与人交谈。16.我阅读英语并以此为乐。20.我将我所听到的和读到的英语做成摘要笔记。

（2）元认知策略

31. 我尽量找机会多阅读英语。32. 别人说英语时，我很注意听。36. 我留心自己的英语错误，以便改正。38. 我尽可能以各种方式使用学到的英语。

（3）情感策略

39. 当我学习英语表现良好时，我给自己奖励。41. 每当感到害怕使用英语时，我尽量放松不紧张。43. 我和别人交流自己学习英语的体会和感受。

这说明学生们使用认知策略、元认知策略和情感策略比较多。

通过对实验组前3名、最后3名和中间层次的3名学生进行访谈，结果表明这9名学生的学习兴趣都有所提高，学习更加主动，养成了一定的阅读习惯，课堂上更加大胆、放松，在参与各种课堂活动展现自己的时候不会那么紧张，并经常会和别人交流自己学习英语的体会和感受。

总之，运用"语感阅读法"对于训练学生学习策略能力，促进学生英语有积极的作用。

（二）成绩分析

在本课题的研究中，笔者收集了三个考试成绩：坪山高中高一年级上学期入学考试（2015年9月6日），龙岗区高一年级上学期期末统考（2016年1月），坪山高中高一年级下学期期中考试（2016年4月24日）。

这三个考试都具有较高的信度、效度和区分度。龙岗区的期末统考和坪山高中的期中考试组织都十分严密，英语试卷分别是由龙岗区教研室以及坪山高中英语科组骨干教师命制，采取统一集中阅卷的方式批阅试卷。

1. 实验前后实验班与对照班学生的英语总体成绩对比分析

实验前两个班英语平均成绩的差异比较（坪山高中高一年级上学期入学考试，2015年9月6日）：

比较对象	人数（n）	平均分（M）	标准差（S）	Z值	差异情况
对照班	54	77.3	13.5	0.545	Z<1.96 无明显差异
实验班	54	76.57	12		

实验后两个班英语平均成绩的差异比较（1）（龙岗区高一年级上学期期末统考，2016年1月）：

比较对象	人数 （n）	平均分 （M）	标准差 （S）	Z值	差异情况
对照班	54	83.68	10.2	2.117	Z>1.96 有显著差异
实验班	54	87.76	9.3		

实验后两个班英语平均成绩的差异比较（2）（坪山高中高一年级下学期期中考试，2016年4月24日）：

比较对象	人数 （n）	平均分 （M）	标准差 （S）	Z值	差异情况
对照班	54	91.5	10.3	2.171	Z>1.96 有显著差异
实验班	54	97.73	8.9		

由实验后两个班英语平均成绩的差异比较表可以看出，实验班学生经过近7个月的语感阅读学习后，英语成绩发生了显著变化，有了很大的提升，逐步拉大与平行班的差距。正如胡春洞所提出的，语言综合技能可以融合教学思想，多种知识、多种技能的综合，综合就是统一、和谐、相互促进、相互配合、相互转化。以上数据说明了通过运用语感阅读法，让学生接触大量的原汁原味的英语文学读本，引导学生进行听说读写融合训练，可以在整体上提高学生综合运用英语的能力，提升他们的英语考试成绩。

2. 实验前后实验班与对照班各层次学生的英语成绩对比分析

由于"龙岗区高一年级上学期期末统考"和"坪山高中高一年级下学期期中考试"这两次考试的试卷难度系数比较接近，所以，对这两次考试中相同分数区间的人数变化情况进行比较，是有一定的科学性的。

实验前实验班与对照班各层次学生分数段的差异比较：

比较 对象	参考 人数	均分	≥110分 人数	≥100分 人数	≥90分 人数	≥80分 人数	≥70分 人数	≥60分 人数	<60分 人数
对照班	54	77.3	4	6	15	13	12	2	2
实验班	54	76.57	4	10	14	11	7	3	5

注：坪山高中高一年级上学期入学考试，2015年9月6日。

比较对象	参考人数	均分	≥110分 人数	≥100分 人数	≥90分 人数	≥80分 人数	≥70分 人数	≥60分 人数	<60分 人数
对照班	54	83.68	0	16	14	11	4	1	8
实验班	54	87.76	7	15	13	9	3	4	3

注：龙岗区高一年级上学期期末统考，2016年1月。

比较对象	参考人数	均分	≥110分 人数	≥100分 人数	≥90分 人数	≥80分 人数	≥70分 人数	≥60分 人数	<60分 人数
对照班	54	91.5	3	16	14	11	7	1	2
实验班	54	97.73	8	16	21	3	5	1	0

注：坪山高中高一年级下学期期中考试，2016年4月24日。

以上数据也证明了运用"语感阅读法"在提高高分段（优秀生）人数方面效果明显，在减少低分段人数方面也有效果。

五、结论与建议

综上所述，本研究得出以下结论：

（1）通过半年多的研究，笔者发现"语感阅读法"对高一学生的英语学习有积极的促进作用，可以显著提升高一学生的英语整体成绩。

（2）语感阅读法对培养学生的学习策略的能力，激发学生学习兴趣和自主学习都有积极的促进作用。

根据本研究结果和已有相关研究成果，本文提出如下启示和建议：

（1）转变观念、提升教师素质。新时期的教学改革关键仍然在教师。教师的主导作用不但不能削弱，而且应该进一步加强。这就要教师转变观念，认识到开设英语文学读本阅读赏析课的必要性和重要性。首先，不能只注重课本学习，搞题海战术，不能片面地认为阅读文学读本会耽误正常的课堂教学进度，或者把阅读赏析课开设成应试的复习课或必修课的补习课。其次，加强自身素质的培养，提高口语能力。英语教师的口语是英语课的门面。特别是在课堂上需要给学生做示范性朗读的时候，教师的口语尤为重要。只有教师发音准确，口语流利，音质优美动听，学生才能享受到语言的美，才会发自内心地去模仿。这样学生学得开心，自然就有成效。

（2）合理选择教材对英语学习也起着至关重要的作用。实践证明，阅读文学读本，特别是由经典名著改编而来的文学读本，拓宽了学生的视野，有利于提高学生学习英语的兴趣和提高英语综合能力，促进学生的全面发展。因为，在听读文学读物时，学生不再是单调乏味地学习单词或句型，而是亲临语言环境，感受不同场合中不同语言的运用。所以，教师应转变观念，构建新型课程结构和多样课程内容，为学生获得多种知识，培养多种能力提供可能。

（3）加大时间投入，营造学习氛围。因课时有限每周只开设了一节课，但光靠课堂上的时间是远远不够的。教师应充分利用早读、午读和晚读时间播放材料，训练学生的听力和朗读能力。同时，学校也应大力支持，为学生创造良好的条件。如定期充实图书馆内的英语原著书籍以及相关有声读物，设立选修课学分，举办校际原著表演舞台剧、原著学习交流会等。

六、结语

"语感阅读法"增强了学生学习英语的兴趣，开阔了他们的视野，加大了英语信息输入量，提高学生的人文素质，是我国中学英语教学改革的发展趋势。在中学英语教学改革实践中，我们要继续探索，真正实现通过英语课程促进学生的全面发展的目的。

参考文献

［1］Oxford, R. L. Use of Language Learning Strategies: A Synthesis Of Studies With Implications for Teacher Training［J］. System, 1989（17）.

［2］Collin J., Slater S. Literature in the Language Classroom: A Resource Book of Ideas and Activities［M］. Cambridge: Cambridge University，1983.

［3］梁亚平.高中英语新课标与英美文学名著欣赏课的开设［J］.课程·教材·教法，2004，24（6）.

［4］陈红.外语教学中的文学观［J］.外语与外语教学，2001（2）.

［5］韩炳华.中学开设英语阅读选修课的尝试［J］.辽宁教育学院学报，1997，14（3）.

［6］徐火辉.中国人英语自学方法简明教程［M］.北京：中国金融出版社，2011.

范例式文本解读视角下提高高中生英语写作能力的探索
——以高二英语Cohension and Coherence 写作教学为例

一、问题的提出

（一）英语写作教学的重要性

（1）《高中英语教学大纲》中明确指出："写是书面表达和传达信息的交际能力，培养初步写的能力是英语教学的目的之一。" 写作是一项很重要的输出技能，是"听、说、读"的综合反映，最能反映考生综合运用英语的能力。

（2）英语写作能有效地促进语言知识的内化。Swain（1985）提出"可理解输出"假设，认为包括写在内的语言产生性运用有助于学习者检验目的语句法结构和词语的使用，促进语言运用的自动化，能有效地达到语言习得的目的。

（3）英语写作能力的培养既是发展学生思维能力和表达能力的有效途径，又是衡量学生学习效果及教师教学效果的标准之一。

（二）当前英语写作教学存在的问题

1. 写作教学的目标定位不够准确

受传统写作教学观念以及英语教材的影响，很多老师忽视了写作的交际功能。老师们错误地认为只要学生写出正确的句子就行了，所以他们侧重文章句子层面的表达，注重机械性的句型操练，严重忽视写作的篇章整体意识。McDonough and Shaw（2004）认为写作的特征是："典型的材料组织原则包括段落安排，尤其是与功能类别相关联，以及一系列的篇章连贯方式，句子层面的语法练习处在一大段具有目的性和较长上下文中。因此，写作主要是以信息为本，语言的交际观就是其必要的基础。"可见，如果只注重指导句子层面的表达，忽视写作理由和对象、忽视谋篇布局思路，对于在写作教学中渗透对学生思维能力的培养方面就更不用提了，长此以往学生就只能是堆砌写作的句子，内容空洞。换句话说，学生没有真正用写作来交流情感和信息，慢慢地他们就失去了对写作的兴趣。

2. 重视程度不够，缺乏对写作过程的具体指导

写作一直是英语教学中的薄弱环节。很多一线老师重结果，轻过程，认为写作根本不需要教，学生多读多写自然就会了。平时按部就班地布置写作任务。学生写完后，要求学生背诵范文。很少会针对不同程度的学生进行写作策略的指导。一方面，写作前，不能有效激发学生的写作欲望；另一方面，也没有给学生提供足够的语言支持（如体裁、时态和必要的词汇句型等）。写作后，较少指导学生进行自我批改、同伴互评，也很少引导学生关注作文体裁、内容的构思、语言表达的修订完善。长此以往，这种无指导、无评价、无激励的"放任式"写作教学模式，脱离了发展英语写作技能的宗旨，很难有效提高学生的写作水平。写作课作为一门课程，连基本的"教学"的可能性、必要性和有效性都成了问题，可见写作课缺少"教学"的严重性。

二、教学理念与设计

（一）教学思想

Webb认为，阅读从某种意义上说是写作的"彩排"，阅读材料为写作提供彩排的道具（董越君，2012）。阅读是一种很好的语言输入。合理有效地利用教材阅读文本，在很大程度上能有效地达到输入和输出的结合。阅读材料其实就是一种很好的范例。通过有效阅读文本，挖掘出文本的篇章结构，深入分析文本是如何谋篇布局，如何衔接不同内容点以及有针对性地输入话题所需的词汇、句型，对学生进行写作技能的指导，帮助学生在模仿文本的基础上进行写作。这也正是范例式教学模式的精髓所在。

本节课挑选了两篇在文章结构方面具有典型代表性的阅读文本，侧重分析其中心句、过渡词，画出篇章的概念图给学生以直观感受。同时通过挖空补句的练习形式进一步强化学生的篇章意识。在这两个不同训练阶段，所选阅读材料具有典型性，有助于学生的理解。整节课思路如下。

理论层面 → { 范例1 / 范例2 } → 总结学习文章篇章结构特点 { 中心句 / 过渡句 / 过渡词 }

实践层面 → 练习1 → 训练学生语篇意识，根据篇章结构特点，选出
正确的中心句和过渡句以使行文连贯

练习2 / 练习3 } → 训练学生写作思维 { 根据篇章结构特点，写出中心句或过渡句 / 根据中心句，写出拓展句 }

（二）教学目标

知识与技能：

Students will learn about the skills on how to analyze the discourse organization from the examples and practice the skills in the real context.

过程与方法：

1. Student will be able to practice writing the topic sentences or transitional sentences based on the discourse organization.

2. Students will practice how to extend the passage based on the topic sentence or the transitional sentence to improve the cohesion and coherence of the passage.

情感态度与价值观目标：

Students will learn to cooperate with their partners and develop theirself confidence by different tasks.

（三）教学流程

Procedures	Activities	Purposes
Step I Guidance	Observe and Discover—Take two passages as the examples	To help students to analyse and understand its basic framework—how is the passage well organized?
Step II Practice	Choose the best sentence to fill in the blank in a context from the given seven sentences	To practice the skills in the real context

续　表

Procedures	Activities	Purposes
Step III Self- practice and Group discussion	Activity 1： Write about the topic sentence or transitional sentence to make the passage well organized. Activity 2： Write about some sentences to extend the paragraph according to the topic sentence or the transitional sentence to make the passage well organized. Activity 3： Share, compare and make comments	（1）To help students to master the writing skills on improving the cohesion and coherence of the passage. （2）To develop students' thinking ability. （3）To learn to cooperate with their partners

三、教学问题解决实施

（一）谋篇布局、框架结构的分析与训练——范例式文本解读法

根据《普通高中英语课程标准（2017年版）》对写作要求的描述，高中学生应具备独立写作的能力，包括收集、起草和修改素材，能使用常见的连接词正确表达顺序和逻辑关系，以确保文章的连贯和统一。同时规定对学生的作文主要从内容要点、语言使用效果、结构和连贯性、格式和语域以及与目标读者的交流五个方面进行评价。所以，思考如何将与话题相关的内容点连贯、合理地贯穿在一起，让人一看就感觉思路清晰、顺畅自然就显得尤为重要。在平时的学习中，依托阅读文本，进行范例式文本解读，厘清文章的逻辑结构将有助于这一目标的实现，切实提高学生的写作水平。在本节课中，主要从以下两个方面对文本进行解读。

1. 了解文章的整体框架结构

这一目标的达成主要是通过训练学生概括主旨大意的能力。主题句是英语段落构成的主要特点。对于结构分明的文章来说，寻找主题句是最好的了解文章整体框架结构的办法。在确定文章框架结构后，老师可用概念图直观地显示段落之间的逻辑关系。比如，在让学生阅读文章之前，我给学生布置的任务就是找出每一段的主题句。接着我给学生呈现了以下的概念图来方便学生去理解文章的框架结构。

Paragraph 1 beginning

> local organizations to help people stop smoking
>
> ↓
>
> Here is an extract from one of their leaflets

Paragraph 3—7 try the four Ds

> 1. Delay
> 2. Distraction
> 3. Drink water
> 4. Deep breathing

Paragraph 8—12 And here are some ideas to help people to give up smoking

> 1. Make a plan
> 2. Set a date
> 3. Keep busy
> 4. Develop new interests

这样的概念图有助于培养学生的逻辑思维能力，是进行有效思维训练的重要教学策略。在平常的教学中，老师要创设条件，通过对不同文体的文章结构进行分析训练来强化学生的篇章意识。在平常的写作中，老师也要培养学生以概念图的形式确定自己文章的框架。长此以往，学生就能慢慢养成列提纲、写主题句的好习惯，再也不会想到什么写什么，也就不会思路混乱了。

2. 分析文章内部的逻辑结构

在勾勒出文章的主体框架后，分析得出文章的内部逻辑结构就是下一步学习的重要内容。老师要指导学生学会观察段落之间的衔接手段，掌握怎样使一段结束后能自然地过渡到另一段，阐述完一个观点后怎样能引出另一个相反的观点或再补充其他的观点。在这篇文章中就出现了很多的过渡衔接语。比如：Example 1是一篇介绍如何戒烟的议论文。一开始介绍了有很多机构组织帮助人们戒烟，由此引出其中一个最受欢迎和最成功的例证。在具体介绍其做法之前，文章中就使用了"Here is an extract from one of their leaflets"引出下文。接着在介绍具体的建议之前，又使用了"When you really want a cigarette—try the four Ds"和"And here are some ideas to help people to give up smoking"来过渡不同的内容。而且在这两个建议之间，作者也使用了and 这个看似简单但作用强大的过渡词。在Example 2中，过渡衔接词句的作用就更加凸显。比如：

There are a number of reasons for this. Firstly, young people from villages usually want to live somewhere livelier and they often move to the towns and do not return. Secondly, people move to the cities to find work, as there are often very few jobs in the countryside. Sometimes villages remain because people from the cities have bought a "second home" in the village, where they come and stay at weekends. The prices of houses go up and people from the area cannot afford to buy a house there. Another problem is that it is becoming more and more difficult for farmers to make money from the farms. So they sell their land and find another job.

All these things mean that many villages in western Europe are fighting to survive. We can only hope that they will remain. The countryside would be a sadder and uglier place without them.

这个段落中使用了There are a number of reasons for this. 这个过渡句，接着使用了Firstly，Secondly这两个连接词，使得文章的叙述层次分明，一目了然。再比如，在最后一段"All these things mean that many villages in western Europe are fighting to survive."这句话中的代词"All these things..."起到了总结上文的作用。

由此可见，段落之间以及同一段落中的句子都不是随意堆积的，而是按照一定的逻辑关系组织起来的。在写作过程中，巧妙地使用衔接语，能使文章看上去逻辑清晰、结构合理、流畅自然。

（二）梯度练习的有效设计——抽象思维能力的培养

课堂上老师讲授完知识后，及时进行巩固练习。这一教学环节，是提高教学质量切实可行的好办法。及时的练习是巩固新授知识、形成技能技巧、培养良好的思维品质、发展学生智力的重要途径。所以，练习要进行精心设计。在本堂课中，主要设计了选择题和写作题两大类型。选择题是从7句话中选择其中5句话补充全文。写作题包括写中心句和过渡句以及拓展段落。这两个练习的设计体现了以下几个特点。

（1）练习的设计紧扣了教学目标。一道优秀的作业设计能促进教学目标的达成，两者紧密相关。巩固练习，不仅给我们揭示了教学的目标，同时也提示了达成目标的途径。可以说，本堂课设计的课堂练习能有效地达成教学目标。

（2）练习设计体现了阶梯性和系统性。阶梯性是指布置作业要贯彻循序渐进的教学原则，以从易到难，由浅入深，由基本到变式，由低级到高级的发展顺序去安排，让不同层次的学生都能练有所得。正如本堂课的练习，第一层是基本性练习，目的在于检查学生是否明白中心句及过渡词句的作用，明白段落衔接的基本特点和基本构成。第二层是应用性练习，目的在于让学生能运用中心句和过渡句完成写作。第三层是发展性练习，目的在于帮助学生深化和扩展知识，提升能力。从另一个角度来说，这三个层次练习的设计也体现了多样性。苏霍姆林斯基说过："学习兴趣是学习活动的重要动力。"只有学生对练习感兴趣，才会积极主动地探究。所以，老师在设计练习题时，要注意对同一项知识或技能的训练设计形式多样的练习。

（3）练习设计有助于激活学生思维。抽象思维是人们在认识活动中运用概念、判断、推理等思维形式，对客观现实进行间接的、概括的反映的过程。高中阶段的议论文写作要求学生有较高的抽象思维能力，即逻辑思维能力。写作是思维的运动过程，议论文写作教学需要从思维的角度来指导学生，才能从根本上帮助学生提高议论文写作水平。练习写好中心句和过渡句正是培养学生的抽象思维能力的手段之一。殊不知，英语思维呈现"直线型"的特点，因为西方人喜欢直截了当，习惯上把主要信息置于开头，然后再将其他信息补进。所以语言表达往往都是开门见山，直奔主题，以主题句（论点）开始，层层展开论述。所以要使学生的作文更具有英语味，要想提高学生的抽象思维能力，写好主题句和中心句是重要的第一步。

四、教学问题解决成效分析

（一）问题研究方法

教学完成后，采用学生问卷调查法，从"知识与技能""过程与方法""情感态度与价值观"以及"教学方法"4个方面调查学生对本节课的反馈与评价；通过纸笔测试法评价学生学习的效果，从而获得定量的数据。定量数据采用SPSS 16.0进行分析。

选取深圳市某中学50名高二理科实验班学生作为被试，整体学生基础较好。调查问卷共10题，采用李克特式5点量表计分法，选项包括：非常同意、同意、一般、不同意和非常不同意，分别记为5分、4分、3分、2分、1分。发放问卷50份，回收问卷50份，回收率100%。

（二）调查结果与分析

学生自评表各题平均分如下。

项目	题号	三维目标的具体项目	学生答题平均分
知识与技能	1	（1）通过本堂课的学习，我了解了中心句和过渡句的主要用途	4.91
	2	（2）通过本堂课的学习，我了解了代词衔接上下文的作用	4.89
	3	（3）通过本堂课的学习，我了解了文章的总—分以及总—分—总结构特点	4.83
过程与方法	4	（1）通过本堂课的学习，我对中心句、过渡词句的作用有了进一步的了解	4.87
	5	（2）通过本堂课的学习，我能自觉关注文章的篇章结构	4.71
	6	（3）通过本堂课的学习，我能把中心句和过渡句运用到写作中去	4.76
情感态度与价值观	7	（1）我喜欢老师通过大量的范例来辅助教学	4.94
	8	（2）本堂课比传统的讲授课更轻松易懂	4.953
	9	（3）我对本堂课的学习总体满意	4.912
	10	（4）我觉得此次教学内容杂而乱，没有主题	0.04

通过以上的问卷结果，可以看出。

（1）本堂课通过大量的范例进行教学有利于学生了解篇章结构特点，理解中心句和过渡词句的作用，也是学生们喜欢并认可的学习方式。

（2）利用小组讨论交流、内部评比的形式丰富课堂，改变老师一言堂，有助于学生对篇章结构特点的学习和掌握。

（3）第5、6两道题反映学生自觉关注文章结构的意识以及运用能力还有待进一步提高。今后要发挥本堂课的辐射作用，利用好每堂阅读课强化学生的语篇意识并加强针对性训练。

五、教学反思与建议

（一）整合课本阅读素材，发挥阅读文本的范例作用，提高学生写作能力

阅读是获取知识最直接、最有效的方法。在语言学习中阅读更是所有其他技能的基础，较强的阅读能力有助于学生对目的语的掌握。听说读写这四项技能在语言学习和交际中相辅相成，相互促进。阅读不仅可以处理为理解篇章，

同样也可以作为很好的语言输入。所以，从某种意义上说，有效利用好阅读教学，发挥阅读材料的范例作用就能有效提高学生的写作能力。但在传统的英语阅读教学中，很多老师忽视了比词句单位更大的语篇结构及语篇的分析，过多地关注一个个单独的词、句，关注语篇表层意义，缺少对语篇资源价值和思想内涵的进一步挖掘。这种阅读教学完全忽略了阅读的真实目的，也不利于提高学生英语写作兴趣和写作能力。对于写作而言，阅读材料就是一个写作范例。所以，阅读教学的目标定位是培养和提高分析语篇、解决语篇问题的能力，增强语言综合运用能力（黄远振，2003）。学生通过阅读，获取文本篇章结构、句式、词汇等写作素材后增加了自己的积累，为其写作水平提升奠定了基础。同时，文本阅读也有助于开阔学生的思维，使其写作能力得到提升。比如在学习故事类文本时，老师可以从故事情节出发引导学生进行思考，引导学生对原有故事进行扩写或续写。在学习观点类文本时，老师可以引导学生总结出议论文写作主体框架，分析出文章的论点以及如何论证再进行仿写。

总之，阅读课绝不是简单地完成一些表层的阅读理解题。我们要将阅读活动的坐标锁定在培养学生的"读者意识"上，充分利用教材文本，开展各种以读促写的活动，通过阅读能力的培养来辐射带动学生写作能力的提高。

（二）转变教学理念，重视过程性写作指导

我们不难发现在实际的写作教学中存在以下几种现象：

（1）写作通常布置成家庭作业，在课堂上老师至多进行几分钟的讨论或直接给学生少量的提示，让学生各自完成写作。

（2）教师指导不够到位，忽略写作内容建构，没有体现写作过程，写作过程缺乏思维能力的培养。

（3）光练不评。

（4）比较偏重批改词汇和语法。

这些做法体现出教师忽视学生在整个写作过程中出现的问题和遇到的困难，也说明教师自身对写作教学的方法、策略缺乏深入细致的研究。长此以往，学生无法掌握写作要领，很难提高其写作能力。实践证明，写作教学改革迫在眉睫。学生写作能力的培养是一个极其考验教师专业知识和人文素养的过程，也是慢工出细活的过程。老师们要从思想上转变观念，重视过程性写作指导，多采取一些技巧和策略。通过自己的切身体验与学生的写作实践进行面对

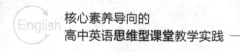
面的碰撞，在学生的思维上产生影响。

  总之，教师不应失去发现教学问题的眼光，不应忽视诊断和反思写作教学的行为，只有教师运用得当写作的教学策略和方法，加以示范和渗透，才能春风化雨、润物无声，那么学生写作能力的进一步提升也将指日可待。

参考文献

［1］董越君.利用阅读文本有效拓展写作教学［J］.中小学外语教学（中学篇）.2012，35（6）.

［2］黄远振.新课程英语教与学［M］.福州：福建教育出版社，2003.

［3］中华人民共和国教育部.普通高中英语新课程标准(实验稿)［S］.北京：北京师范大学出版社，2002.

［4］McDonough, Jo & Shaw, Christopher. 英语教学中的教材和方法：教师手册［M］.北京：北京大学出版社，2004.

［5］Swain, M. Communicative Competence: Some Roles of Comprehensible Input and Comprehensible Output in Its Development［C］//Gass,S. M. & Madden，C. G. (eds.). Input in Second Language Acquisition. Rowley, MA: Newbury House, 1985.

基于英语学科核心素养下的读后续写教学策略探究

一、问题的提出

（一）广东省新高考方案的实施

  随着新课程改革的深入推进，高考英语试题的命题思路和题型结构发生了巨大的变化。广东省新高考方案中英语试题中写作部分新增了读后续写和概要写作，这两种形式在不同考次不定期交替使用。一道题目，双倍难度。所以，不论是对于一线教师还是高三学生而言，这无疑都是一次巨大的挑战。2021年高考考查读后续写的可能性较大。如何攻破读后续写迫在眉睫！

（二）当前读后续写教学中暴露的问题

通过学生的访谈以及研究分析学生的习作，不难发现学生在读后续写中主要存在以下几个问题。

（1）提供的原文看不懂。

（2）读后续写的结构不清楚。

（3）解读原文不到位，导致续写文不对题。

（4）续写内容天马行空，脱离原文本或者续写内容缺乏创新，言之无物。

（5）续写故事情节欠合理，缺乏连贯，偏离主线，让人不知所云。

（6）续写内容立意不高，续写情节过于偏激或消极等。

（7）语言表达不规范，不地道，语法结构和词汇较为单一贫乏，错句较多，存在很多中式表达。

二、教学问题解决实施

（一）研读读后续写题型特征和《评分标准》

俗话说："知彼知己，百战不殆。"读后续写是什么？它的写作要求是什么？了解这些有助于我们高效备考。

通过研读《考试说明》，我们不难发现读后续写是集阅读和写作于一体的综合语言运用能力考查。它包含了"写作""阅读""分析"和"创造"。要求学生在阅读文本及其作者互动的过程中发挥想象力并创造性地模仿和使用语言。

同时，《评分标准》表明评分时主要从以下几个方面考虑：①与所给短文及段落开头语的衔接程度；②内容的丰富性；③语法结构和词汇运用的丰富性和准确性；④上下文的连贯性。

所以，文本解读能力、创造思维能力的培养是两大抓手，能有效突破写作瓶颈。

（二）文本解读

读后续写是对所读材料进行续写。要完成续写，学习者需要先理解原文，构建情境模式，而后创造续写内容。在创作过程中，学习者需要与原文的情境模式协同，以确保续写的内容和语言与原文连贯。所以一定要多角度解读前文内容，这是至关重要的第一步。那么，如何多角度解读前文内容呢？笔者通过教学实践发现以下策略和方法非常实用。文本的解读一般遵循以下两个视角：要素、细节。

1. 要素

我们知道，记叙文的话题一般更贴近生活，给学生的想象空间更大，语言容易把握，所以读后续写任务主要从记叙文展开。记叙文文本的解读主要关注人物、时间、地点和情节。首先，人物关系要厘清。其次，情节是关注的重点。情节是由一系列展示人物性格和表现人物与人物、人物与环境之间相互关系的具体事件构成，一般包括故事的开端、发展、高潮和结局。我们在阅读文本时，可以有意识地查找时间关键词、地点关键词来梳理整个故事脉络。比如，在2017年6月浙江省高考读后续写的文章中，我们可以列出如下的时间轴："On a bright, warm July afternoon—As Mac pedaled along alone— Then Mac heard quick and loud breathing—But a minute later— Then it attacked the back of Mac's bike—Mac was pedaling hard now— At this moment— A bit later—As they got closer."这一时间轴正好反映出整个故事的开端、发展、高潮和结局，有效地帮助我们获取故事大意，给我们呈现了一个非常有画面感的场景。

再比如，在2016年10月浙江省高考读后续写文章中，我们可以尝试通过关注地点关键词来获取故事的线索。"Camp overnight by a lake in the forest—by the time they reached the lake—After she had climbed to a high place—Jane kept moving—she had to stop for the night—Quickly she followed the sound to a stream—As she picked her way carefully along the stream."顺着这些不同地点转换的线索可以告诉我们女主人公Jane独自离开野营地后在森林迷路以及最后等待营救的故事。lake和stream是故事发生的关键地点。

所以，列出文章的线索，搞清情节的来龙去脉就为后续进一步进行文本解读奠定了坚实的基础。

2. 细节

梳理完故事大概脉络后，我们要继续研读文本。这一阶段我们要从字里行间找到故事续写的切入点。我们要知道，创新是细节的创新，而不是追求情节的离奇。所以，关注细节，找到切入点并厘清情感发展线是进行文本解读最重要的一步。

细节描写可谓记叙文中描写的核心部分，有了细节描写，整个文章才能吸引读者。有了细节描写，我们才能读懂人物。常见的细节描写可以与人物相关或者与场景、环境有关。在阅读原文时，我们要有意识地关注人物所看、所说、所做、所闻、所想和所感。其中，体会人物的所想和所感非常具有挑战性，但也是最有效的途径。人物的内心世界非常地丰富。通过人物的所想、所思、所感，我们可以体会到人物内心的喜、怒、哀、乐、思念、痛苦、怨恨、嫉妒等各种复杂的情感变化。而这些人物思想情感的变化正好又能推动故事情节的发展。当我们抓住人物情感变化主线时，往往也就厘清了文章的情节，这样就能合理地预测并续写故事。

再次以2016年10月浙江省高考读后续写文章为例，我们来关注对主人公Jane的一些细节描写。

第一处：By the time they reached the lake, Jane was so angry that she said to Tom，"I'm going to find a better spot for us to camp." and walked away. 从中看出Jane was bad-tempered and stubborn。

第二处："Tom！" she cried. "Help！" " The farther she walked, the more confused she became." 从中看出Jane was frightened and confused。

第三处："She wanted to hold him and tell him how much she loved him." 从中看出Jane was regretful and deeply loved her husband。

第四处："Quickly she followed the sound to a stream." "Feeling stronger now, Jane began to walk along the stream and hoped it would lead her to the lake." "Jane took off her yellow blouse, thinking that she should go to an open area and flag them if they came back again." 从中看出Jane was very clever and experienced。

文章中Jane 的情绪变化贯穿始终：从bad-tempered—frightened and confused—regretful—clever and experienced抓住了这些细节，我们续写的故事最终肯定就是她被成功营救，同时他们夫妻和好如初，感情更加的深厚这一美满的结局了。

（三）创作

深入解读文本之后，发挥学生的创造性思维，进行巧妙的构思就是最后的产出了。那么，如何合理巧妙地构思故事情节呢？ 我认为要做好以下几项专项训练。

1. 解读续写段首句，大胆设问，进行多维度衔接

续写部分所给的两句首段开头句规划了写作思路和框架。它们是基于原文背景下的顺延。这两句首段开头句起到提纲的作用，是非常有效的支架，所以在开始正式写作之前我们必须仔细研究两段的开头语。基于原文本和首句提供的信息，围绕中心词引导学生积极思考，展开合理的想象，大胆地设问，最终形成合理的故事情节线。学生提出的各种想法是否合理取决于学生对于衔接这个写作技法的掌握程度。我们知道，衔接是一种使上下文之间取得连接与过渡的写作技法，主要作用是使文章保持意义上的连贯、文句的流畅和行文的变化。

正如程晓堂、郑敏所说的，一篇好的文章不仅需要丰富的内容，巧妙的构思和规范的表达，还需要具备把这些内容联系起来的语篇衔接手段。在平时的教学中，老师们可以分阶段地通过不同的训练形式来引导学生关注续写内容与原文的逻辑衔接，关注续写内容与所给段首句的衔接，关注续写第一段段末与第二段段首的衔接以及关注续写段落之间的衔接。实践证明，学生往往最容易忽视续写第一段段末与第二段段首的衔接。因此，只有不断强化学生对衔接的认识，对这四个层面进行反复的训练才能培养学生进行多维度衔接的能力，才能有助于打开学生的思绪，产生更多合理可行的想法。

2. 讨论评判，碰撞思维火花

学生们通过头脑风暴有了各种不同的想法后，在课堂上，组织学生进行讨论和评判是非常重要且有必要的。首先，我们要鼓励每个同学都要大胆发挥想象力，写下自己的想法。学生只要写出来，老师们都要及时地给予肯定，不能打消学生的积极性和自信心。接着，以小组为单位组织讨论，让学生之间相互评判，碰撞出不同的思维火花。学生们既可以欣赏到一些逻辑性强、言之有物的想法，也可以发现一些欠合理、存在漏洞的想法。不管怎样，学生的创造性思维和批判性思维都能得以训练提升。

3. 精彩收尾，升华情感

一个故事的精彩与否和故事的结局存在很大的关系。而设想一个合理的结局往往是最容易被忽视的一部分。通过分析学生的习作，我们发现主要存在以下问题：①结局不合理；②完全没有凸显主题，升华情感；③主题升华牵强或跑偏。

在读后续写中，结尾发挥着至关重要的作用。能顺着原文中所描述的情节自然发展下去，以它的必然结果作为结尾，没有套话，没有空话，简单、自然，能让读者感受到"意料之外，情理之中"，能将整个故事补充完整就是好的结尾。换句话说，好的结尾一般都是与原文中埋下的伏笔照应，使人觉得在情理之中，或者与原文形成对比，点明主旨，深化主题。但同时，如果在结尾处能揭示故事背后蕴含的深刻哲理，能做到以小见大、从物到人、由事及理、由一及众来升华主题的话，那这样的结尾一定就能起到画龙点睛的作用，成为文章的增分点。

以The Last Delivery范文为例：

Upon hearing this, the husband had tears in his eyes and turned to his wife. "He was hungry, he was poor, but he was an honest man. "the husband said with a trembling voice. Hearing that, the wife felt quite ashamed that she had been angry with her husband's decision. And yet, she had no courage to look straight at her husband. Through all these things, she came to realize that honesty has no class and she should respect everyone regardless of their financial and social status.

最后一句妻子的幡然悔悟是对整个文章进行了一个主题上的升华，这对有钱的夫妇受到老人的品质的感动，他们的改变给故事画上了圆满的句号，也启发我们善良的品质能够感染他人。这就是我们所说的精彩收尾，升华情感的妙处。

三、教学反思与建议

（一）改革阅读教学，渗透思维能力培养

读后续写，读是基础，读是核心。读的深度决定写的高度。换言之，读后续写题型对阅读教学提出了更高的要求。阅读是获取知识最直接、最有效的方法。在语言学习中阅读更是所有其他技能的基础。所以，读后续写能力的提升很大程度上取决于学生的阅读能力。为什么读？ 读什么？怎么读？这几个问题是我们平时阅读教学中要着力思考的问题。我们的阅读教学一定要改变之前那种过多地关注一个个单独的词、句，关注语篇表层意义，而缺少对语篇资源价值和思想内涵的进一步挖掘的这种错误的做法。阅读教学的目标定位是培养和提高分析语篇、解决语篇问题的能力，增强语言综合运用能力。阅读是写

作的基础，阅读教学服务于写作。通过阅读教学，老师们要帮助学生将所读的内容迁移到写作中。Shanahan和Lomax（1986；1988）的研究表明，阅读与写作教学同时进行能够促进学生学习效率的最大化。所以，教师要具有读写结合的教学意识，有意识地在阅读教学中融入写作活动，并在写作活动中融入阅读活动。同时，对于写作而言，阅读材料就是一个写作范例。在平时的阅读教学中，老师们还可以引导学生在阅读记叙文时去把握记叙文的语言特征。寻找一些美句，尤其是寻找细节描写的语言，让学生们进行模仿和背诵，积累大量的语言素材，以备实现语用知识的迁移。最后，要把思维的培养和发展放在读写活动的中心位置，因为不管是阅读还是写作，思维都是关键。思维的层次决定了写作内容的层次。

（二）跨文化意识的储备

英语学科核心素养主要包括文化意识、思维品质、学习能力和语言能力四个方面。而文化意识素养的培养是英语学科核心素养的关键部分。另外三个方面的素养归根结底还是服从于文化意识。在英语教育中，跨文化意识不可或缺。具有这种思维能够保证不同文化影响下的人们之间的正常交流。在故事续写中，如果对于文本所承载的文化背景知识不了解，对于国外的文化不是很了解，就会导致情节不合理，甚至闹出笑话。所以，在课堂教学中，老师们可以利用各类文本材料，采用合适的教学方法，对比各国文化差异，注重培养学生的跨文化意识，对西方文化背景知识进行渗透，防止学生出现文化定型，对外来文化产生歧视。

读后续写是新挑战，更是新机遇。面对这一新题型，我们需要更多的实证研究和实践探索，为读写结合的教学找到更加清晰的路径。

参考文献

［1］王敏，王初明.读后续写的协同效应［J］.现代外语，2014（4）.

［2］成昭伟，朱晓梅.跨文化意识的培养：问题与对策［J］.辽宁医学院学报（社会科学版）.2009（4）.

［3］任丽燕.浅谈英语学科核心素养下的文化品格素养［J］.海外英语，2017（6）.

［4］Shanahan, T. & Lomax, R. G. An analysis and comparison of theoretical models reading writing relationship［J］. Journal of Educational Psychology, 1986, 78（2）.

［5］Shanahan, T. & Lomax, R. G. A developmental comparison of three theoretical: the reading-writing relationship［J］. Research in the Teaching of English, 1988（22）.

基于核心素养下的高中英语校本课程设计研究

一、问题的提出

在教育部号召下，各地学校和教师积极开发具有地方特色的校本课程，涌现了不少内容丰富、形式多样的校本课程。课程开发虽已起步，但仍然存在一些误区。

（1）学生边缘化。由于部分老师的师本位思想及其对教学的理解偏差，校本课程开发与运用在无形中将学生排斥在外。不管是校本课程内容开发、课程评价，还是在具体的教学实践过程中，学生更多的只是观望或追随。

（2）课程设计目标定位不准确。校本课程开发的目的是推进学生的发展。所以，课程规划的中心点是学生的发展。教师更多地要在充分了解学生需求基础上进行课程设计。

（3）课程开发与实施较形式化或者空心化。很多课程由于后期缺乏监管，上课只是流于形式，质量不高，学生参与度不强。

（4）在校本课程开发的实际评价中，学校和教师成了评价的主体。学生并没有参与到评价之中，或者就只是通过表格等方式提供一点反馈信息。

二、校本课程开发的理论基础与背景

基于以上存在的问题，笔者认为课程开发就是为人的学习活动进行计划、实施和总结反馈的过程。所以，任何课程开发都要针对时代特点、实际需求和开发者主观取向等因素来具体操作。学生是课程开发与运用的主体，课程开发与运用必须以学生为中心。学生才是课程开发与运用的中心地位。

与此同时，《普通高中英语课程标准（2017年版）》（以下简称《课程标准》）中提到，普通高中英语课程是高中阶段全面贯彻党的教育方针、落实立德树人根本任务，发展英语学科核心素养、培养社会主义建设者和接班人的基础文化课程。《课程标准》还指出，根据高中学生的心理特征、认知水平、学习特点以及未来发展的不同需求，开设丰富的选修课程，设计具有综合性、关联性和实践性特点的英语学习活动。在课程评价方面，《课程标准》指出评价应聚焦并促进学生英语学科核心素养的形成及发展，采用形成性评价与终结性评价相结合的多元评价方式。

所以，校本课程的开发也要以此为指导思想，构建指向英语学科核心素养的高中英语课程目标，注重提高学生语言能力、文化意识、思维品质和学习能力，并引导学生学会监控和调整自己的学习进程，重视评价的促学作用。

三、校本课程的设计

笔者所在的学校学生大部分英语基础相当薄弱，缺乏对英语学习的兴趣和积极性。只学习基础课程不利于激发学生学习英语的热情，所以开设适合学生学习水平的校本课程是一个很好的抓手和辅助手段。通过问卷调查和访谈，学生们表达了不同的学习愿望。综合学生们的需求，笔者开发了"合美英语"为主题的校本课程。此校本课程有着丰富而深刻的内涵。

（1）课程之美。科学、整合、选择和多元是"合美英语"的基础。生本、求真、灵动和创新是"合美英语"的核心。

（2）学生之美。至真乐美、至新创美是"合美英语"的灵魂，重在提升学生核心素养，化育希望。

（3）教师之美。敬业和专业是教育品牌的根本。通过系列校本课程的开发旨在加强队伍建设，进一步提升教师素养，成就卓越。

下面简要地谈谈本课程的设计方案。

1. 课程目标

以"人的发展"为基点是新课程改革的精髓所在。"合美英语"为主题的英语校本课程开发致力于培养学生的英语学习兴趣，在活动中提升学生的英语学科核心素养。教师将帮助学生去发现语言之美，不断创造出新的知识。

2. 课程内容

本课程共分为"走进英语诗歌""英语故事大王""英语趣配音"以及"英文歌曲大比拼"4大模块，最后通过自创报刊来展示学生各类作品。每个系列都包括单元说明、学习目标、内容描述和学业标准。我们融知识性与趣味性为一体，力求加强课程的综合性。在课程内容的设计中既注重学生的智力发展也关注学生的需求和自信心的培养，让学生在各种活动中都能找到自身的闪光点，从而激发学生学习英语的兴趣。

3. 课程实施与评价

本课程的内容设置决定了学生不再是知识的"被动接受者"，而是成为知识意义的主动建构者和创造者。在整个课程的实施过程中，我们鼓励学生多动手、多实践。在课程评价方面，我们采用一种多元的、开放性的评价机制，不断地根据实际情况建构学生评价的标准和方式。通过质性评价、表现性评价等方式来记录学生参与课程的整个活动过程，突出强调对学生学习过程的评价，尊重学生的个性差异，保证学生评价能始终处于发展的状态，以此来推动教学过程的生态发展。

四、创新之处

1. 英语学科核心素养在本课程中的渗透

本课程的4大系列始终紧扣发展学生的语言能力、文化意识、思维品质和学习能力，树立发展学生核心素养的意识，做到了重视学生能力的培养。以"走进英语诗歌"这个模块为例，教师通过导—学—评这三个教学环节有效地渗透每一项核心素养。学生学习诗歌的方式主要有：读，悟，述，品，评，诵和仿等。"读"的任务就是大体把握诗歌含义，初步想象诗歌描述的情境，体会诗人的情感。在诵读的基础上，反复琢磨品味，激发学生自己去想象，走进诗歌的情境去体验，提高学生的感悟能力。接着引导学生借助想象，将自己头脑中那幅画面描绘出来。这一步既培养学生思维的连贯性，也培养学生大胆说的能力。"品"是领悟诗歌的神韵。教师要引导学生去品味诗歌的语言，为后续模仿创作诗歌奠定基础。"评"是让学生谈谈对诗句的看法，阐述自己独到的见解。它有利于提高学生评价能力，增强创新意识。"诵"要区别于之前的"读"，这个阶段的朗诵一定要让学生进入角色，把原作品创作时燃烧着的思想感情再一次地燃烧起来。最后一个环节"仿"是本模块课程的点睛之笔。老师鼓励学生大胆进行创作，让学生在做中学以提高他们的创造性思维品质。

2. 课程开发的内容具有生本性

课程设计不仅要渗透核心素养，更要具有生本性。脱离学生实际而开发的校本课程不仅会造成学生在国家课程和地方课程之外的负担，还会影响学生的学习情绪，直接影响到学生的学习。这样的课程开发不仅浪费了人力物力还带来了负面的影响。所以，校本课程的最终归结点是学生。学生是发展的鲜活的生命体，而不是毫无自我的课程知识的接收对象。与此同时，在课程设计中教师们关注了情境的创设，基于情境来开展教学和评价。本课程的4大系列强调以学生的实际发展状况，以学生的学习能力、课外阅读能力为依据，通过梯度式、阶段性活动的设计来逐步培养和提升学生的英语学科核心素养。

五、结语

综上所述，校本课程开发任重而道远。一线教师不要偏离校本课程开发的初衷，注重课程开发目标的发展性、课程内容选择的生本性、课程实施的达成性以及课程评价的多元性，回归校本课程开发的本真和初衷。

参考文献

［1］徐玉珍.校本课程开发：概念解读［J］.课程·教材·教法，2001（4）.

［2］施良方.课程理论：课程的基础、原理与问题［M］.北京：教育科学出版社，1996.

［3］王贝贝.基于情境模式的校本课程开发：以红色历史人物为例［J］.青春岁月，2017（23）.

［4］中华人民共和国教育部.普通高中英语课程标准（2017年版）［S］.北京：人民教育出版社，2018.

高考英语读后续写命题特点分析与读写结合教学启示

2021年全国新高考卷英语学科命题以习近平新时代中国特色社会主义思想为指导，贯彻党的十九大精神和全国教育大会精神，落实立德树人根本任务，依据新课程标准和高考评价体系对高考英语考试内容进一步深化关键能力考查，有效鉴别学生的思维品质和发展潜能。本套试题注重联系社会生产生活实际，增强情境的时代性，提升考查学生核心素养的有效性。这点在新题型读后续写中较为突出。读后续写题考查学生能否运用英语基础知识准确理解文章故事情节，并结合所给的文本材料及两个段落的首句，发挥其独立思考能力，展开合理想象，运用英语词汇、语法等基础写作知识技能，完成一篇与给定材料有逻辑衔接，情节和结构完整的短文。

读后续写创造性地将阅读和写作深度结合，在巩固应用文写作能力考查的基础上，进一步加强了对英语语言书面表达能力的考查，更有效地考查学生是否具备高质量地认识问题、分析问题和解决问题的综合素质，全面考查英语核心素养，充分体现基础性、综合性、应用性和创新性的融合。这个新题型能够较全面客观地反映高考评价体系中"四层"的考查内容和"四翼"的考查要求。本文试从语篇结构、语言特点分析、写作构思三个维度进行定性分析，探讨高考读后续写命题趋势和对教学的启示。

一、读后续写的命题分析

1. 语篇分析

读后续写提供的语篇材料一般都是具有正能量而且故事性比较强的文章。体裁一般是记叙文，或叙议结合。文章一般通俗易懂，故事线索逻辑性较强，按照情节或时间发展顺序推进，有利于正面引导考生，充分体现高考坚持立德树人，促进核心素养落地生根的激励导向目标。与2020年读后续写相比，语篇不论在文章体裁还是主题语境方面都有相似之处，具有延续性。考生不仅能够读得懂，还可以产生共鸣与联想，从而写出恰当的续篇。

语篇分析		2020年读后续写	2021年读后续写
语篇长度		8段，334词	3段，308词
语篇类型		记叙文	记叙文
主题语境		人与自我：做人与做事；优秀品行，正确的人生态度 人与社会：良好的人际关系与社会交往，助人为乐精神，社会文明和谐	人与自我：做人与做事； 人与社会：家庭、朋友和周围的人；良好的家庭成员关系
语篇话题		本文讲述三个孩子在母亲的影响下，想办法帮助镇上一户贫困家庭的暖心小故事。大儿子想出了制作爆米花让那个孩子去卖的好主意，得到了大家的认同支持。通过大家齐心合力，他们最终成功帮助Bernard一家渡过生活难关	本文讲述两个孩子在母亲节当天想给母亲一个惊喜，为母亲制作早餐。一开始都挺顺利的，直到杰夫开始煎面包。因为锅太热，面包烧焦了。后面小事故频发：粥喷出来了，杰夫的手碰到了煤气头，锅里煎的第二块面包又烧焦了……整个早上他俩搞得一片狼藉
"四层"分析	核心价值	原文中提到小镇居民受经济萧条影响，生活窘迫但依然互帮互助，共克时艰，这给文章脉络定下了主题基调，暗示了故事所要体现的核心价值。通过友善的行为引导学生发扬乐于助人的精神，践行社会主义核心价值观，体现了语篇的德育价值	原文中提到两个孩子给母亲制作早餐，因没有实践经验导致小事故频发。通过这个故事能引导学生形成热爱劳动的观念，在实际的生活中宣扬劳动精神，积极参与劳动
	学科素养	通过设置学生相对熟悉的语篇语境，要求考生分析篇章情节脉络，发挥独立思考能力，展开合理想象，考查学生的交际、学习和思辨素养	
	关键能力	有效考查学生综合语言运用能力、思维能力、学习能力和书面表达能力	
	必备知识	语篇分析知识以及词汇、语法等基础语用知识	
"四翼"分析		原文通过设置真实的问题情境，材料内容贴近日常生活，情节简单清楚，语言通俗易懂，考查考生能否读懂故事并准确理解文章故事情节；故事开放式结尾需要考生发挥想象力和创造力，灵活运用所学知识技能，创新性地分析解决问题，这充分体现了高考评价体系所倡导的基础性、综合性、应用性和创新性的考查要求	

2. 特点分析

（1）词汇

笔者使用语料库检索工具AntConc3.5.7w，导入了2020年和2021年新高考卷读后续写文本，可以看到2021年语篇相比2020年词汇的难度不大。而且文中的名词和动词功能性很强。通过这些名词和动词就能非常清楚地读懂故事。文中的名词大多属于烹饪类话题词汇，包括用具和食材。文中的动词则具体告诉读者两姐弟如何做早餐。

（2）句式

2020年句式分析	2021年句式分析
以简单句五种基本句型为主（10句）	以简单句五种基本句型为主（16句）
含to do 表目的状语的结构	含and连接两个并列谓语动词（5句）
含but/ and并列句（4句）	含so/ and连接的并列句
含as 原因状语从句	what to do 结构作宾语
含when /after时间状语从句	含to do 表目的状语的结构
含what 引导宾语从句	含as / while/until时间状语从句；
含who/ that省略连词的定语从句	How感叹句
It句型	

通过以上句式分析，2021年语篇以简单句为主，长难句较少，这在一定程度上降低了阅读的难度，同时也利于考生的仿写。

3. 写作构思

在获取原文文本大意，了解了故事情节走向后，考生就要仔细研读所给段落开头语了。对比2020年和2021年读后续写所给段落开头语，发现命题思路是完全吻合的，一定是按照如下标准进行命题。那就是第一段开头语与原文最后一句紧密衔接，第二段开头语一定可以预知续写第一段的结束语。与此同时，两段给出的开头语本身就含有提示词，考生要善于抓住句子中的题眼来帮助构思。例如：2021年读后续写题第一段的开头语中的题眼就是"in disappointment"和"their father appeared"。第二段的开头语中的题眼就是"carried the breakfast"，那么，在这几个关键词的提示下，考生很容易能够展开续写：在他们爸爸的帮助下，两姐弟成功地做好了早餐，喊妈妈起床。妈妈看到早餐后，脸上露出幸福的笑容并夸赞两姐弟。所以，从一定程度上讲，2021年读后续写题在内容构思方面是相对容易的。考生只要厘清文章情节脉络，就都能有话可说。

二、教学启示

读后续写这一新题型是全国新高考改革的一个重要表现，为我们指明了英语学科教学和学习的方向。读后续写题所考查的是学生的理解信息、语言运用、逻辑关系和创造性思维等能力，这正好呼应了英语学科核心素养的四个方面。读后续写需要先阅读，后续写。这说明读后续写更看重的是阅读的"整体性"，解题的关键是理解整个故事。如果平时不注重广泛的阅读，没有地道语言的积累，且不说拿高分，就连读完原文阅读的材料，理清头绪都将是空谈。如果只是注重考试技巧，就好像考前临时抱佛脚，纵使有时能过关，但没有日积月累的付出，也绝对无法答好读后续写题。所以，教师可以在平常的教学中就深度阅读与写作练习开展对应的教学活动，训练学生的各种语言微技能，为应对读后续写题型做好准备。

1. 词汇是阅读的基石，量的积累才能带来质的飞跃

自然教学法的倡导人特蕾西认为：词汇学习对于理解语言和言语输出都至关重要。有了足够的词汇量，即使对结构的了解几乎等于零，也可以理解和说出大量的第二语言。魏尔金斯更是精辟地指出：没有语法不能很好地表达，而没有词汇则什么也不能表达。可以毫不夸张地说，词汇量是制约外语学习效率的最重要因素。不要指望词汇基本功不扎实的人能够考出高分。拥有大量词汇与语言运用的各个方面都呈正比例。词汇的学习是一个质与量并举的系统。语言是动态的，只有我们掌握了词汇，才能驾驭语言。

有研究表明：外语学习者如果拥有5000个词汇量，阅读正确率可达56%，词汇量达到6400个，阅读正确率可达63%。所以，词汇是阅读理解的基石。在英语教学中，教师们要转变观念，要首先重视和研究词汇教学。除了直接词汇教学，教师们要强化词汇网络和词义层级关系，还要思考如何通过一系列听说、阅读等交流活动来创设语境帮助学生们记忆并灵活运用词汇。教学中，教师们还可以要求学生围绕单元主题使用所学的相关主题词块进行创造性写作。

这种通过习得的认知经过多次重复后，学生日积月累就自然而然地识记了很多词汇并能更好地使用这些词汇。

2. 关注深度阅读教学，以深度阅读培养学生的思维能力

有了丰富的词汇量，才会有流利的阅读。根据《普通高中英语课程标准（2017年版）》对语篇知识的内容要求，引导学生展开深度阅读至关重要。在平常的教学中，教师们不能只让学生完成一些肤浅的阅读理解题。教师们要通过文本分析帮助学生去理解篇章结构、文体特点，要把语篇分析、语体应用融入日常课堂教学中。根据读后续写的特点，培养学生梳理分析文本的关键信息和语言特点是关键的第一步。文本分析往往是很多教师最容易忽略的环节。在阅读教学过程中，教师们可以从文本内容、写作目的和组织结构三个方面来考虑，可以通过回答what、、why 和how 问题的方式来分析和解读文本。换句话说，阅读的目的就是对阅读材料的深层次理解和欣赏，从写作者视角把握文本的主题和内在逻辑，从而领会文本的写作方法，为写作做好准备。此外，教师们还要尽可能给学生创造提问的机会，让学生与文本、学生与学生、学生和教师之间进行更多深入的互动。最后，在引导学生正确理解文本内容之后，教师们要进行一定的应用实践类的活动。例如，利用思维导图让学生对这些图进行基于文本的描述与阐释或者角色扮演活动。这可以为读后阶段的预测、想象和创造类活动奠定语言知识和语篇结构的基础，发展学生的思维能力，提升学生的文化意识。

3. 训练仿写能力，提高语言水平

读后续写要求考生能准确、恰当地使用所学词汇和语言结构续写文章，最终还是考查学生的写作能力。续写不能乱编，它需要延续之前的情节发展，要与原文的语言风格保持一致，这无疑对平时鉴赏和写作提出了更高层次的要求。这就十分考验学生的学习能力，特别是仿写技巧。所以，建议教师们从高一开始就训练学生的仿写能力。在写作教学中不应要求学生死记硬背、套用语言模板，而应该将写作能力的要素融合在阅读和语言知识的教学中，采用读写结合、读以致写的方式进行课堂教学活动，引导学生学习并使用文本中新颖的词句，模仿文本中的关键句式，从而提高语言水平。仿写可以是从单句入手，也可以是模仿阅读文本中某个精彩段落。只有这样层层推进，才能提高学生思维质量，加强学习能力，为读后续写打好坚实的基础。

三、结语

高考英语引入读后续写对学生的综合语言运用能力提出了更高的要求，所以一线英语教师要积极适应转变，调整一些固有的教学理念和方法，以新的视角和思路推动教学改革。

参考文献

［1］中华人民共和国教育部.普通高中英语课程标准（2017年版）［S］.北京：人民教育出版社，2018.

［2］陆正琳.高考英语读后续写题型写作策略探究——以新高考山东卷和浙江卷为例［J］.福建教育（中学），2020（41）.

［3］张献臣.加强英语语篇教学，提高英语阅读效率［J］.课程·教材·教法，2009（6）.

［4］王初明，亢鲁霞.读后续写题型研究［J］.外语教学与研究，2013（5）.

［5］王初明.读后续写——提高外语学习效率的一种有效方法［J］.外语界，2012（5）.

［6］朱向荣.英语写作教学中学生体裁意识的培养［J］.教育理论与实践，2011（21）.

基于语篇意识的高考英语"七选五"教学探究

一、引言

2022年高考英语全国卷的选材思路与2021年的试卷想法一致。总体而言，试卷"融入中华优秀传统文化，加强体美劳教育引导，关注时代发展"，与2021年选材一脉相承。试卷整体阅读部分选取的材料题材丰富，涉及三大主题语境。运用真实、地道、典型的现代英语素材，进行了适当的删减和改写，尽量符合学生的实际语言水平。阅读理解七选五是高考阅读题型之一。《考试说明》要求，根据短文内容，从短文后给出的七个选项中选择可填入短文空白的五个最佳选项，使补完后的短文意义畅通，前后连贯。这种新的阅读题对考生提出了更高层次的要求，不仅要考查阅读速度，还要考查对文章总体内容和结构以及语境逻辑意义的理解和把握。也就是说，这个题型是对语言能力和阅读能力的综合考查。根据"服务教育评价、反馈教学和促进教学"的宗旨和原则，笔者对近两年的七选五试题进行了初步归纳和分析，并探讨了对高中英语教学的启示。

二、试题分析

		2021新高考I卷	2022新高考I卷
七选五	主题语境	人与社会	人与自我
	体裁	说明文	说明文
	话题	旅游休闲：巴黎一周游的发现	体育：寻找健身搭档
	字数	267个+70个	257个+70个
	选项	全部都是完整的句子	全部都是完整的句子
	考查项目	段首句1个；段中句4个	段中句4个；段尾句1个

与近两年全国新高考I卷七选五题型相比，不难发现以下特点。

（1）体裁都是说明文，文体一致。话题联系生活实际，符合绝大多数高中生的认知特征。体现较强的实用性，能够真实培养学生的生活技能和综合素质，关注情感价值的培养。2021年七选五主题是以第一人称介绍作者夫妇对正宗巴黎生活方式的体验，文体属于散文风格的旅行日记，作者的语调具有幽默感，对学生的跨文化理解能力有很高的要求。2022年七选五文体是典型的说明文体，对如何选择健身伴侣提供了切实可行的建议，为高中生的人际关系提供了帮助。

（2）从命题角度来说，命题方式和考查方式都比较稳定，都关注考查语篇结构，注重语篇分析。文章结构严谨，段落层次明显，逻辑性较强。语句之间的连接在语义和逻辑上都非常一致。设空位置主要以"段中句"为主，考查注重语境逻辑意义的注释性句子。两篇文章的结构相似，各层次、各段落之间的内容紧扣全文的中心，句子与句子之间存在一定的语境。以2022年的主题为例，第36、40题都起着承上启下的作用。第37题和空后or引出的句子是并列关系，用提问方式向读者提示考虑想从健身伙伴那里得到什么，起到继承上述句子的作用。第38题是为了引出下文。

三、对高中英语教学的启示

（一）侧重语篇分析，培养学生结构意识

七选五试题注重考查学生的英语阅读能力和语篇理解能力，所以平时课堂上的阅读教学是一个很好的平台和突破口。但目前高中英语阅读教学中仍存在少数教师过分强调单词、语法等语言知识的教学，缺乏阅读策略、阅读方法、阅读技巧等非语言能力的训练和培养，造成阅读教学模式化、学生的阅读能力无法得到实质性提高的现象。因此，今后阅读教学的重点应从简单的阅读技巧训练转向解析语篇，把握主题意义，挖掘文化价值，分析文体特征与语言特征及其主题意义的关联，最大化语篇的意义和价值功能。文本解读要进入思维领域，面对文本，引导学生通过观察、比较、分析、思维等活动，发展思维品质。教师们从解读文本体裁入手，建议帮助学生理解文本体裁结构和篇章模式，把握文章的主体脉络，进而掌握不同文体的阅读方法。另外，在平时的教学和练习中，设计概括大意、概括段落大意、分析篇章结构、推测作者的写作意图等问题来指导学生，关注整篇文章的结构，分析段落与段落的关系以及段落的功能等，以训练学生理解和获取信息的能力，进而提高学生七选五的解题能力。潜移默化中也培养了学生为了学习而阅读的习惯。

（二）加强读写结合的写作课堂的实效性，培养语篇意识

在所有的语言技能中，写作是高中生非常重要的语言技能。但从目前的英语教学来看，写作课取得的效果最不理想。"写作"成为学生最薄弱的英语技能。客观地说，目前不少一线教师很辛苦，每周都布置学生写作文、精心批改、耐心讲解，但实际上写作教学效果甚微，学生写作能力很难提高。

阅读和写作看似相对独立，但是他们之间是相互依存、相辅相成的。所以，阅读与写作教学应该结合在一起，这样才能顺应这两种技能内在本质关系的规律。一线教师以阅读课文为例，建议利用思维导图引导学生关注阅读课文的语篇结构与语境的连贯性。在阅读中让学生积累，这样学生在写作时就会有

创意。严格挑选结构严谨的阅读材料，使涵盖中国文化、体美劳教育、环保、和谐人际关系、科技发展前沿等话题的文章尽可能丰富多样。同时，重视赏析范文。实践表明，阅读材料就是很好的学习范例。教师多引导学生关注语篇的结构、连贯性，让学生对其进行模仿和实践，创作出类似结构的文章。这样，学生们自然会将这些领悟到的语篇知识内化为自身的知识结构，提高学生的谋篇布局的能力，这对阅读七选五文本结构非常有帮助。

（三）创设活动培养英语思维，加强学生深度学习，促进学生英语核心素养的发展

《新课标》中强调语言学习是一项有意义的主题探究活动，体现了以学生为主体的学习过程，通过学习理解、应用实践、迁移创新等相互关联、层次性的进步，并通过集语言、文化、思维于一体的实践活动，实现学生逻辑、批判和创新思维的培养，落实学科育人。基于此，在平时的教学中，一线教师应结合学生主体的需要，对教材进行深入解读，确定整个单元的教学思路。设计丰富有意义的学习活动，引导学生积极进行意义探究，由浅而深地实现思维发展升级，推动核心素养落实课堂。当然，除了常规课程外，老师们还可以积极探索多种形式的英语课程，包括英语诗歌鉴赏、戏剧、英语演讲和辩论。通过开设这些校本课程能在一定程度上增强英语学习的开放性和实践性，有利于学生综合素养的培养，自然也能推动学生思维品质的提高。

（四）高中英语教师高阶思维水平的提升

客观来说，教师的教学质量很大程度上决定了学生的学习质量。目前，基础教育英语课程呼吁培养学生思维品质，这势必要求中小学一线英语教师在思维品质方面具有更高的能力水平。但教师自身思维品质的发展和提高不可能一蹴而就，需要长期的规划和持续的积累。建议学校加强学科建设，开展专题培训活动对一线教师进行理论指导。建议教师们尊重学情，根据学生所拥有的语言基础进行课堂设计。因为语言是思维的外壳。学生的语言水平制约了其表达思维、生成思维的水平。首先，教师在平时的教学中，通过逻辑清晰的教学流程、环环相扣的教学活动来训练自身的逻辑思维能力，进而保障学生学习的有效性。其次，教师善于用发现的眼光寻找教材中学生思维的发展点，并将其作为逻辑起点加以拓展，这也是有效提高教师思维水平的策略之一。最后，教师要加大对教学实践的反思力度，反思自己的教学理念是否在教学策略中得到体

现，探讨背后的影响因素，分析得失，这也有助于提高教师的思维能力。

四、结语

由于"七选五"属于篇章阅读，一线教师要始终具有"语篇意识"，任何教学设计和活动都要把上下文语境放在第一位，对学生进行有效的指导。这样，才能真正提高学生的语言能力，让他们感受到学以致用的快乐。

参考文献

［1］中华人民共和国教育部．普通高中英语课程标准（2017 年版）［S］．
北京：人民教育出版社，2018.

［2］武尊民．英语测试的理论与实践［M］．北京：外语教学与研究出版社，
2008.

［3］王蔷，罗少茜．英语学习与思辨及表达应融为一体［N］．中国教育报，
2014-06-12.

［4］杨志宏．英语思维教学模式研究［J］．国外外语教学，1999（1）.

英语学习活动观视角下高中英语语法教学探究

一、问题的提出

2020年实施新高考以来，英语学科试卷全面贯彻《中国高考评价体系》"一核四层四翼"的整体框架，以立德树人、服务选才、引导教学为核心功能，以核心价值、学科素养、关键能力和必备知识为考查内容，充分体现基础性、综合性、应用性和创新性的考查要求。新高考试题更为侧重考查学生在特定语言环境中的综合语言运用能力。它弱化了对单纯的语言知识记忆的考查，"为知识而知识"的题目也在不断减少。今年高考题型中的语法填空题较以往在命题模式（挖空设置）和所给提示词方面都有新的"变化"。具体表现在以

下几个方面。

1. 设空的变化

2022年新高考I卷语法填空的设空模式首次采用了"四六开"，即4个纯空白填空题和6个给提示词填空题。而以往都是采用"3个纯空白题"和"7个给词题"。这种变化加强了对"虚词"的考查，涉及冠词、并列连词、介词和关系代词。这些虚词实际上正是学生学习中的难点，也是极易出错的知识点。

2. 长难句的设置

2022年新高考I卷语法填空出现了两句超过35个词的长句子，挖两个空设题，这是以往所没有的。长难句的增多无疑增加了考试的难度，需要学生在具体语境中分析和理解句子。

综上所述，新高考更加注重考查学生的思辨素养和学习素养，关注思辨中的理解能力，尤其是学生对语言知识的掌握程度是否全面和牢固。这一变化也对今后的语法教学提出了更高的要求。如何实施并提高语法教学的效益成为教师们亟须思考并解决的难题。

二、理论依据

语法是语言的基本框架，是语言理解与表达必须遵循的规则。所以，语法教学在高中英语教学中占有重要地位。但是在实际教学中，有相当多的教师尽量淡化语法教学，一提到语法教学就认为是在走老路，与教学改革背道而驰，这显然是不对的。

《普通高中英语课程标准（2017年版）》（以下简称《新课标》）中指出要改变英语课程中过分重视语法和词汇知识的讲解与传授，忽视对学生实际语言运用能力的培养的倾向，但是这并不是全盘否定语法教学。《新课标》中还提出了指向学科核心素养的英语学习活动观，倡导以语言运用为导向的语法教学，要求教师围绕主题情境和不同类型的语篇设计不同层次融合语言、思维和活动的教学活动，指导学生在主题意义探究的过程中获取、操练及运用语法知识，进一步增强学生的语法运用能力，发展他们的核心素养。

三、教学问题解决实施

依据《新课标》的基本要求，为切实提高语法教学的质量，教师需要改变原来陈旧的语法教学观念，积极开展活动观视角下的语法教学，将语法教学与主题和语篇紧密结合起来，通过在输入、互动和输出环节进行教学干预，让学生在主题意义探究的过程中获取、练习和应用语法知识。下面以外研版选择性必修第一册Module 1 Laugh out loud 为例，本单元的语法主题是非限制性定语从句（where、which 、who 等关系词的用法）。通过创设一系列学习理解类活动、应用实践类活动和迁移创新类活动，尝试探索基于英语学习活动观的高中英语语法教学策略，旨在提高语法教学课堂实效性的同时提升学生的英语学科核心素养。

（一）基于语篇，以阅读教学为载体学习语法知识

语篇为语法学习提供了内容载体。语法学习应与阅读活动紧密结合。教师应搭建阅读教学和语法教学之间的联系，在阅读语篇中渗透本单元语法项目的相关用法，引导学生把语法点放入语篇中，让学生在阅读中找出文章中所有非限制性定语从句，分析这些语法现象并自己总结归纳语言，加深对语法知识的理解。

T: We've learnt about a passage about Larry, who is a clown doctor. Let's recall some main contents. First, what is this crown doctor's working environment like?

S: I walk through the doors into the waiting area, where there's a familiar atmosphere of boredom and tension.

T: Which patient is in need of the clown doctor's attention?

S: I speak with the on-duty nurse, who tells me that Lara's parents rushed her to the hospital after she fell off her bicycle.

T: Why the clown doctors can be helpful?

S: Scientific studies show that laughter produces chemicals to make people feel better, which means clown doctors can be helpful.

T: Why did Larry choose to be a clown doctor?

S: I chose this career because of my experience of going to hospital when I was a child. ...I spent much of the time when I was there feeling frightened and more than a little bored.

T: What are the responsibilities of a clown doctor?

S: ... We have to be very sensitive and work closely with the doctors and nurses, who keep us updated on each patient.

之后，教师对单元目标语法项目的形式、意义及其功能进行必要的讲解、适当的补充拓展。

T: Great. Observe all the sentences again, make a comparison and find out the differences among them.

阅读的语篇就是最好的范例，让学生在具体的情境中初步感知体验语法知识，对输入强度和输入频次进行操控来凸显目标语言形式，为后续的语言实践活动做好铺垫。

（二）设计不同层次的实践任务，搭建操练语法知识的平台

学生通过语篇阅读的分析与综合获取了语法知识后，需要通过不同形式的聚焦手段引发学生对目标语言形式的注意。在互动阶段，教师可以设计一些有意义的语言活动让学生深入了解所学语法知识的意义和功能。语法操练活动不应仅局限于传统的单选题、造句和句子翻译等。教师仍然以语篇为依托，借助思维导图、问题群、图片、视频等帮助学生对语篇进行描述、复述、分析和综合或者引入一篇主题一致、内容相关的新语篇，通过讨论、角色扮演等形式帮助学生内化所学的语法知识。

T: After reading the whole passage, please think of the following two questions and try to express your ideas using as many non-defining attributive clauses as possible：

（1）What are the differences and similarities between clown doctors and medical doctors?

（2）Would you like to work as a clown doctor? Why or why not?

（3）What's your future ideal job?

T: Well done! Many students have expressed their own ideas. I think what Larry did will definitely have a great effect on the choice of your future job. Now let's read a joke on page 5 and complete the joke with the sentence parts using who/ which and put commas in the correct position.

T: After finishing completing the joke, please finish the tasks：

（1）What does the joke mianly talk about?

（2）What do you think of Sherlock Holmes react to Dr Watson?

（3）Act it out. Then let's see which group will perform the best.

（三）设计迁移创新类语言活动输出语法知识

学生围绕单元话题和语篇完成了语法知识的输入后，接下来在输出环节要创设交际性情境，设计不同的迁移创新类活动来促进学生目标语言使用的自动化。这一阶段较之前的输入性互动阶段而言，它更加侧重交际性和创造性，有助于学生在潜移默化中自然地习得语法知识。老师通过引入新的交际性情境，呈现新的问题，让学生进行小组合作学习，完成语篇层次的整体输出活动，如书面写作、口头表达、观点分享、作品展示等最终完成语法知识的灵活运用。

T: Now think of a joke you find funny or a story you find impressive and work together with your group memebers to write it down using non-defining attributive clauses where appropriate. Then share your joke with the class and finally let's vote to choose the funniest joke or the most impressive story with more non-defining attributive clauses.

与此同时，教师还利用形成性评价量表（如下表）来引领学生学会学习、学会竞争和合作，充分发挥学生学习和评价的主体地位，促进教、学、评三者融为一体。

活动	评价标准	评价等级	学生自评	小组互评	教师评价
讲笑话/故事	顺利创作一篇笑话或故事；语句通顺；内容诙谐有趣；能正确使用若干个非限制性定语从句；借助连接性词语，建立句子及段落之间的逻辑关系。口头语言表达清晰流利，声情并茂，能有效吸引听众	优秀			
	较好地创作一篇笑话或故事；语句较通顺；内容完整；能较好地使用若干个非限制性定语从句；较好地借助连接性词语，建立句子及段落之间的逻辑关系。口头语言表达清晰，基本能顺利讲好笑话或故事	良好			
	基本创作一篇笑话或故事；语句较通顺；内容不够丰富；使用较少的非限制性定语从句；句子及段落之间的逻辑关系不够清晰。口头语言表达较清晰，感情较平淡	合格			

教育心理学研究发现，教学效果和学生的参与深度成正比。适当引入小组竞赛和合作能有效提高学生参与的积极性，对于挖掘同伴资源和团队智慧，提

升教学效果都大有帮助。语法"非限制性定语从句"课后学习效果自我评价表如下：

学习效果自我评价表				
评价内容	优秀	良好	合格	需要改进提升的地方
我能梳理出阅读文本的结构框架并找出文本中所有的非限制性定语从句				
我能使用非限制性定语从句准确地表达观点				
我能谈论自己未来的理想工作				
我能正确使用对应关系词完成语篇				
我能使用非限制性定语从句创作笑话或故事并分享				

在教学评价中，教师可以多维度检测学生基于活动观发展核心素养的过程，及时提供必要的指导和反馈，确保核心素养目标在课堂落地。

四、教学反思与建议

（1）英语语法教学必须从"用"的角度出发。语法并非一套关于结构的僵硬规则，而是一套有意义的、动态的系统，所以语法教学必须与英语语用的学习紧密结合，必须关注语言使用的体验性。

（2）任何课堂活动设计应依据学情，制定合理的教学目标，不能完全不顾学生实际水平设计一些高屋建瓴的活动让学生无法体验活动的乐趣和获取成就感。没有学情分析的活动是难以落实的，最终导致课堂成为教师个人的表演。

（3）活动观视角下的英语语法教学必须关注学生核心素养的培养。从分析与处理教学素材到制定教学目标再到设计教学活动都必须基于核心素养的理念。

（4）关注学生在整个语法学习过程中所表现出的情感、态度和价值观，在课堂上采用形成性评价框架，融入多种形成性评价策略，从而促进学生主动参与学习过程，培养积极向上的内驱力，为其终身学习和发展奠定基础。

参考文献

［1］中华人民共和国教育部.普通高中英语课程标准（2017年版2020年修订）［S］.北京：人民教育出版社，2020.

［2］章策文.英语学习活动观的内涵、特点与价值［J］.教学与管理（中学版），2019（19）.

［3］吴琦.基于学习活动观的高中英语语法"五环三段两评"教学模式构建与应用［D］.厦门：集美大学，2020.

［4］王蕾，孙薇薇，蔡铭珂，汪菁.指向深度学习的高中英语单元整体教学设计［J］.外语教育研究前沿，2021（1）.

课程改革前后课堂教学之反思

新课程，新理念，新教材给英语教育发展带来了机遇和挑战。英语教学要回归生活，回归时代，还语言教学本来面目，正成为广大英语教师的共识和教学行为。在一系列课堂教学改革措施的促动与指导下，广大教师的课堂教学发生了实质性的变化。

一、实施新课程后的课堂变化

1. 师生角色的转换

过去，老师们普遍采用的都是"保姆式"的"满堂灌"的教学模式。"满堂灌"即指老师在一节课或一节课的大部分时间向学生传授知识，以知识的讲解为重点。由老师把持着讲台，学生只有接受的份儿，"理解的要听，不理解的也要听""喜欢的要听，不喜欢的也要听"，学生成了装"知识"的"桶"。如今，在新课程理念的指导下，大部分老师改变了这种传统的讲授式课堂教学模式，而采用师生互动和师生共同参与的课堂教学模式，注重培养学生的独立性、自主性，引导学生质疑、调查、探索，在实践、探索中学习，使学习成为在教师指导下的主动的、富有个性的学习过程。提倡开放性的学习方式，鼓励学生创造性地学习，营造平等、民主、宽松的学习气氛。

在开放的课堂中，学生成为了主体。教师通过创造各种各样的活动，选择多样的题材，让学生积极参与，让学生有更多的选择、更好的机会说他们想说的话，从而营造出一种互动的课堂效果和交互的情感气氛。同时教师也融入其中，参与这些活动，从而使合作学习成为学生间、师生间合作交往的主要形式，有利于发展良好的人际关系。

2. 课堂组织形式和教学方法的转变

在开放的课堂中，小组活动成为主要的课堂组织形式。一般把学生分成4人或6人一小组，学生的座位可以根据教学的需要而随时随地地重新组合，把"秧田式"拉开，变成"马蹄"形、"蜂窝"状、"半圆"状或"圆"形等，以加强学生群体间的交流，有时候还允许学生上讲台或离开座位进行非正式群体的自由研讨。

"任务型"和"情景交互式"教学方法成为主旋律，颇受教师们的关注。我们不难发现，现在的英语课堂不论是上什么课型，老师们普遍的做法都是围绕特定的交际和语言项目，设计出具体的、可操作的任务。学生通过表达、沟通、交涉、解释、询问等各种语言活动形式来完成任务。学生完成任务的过程加强了学生对语言的运用，营造了一个有利于学生将语言运用转化为言语技能的环境。

二、新课程实施中存在的问题

《新课标》实施几年后，英语课堂已经发生许多积极的转变，也取得了一定的成效。但是，我们必须清楚地认识到在实施《新课标》的过程中，英语课堂教学也产生了一些新的问题。这主要表现在如下几个方面。

1. 过分突出学生的主体地位，忽视了教师的主导作用

很多年轻教师未能真正理解"任务型"教学和"开放式"课堂的本质。他们的课堂没有一个贯穿始终的主线，重点不突出，整堂课就是大量的任务的堆积。很多时候，老师们就是按顺序一个个地呈现任务，然后要求学生在规定的时间内逐个完成，任务完成后就让学生来试讲。老师所做的只是对学生答案进行一个简单的判断，忽视了相应的基础知识的讲解以及学法指导。

他们觉得通过设计课堂任务让学生去完成就算是贯彻和实施了"突出了以

学生为主体的"教学思想。其实这是很片面的。以学生为主体并不意味着放手让学生自己搞，并不意味着老师讲解的东西就要少。我们不提倡"满堂灌"，但这并不意味着就要将其"一棍子打死"。许多新知识学生只有在教师的分析讲解后才能深入学习。过分突出学生的地位实际上是暗中否定了教师的主导作用。老师是课堂的总指挥与裁判员，更是英语知识的有效传授者。要解决这个问题，就要讲究讲解的艺术性和科学性。我们要做到：

（1）不断提高自身驾驭教材的能力。把课讲活的关键是具有高超的驾驭教材的能力。只有深入挖掘教材的内涵，深刻领会教学内容的本质，我们才能把握学生学习中的疑点、重点和难点，突出讲解的针对性。

（2）优化讲授形式，训练语言的提炼能力。课堂讲解的语言必须做到清晰、透彻、简单、明了，千万不要拖泥带水，黏黏糊糊。一句话，要做到把最难最复杂的东西讲得简单明了。

2. 只注重课堂气氛，忽视了教学效果

我们必须承认现在的课堂的确比以前热闹了。我们经常会看到在热闹的课堂上有的学生活动时很活跃，大声参与，但同时有的却躲在一边开小差。学生活动的时候，有些老师只是站在一旁；有些只是来回走动，却没有参与到学生活动中去。透过这些现象，我们不难看出热闹的背后存在着很大的隐患。如何掌控课堂纪律并能有效监控到每个学生的一举一动成为了摆在我们面前的一大难题。如果老师只注重课堂气氛，不管课堂纪律，不讲究教学效果，那么这样的课堂其实是无效的。要避免该问题的发生，我个人认为要注意以下几点。

（1）老师要有敏锐的观察能力和课堂的驾驭能力，学会及时制止并灵活处理课堂的违纪事件。

（2）老师要动起来。学生活动时，老师不能只站在一旁看着，仅仅走动是不够的。老师一定要参与到每个小组的活动中去，引导和帮助学生去开展课堂活动，并检查各个小组任务的完成程度，及时进行表扬和督促。

（3）关注后进生。每个班都有一定数量的后进生。在课堂上，我们绝对不能仅仅关注优等生，而忽视了对后进生群体的培养。对后进生放任自流的话，一方面会对课堂纪律带来破坏，另一方面会影响整体的课堂效果。所以老师应考虑到后进生的实际情况，通过分层教学，给他们分配任务，让他们做一些力所能及的事情，给他们创设参与团体学习活动的机会，通过有趣的学习活动让他们自然而然地融入集体中。

3. 教学活动时间分配不合理或教学设计缺乏科学性，导致课堂教学的低效或无效

为急于完成教学任务，有些教师在布置小组讨论后2分钟就让各小组进行汇报。显然，在如此短的时间内学生根本无法对话题相关信息进行充分的组织和交流。课堂活动是学生进行实践、体验、探究、合作与交流的学习活动和思维活动，思维需要语言，思维更需要时间。除此之外，在活动任务设计中也出现了"为活动而活动""为问题而问题"现象，教学活动有效性明显缺失。比如，在阅读课上，我们经常会听到老师布置这样一个任务："Listen to the tape and find out the main idea of each paragraph."面对较长的语篇，让学生在听一遍录音后迅速概括出每一段的主旨大意显然是不合情理的。

要解决这个问题，有效备课就显得至关重要。要做到有效备课，必须做到以下两点。

（1）时刻牢记学生是课堂的主体。一堂课所制定的教学目标一定是从学生的实际出发，而不是从书本出发。教学活动也是依据学生的学习需求和学习能力来设计，要让教服从于学，而非让学硬性服从于教。这样才能保证教学活动的科学性和合理性。

（2）充分发挥教育智慧，前瞻性备课，预设可能的教学备选方案。

有时候，我们一味坚持按事先设计的方案授课，结果往往会出现一些教学失效的问题。所以我们要实现由"死课"到"活课"的转变，活用教学方案，提高自身在课堂教学中的应变能力和引导能力。老师们在备课时要具有前瞻性，学会预估可能出现的趋势和问题，在备课中做好应对措施的预备方案。另外，在授课时间上要留有充分余地，留出机动的时间解决应对实际授课中出现的即时性问题，真实地体现学生在学习过程中的主体性。只有这样，老师们才能有效地把握课堂节奏，灵活地分配各个教学活动所需要的时间。

课堂教学的本质就是课堂的有效性。一切教学形式和手段都必须服务于这个理念。课堂的有效性归根结底就是通过老师的教能使学生在有限的课堂时间内尽可能多地学到知识，发展能力。学生学的效果是判断一节课是否有效的重要指标。任何改革的过程都是一个不断发现问题和解决问题的过程，只要广大英语教师在这一过程中牢牢把握新课程理念，不断反思，就一定能在英语教学中取得长足的进步。

参考文献

[1] 杨良雄，黄远振.中学英语课堂教学活动的有效性研究 [J].中小学
　　外语教学（中学篇）.2007（1）.

[2] 吴松年.有效教学艺术 [M].北京：教育科学出版社，2008.

[3] 广东省教育厅教研室编.普通高中新课程英语教学与评价指导 [M].
　　广州：广东教育出版社，2006.

论高中英语学习动机的激发

我们知道，英语属于高中学生的必修课，在高考中占据着重要的位置，因此学好英语对于高中生来说至关重要。而今，众多高中生对英语学习不感兴趣。老师们经常会注意到有些同学厌倦学习、逃避学习，上课不认真听讲、不积极思考、不愿参与小组活动，无精打采，总是抱怨上课听不懂，不配合老师的教学，而且他们容易注意力分散，对学习以外的事反而兴致勃勃，不惜花时间，常常喧宾夺主、主次颠倒。还有些学生焦虑过度，缺乏自尊和自信心，上课从来不讲话，成为了被遗忘、被忽视的小群体。其实这些都是缺乏学习动机的表现。这些学生没有学习的乐趣，也体验不到成就感。这时又怎么奢望他有兴趣去钻研，怎么奢望他有学习的动力！

美国教育部前部长泰洛尔·贝尔（Terrell Bell）曾说："关于教育，有三件事要牢记—— 一是动机，二是动机，三还是动机。"可见，动机对于促进学生学习起着决定性作用。动机是激励或推动人去行动以达到一定目的的内在动因。学习动机是直接推动学生学习的内部力量，也是一种学习的需要。学习动机就像汽车的发动机和方向盘，有了它，才能朝着既定目标奋勇前进。没有它，就像机车没有发动机停步不前。在碰到学生不学习的情况下，老师们不能仅仅靠简单的说教，不能认为天天告诉学生"你能行"或者"只要你努力就一定能成功"之类的话，学生的成绩就能提高。在学生学习过程中，学生的学习动机是学习过程的核心。此时，解决问题的关键就是要激发出学生的学习动

机，使学生的学习从被动地学习转化成主动积极地学习。因此，培养和激发学生的学习动机是教师的一项重要任务。

许多心理学家认为人类本身具有去寻找和战胜挑战的内在动机。而寻找和战胜挑战的欲望是课堂学习内在动机的核心。美国James P.Raffini指出要激发学生寻找和战胜挑战这一欲望，精髓就在于满足学生的自主需求、胜任需求、归属感与联系感需求、自尊需求和参与与享受需求。换句话说，即要想学生能主动积极地学习，首先就要放手，让学生有独立探索、接受挑战的机会。其次，要让学生在做一项活动时感受到成就感。再次，强调团队意识，在团队的合作中每个人都自我感觉良好，体现出每个小组成员的价值，相互接纳，共同进步，获得自尊。最后，在做的事情中学生能找到快乐。

反思平常的教学，我们不难发现很多老师的一些做法是有违于这一理论的，并有碍于激发学生的学习动机。具体表现在：

（1）在课堂上，老师常用简单的惩罚来控制学生的行为。学生一犯错，老师就进行说教并给予惩罚。忽视对学生的鼓励性评价或鼓励性评价泛而不到位。殊不知当老师越坚持把自己的意志和决定强加于学生身上，学生就越抵制。著名瑞士心理学家皮亚杰认为，当使用奖励或惩罚影响儿童的行为时，成年人在逐渐弱化儿童自主能力的发展。

（2）不能因材施教，实行分层教学，未能对不同学生采用不同的评价标准。课堂上，老师更多关注的是优等生，较少注意学生个体之间的差异，故而无法真正做到使每个学生都能有不同程度的提高，容易出现两极分化的现象。

（3）小组合作流于形式。小组成员之间凝聚力不强，学生沟通存在选择性。我们不难发现，学生在小组活动时很多时候都未能进行有效讨论，活动的主体一般都是那些成绩较好的学生。老师们在课堂上更多关注的是热闹程度，只是一味地鼓励学生开口，而无法真正地监控到每个小组成员的表现。其实，很多学生都没有参与到活动中去。小组合作就是形式大于内容。

（4）教学缺乏创新。方法单一，内容枯燥。我们经常听到有些学生会抱怨某些老师上课太没意思，教学形式固定化、程序化，就像是催眠曲，觉得学习太没乐趣，所以一上课就睡觉了。长此以往，还谈什么学习呢？

以上现象，提醒着老师们要不断反思，改革创新，做个思考型和智慧型教师。激发学生学习动机成功与否关键在老师。所以，在平常的教学中，老师要积极地激发和满足学生的五大需求来营造课堂氛围支持学习目标和内在动机。据此，笔者谈以下建议以供参考。

一、任务

语言的学习绝不是让学生被动地接受。不是说老师讲得多、讲得好，学生就能学得好。学生自始至终是要通过完成具体的任务来学习语言的。在完成特定的任务过程中获得并积累相应的学习经验，享受成功的喜悦。所以说，英语课堂一定要以学生活动为主体，以发展学生听说读写能力为目标。而如何合理设计任务是成功地开展课堂教学的关键。

（1）设计任务时要提供给学生明确、真实的语言信息，语言情景和语言形式要符合语言实际交际功能和语言规律，同时也要符合学生的个性特点，在设计中掺入有趣易懂且贴近生活的内容话题。要使学生在一种自然、真实或模拟真实的情景中体会和学习语言，这样才便于激发学生的学习兴趣。

（2）所设计的任务应由简到繁、由易到难、前后相连、层层深入，形成由初级任务到高级任务，再由高级任务涵盖初级任务的循环。这样才能有助于培养全体学生的成就目标，为学习较快的学生和学习较慢的学生都能提供挑战。只有变化学习任务的结构，学生才能体验到通过合理的努力取得的成功，从而保证为取得学习结果而不断前进。

二、奖励

为加强学生的成就感，课堂上老师要给予学生必要的奖励，要向所有学生提供充分的、积极的反馈信息。但奖励也不能滥用。根据Epstein的观点，当奖励被用来传递在活动中学生能力的信息时，奖励才能加强学生的学习动机。所以，奖励要用得恰到好处。我们不能只看结果来给予奖励，也不能只凭印象来给予奖励。我们要向每个完成任务和取得成绩的学生表示祝贺，绝不能只对成绩好的学生慷慨而对成绩差的学生吝啬。老师们可以试着记住学生过去的成就和技能、学生正在为之努力的计划或目标、学习结果或实际技能。通过比较，才能更公平合理地奖励学生的进步，而不至于疏远和破坏其他学生的努力。我们可以因灌木丛中有玫瑰扎人而抱怨，也可以为灌木丛中有玫瑰花而欣喜。

三、权力

在过去的传统教学中，老师是主角，是说评书的，整堂课下来"满堂灌"，按部就班地讲解事先准备的教学内容，而学生是听众、是记录员，完全被老师牵着鼻子走。这种课堂权力分配形式只能导致英语教学枯燥无味，教学效果低下。这就好比把课堂教学比作哄小孩吃饭，任凭家长把饭食夸耀得多么香、多么甜、多么有营养，如果孩子不愿把饭食吃下去，孩子还是胖不起来。这个比喻既形象生动，又通俗易懂地告诉我们，课堂教学说到底还是学生自主学习的活动。如今，在新课程教学理念的指导下，一节课相当于一场戏，教师是导演，是引导者、策划者。学生是演员，是主体参与者。要演好这场戏，导演导好是关键，而演员演好更为重要。也就是说，教师引导策划好，学生在课堂舞台中充分参与表现，这堂课才能算是成功。所以，我们要学会转变角色，学会适度地放手，把权力交给学生，把课堂这个舞台真正还给学生，这样才能培养学生自主学习的能力，提高课堂学习效率。那么，要想真正体现学生的主体性，在课堂上我们就要做到：

1. 给学生足够的时间空间和自由

要给学生足够的时间和自由，就要做到合理地分配课堂时间。有效利用课堂时间是提高教学效率的关键。老师千万不能占用大量时间，要尽量减少说话时间。教的本质在于引导，"为师之道，贵在于导"。教的职责之一在于启发诱导学生去理解，积极鼓励督促，而不是给以牵制。所以，在进行课堂教学时，要把话语权更多地交给学生，要给学生充足的练习时间，要给学生更多的提问和内化的时间。通过自主思考，主动探索，除了印象深刻彻底理解外，还增加了学生学习的兴趣和自信，一举多得。

2. 重视培养学生的合作能力

学生间相互协作，共同探讨，分享彼此心得，有助于相互的进步和信心的增加。所以，我们要充分利用小组合作的优势，发挥其应有的作用。学生在小组活动中，老师要走入学生当中，给予必要的指导和监督，促进合作学习的有效性，尽可能地改变课堂上少数优生展示才华，大多数学生作陪客旁观的普遍现象。教师们应注意掌握合作学习的规则，抓住一切教育契机让学生间团结互助，培养学生的团队意识，增强小组凝聚力。老师们要重点关注每个小组中的差生，要充分了解每个差生的优势和劣势，从而创设条件给差生展示才华，让他们感受到自身的价值。另外，定期评选出优秀小组和最佳表现者并给予必要的奖励也能激发学生的学习动力。

总之，课堂是学生获得知识的主渠道。课堂上学生的学习积极性、主动性以及注意力集中的持久性都直接影响着学生的学习效率。因此，在教学中，我们教师应该树立以人为本的教育思想，从实际出发，从效果出发，想尽一切办法激发学生的内部学习动机，从而让学生自主地去学习，去探究，去学会解决问题。请记住泰洛尔·贝尔说过："关于教育，有三件事要牢记—— 一是动机，二是动机，三还是动机。"

参考文献

［1］梁平，宋其辉.这样教学生才肯学：增强学习动机的150种策略［M］.
上海：华东师范大学出版社，2010.

［2］李彬.浅谈学习动机对英语学习的影响［J］.科技信息（科学教研），
2008（12）.

［3］李泉源.论中学生英语学习动机的培养和激发［J］.中学英语之友（下旬），2010（7）.

英语生本教学之杂谈

高考英语新政中提到外语将实行社会化考试，一年两考。这意味着考生可以在他们英语水平最好的时候把握时机，尽早考出最好的成绩。与此同时，这一改变对于老师的英语教学提出了更高的要求。英语教学改革势在必行，提升教学质量显得尤为重要。

一、课堂教学改革的必要性

随着新课改活动开展得如火如荼，一系列课堂教学改革相关的问题也应运而生。我们不难发现，英语课堂教学存在不少典型性问题。具体表现如下。

1. "满堂灌"现象

"满堂灌"是指老师在一节课或一节课的大部分时间向学生传授知识，以知识的讲解为重点。由老师把持着讲台，学生被动接受老师所讲内容。这种以老师为中心的传统的讲授式课堂教学模式只注重了知识的传授，不符合新课标的理念，不能有效提升学生综合运用能力。

2. "热热闹闹"现象

在开放的课堂中，小组活动成了主要的课堂组织形式。很多老师不管三七二十一，每堂课都设计了小组讨论这个环节，根本不考虑其有效性，给人一种为了搞活动而搞活动的感觉。看着课堂上热热闹闹，殊不知有多少假象啊！我们经常发现，在热闹的同时，小组内有些学生无精打采，不愿参与小组活动；有些学生上课从来不讲话，成为被遗忘、被忽视的小群体；更有甚者，有些学生自成一个团体，积极地讨论着一些跟学习无关的事情。所以说课堂质量很难监控。

这些典型现象说明了老师们忽视了学科特点，没有有效教学。忽视了生本教育，没有以学定教。生本教育理论认为："教育的目的在于生命的发展，教育的基本动力最重要的资源来自生命，教育的核心过程发生在生命活动之中，教育最终和基本上依靠生命。"它提出遵循自然，尊重生命，从人的生命的角度来激发和唤醒学生的原始学习欲望，从根本上解决了学生持续学习动力的源头问题。从本质上讲，生本教育就是"为学生好学而设计的教育"。

二、改革应尊重学科特点，遵循客观规律

英语学科要做到生本教育，首先要遵循规律，尊重学科特点。英语是一门语言。语言的学习重在语感的培养，而语感的培养重在语言的积累。Krashen的二语习得理论中提到如果学习者接触到的语言输入具备以下四个特点：可理解性、既有趣又有关、非语法程序安排、足够的输入量，那么学习者就能自然获得必要的语法知识，自然习得语言。克拉申认为，只有语言习得才能直接地促进第二语言能力的发展，才是人们运用语言时的生产机制。可见，语言积累的重要性。可以说，语言积累不仅是一种意识、一种习惯，也是一种能力。

《普通高中英语课程标准（2017年版）》指出，我国高中英语课程的总目

标是在义务教育的基础上"进一步发展学生综合语言运用能力，着重提高学生用英语获取信息、处理信息、分析问题和解决问题的能力，特别注重提高学生用英语进行思维和表达的能力"。英语课程要为每个学生的可持续发展奠定基础。可见，英语学习的目标是培养学生的综合能力。从本质上讲，学校范畴内的英语学习就是在语言积累的基础上发展学生的综合实践能力。

三、打破传统束缚，将改革进行到底

根据英语学科自身的特点，我们知道英语归根结底就是听、说、读、写四项基本技能的学习与训练。它强调了语言的积累与运用。所以，一线英语教师应打破传统束缚，不拘泥于形式，不受限于课型，不能简单地把英语教学就定位为上阅读课、语法课、听说课等。英语教学应该是以训练学生听、说、读、写技能为目标，提高学生的语言综合运用能力。仅仅是课堂上的讲授是远远不够的，指导学生进行课外的学习也同等重要。也就是说，只有实现课内外学习的融合，只有实现语言积累和语言能力提升的融合才能可持续地提高学生的英语水平。为了实现这一目标，我个人觉得英语教学应该要注重以下几个方面能力的培养。

（一）自学能力的培养

自学能力即自主学习的能力。培养学生良好的学习习惯与自主学习的能力十分重要，特别是在英语教学的起始阶段。同时，也是全面贯彻素质教育在英语学科的具体体现。在高中阶段，学生除了需要学好课本知识以外，还必须广泛涉猎各种语言材料，包括所学语言国家的历史背景、人文等方面的知识，而这些都需要一定的英语自学能力。要培养学生的英语自学能力，老师们要训练学生以下能力。

1. 查字典

北京外国语大学的张载梁教授就说过"多一本词典，多一位老师"，说明词典对英语学习的重要性。词典在外语学习过程中发挥着重要作用。首先，它能帮助我们确切了解读音、词性、词义、搭配和多种解释以及在句子中的用法等，同时也有利于学生自主的词汇学习。其次，能丰富知识，锻炼思维。经常使用词典无疑会增长学生的知识和提高其思维能力。俗话说"授之以鱼不如授之以渔"。所以，学会查字典是英语学习者必须掌握的一项技能，是培养自学能力的基础。在课内外，老师应适当学会放手，让学生养成使用字典的习惯。

2. 拼读音标

拼读音标是语言学习的基础，而且也是一种能力。学好音标可以提高英语发音的准确性。这是非常重要的一点，因为发音是最直观地评价英语水平高低与否的标准。另外，学好音标可以使以后对大量词汇的学习和背诵相对更轻松容易。这对将来的英语学习也是非常有好处的。所以，教会学生拼读音标是老师们教学的重要内容，也是传授给学生的重要技能之一。学生掌握了音标后，老师们也可以从中解放出来。

3. 预习

课前预习既是一种科学的学习方法，同时也是一种良好的学习习惯。它可以有效地提高学生的自学能力。预习能够让学生明确当堂课的学习目标，有利于学生有针对性地检查学习目标是否完成。只有预习充分，才能提高听课的效率。所以，老师要重视这个环节，帮助学生养成预习的习惯，加强预习方法的指导，教给学生问"问题"方法，使学生善于问"问题"。同时，制定一套行之有效的检查措施。巴尔扎克曾经说过一句话："问号是开启任何一门科学的钥匙。" 所以，在平时的教学中，老师们要通过课前预习活动，引导学生逐步建立问题意识，促进学生在预习中发现问题、提出问题，这样才有利于学生真正地自主学习和合作学习。

（二）模仿能力的培养

英语学习以积累为本。学习的基础阶段，语言积累的重要途径和方法就是"模仿"。通过模仿可以培养语感。而语感的培养恰恰是提高英语水平的有效途径之一。语感是什么？语感，即人对语言的领悟感应能力，是语言训练到熟能生巧的表现。美国著名语言学家乔姆斯基说："后天经验是决定语感的变量。"英语语感之于学习者而言，就如乐感之于舞者、灵感之于作家、美感之于画家、球感之于球员一样，对促进英语学习者的听、说、读、写等基本技能的提升和发展，有着神奇的推动作用。

在平时的教学中，老师可以通过以下几种手段来培养学生的英语语感。

1. 模仿朗读和背诵

朗读和背诵可以说是我国语言学习的传统方法。在古代，学生集中识字以后，就开始诵读经典文章。学生学习主要靠自己在"诵"上下功夫，朝夕吟读，甚至背诵，文字读顺了，文章的大意也就把握了，从而达到无师自通。这同样也适用于英语学习。通过朗读训练和背诵来培养语感。朗读英语是培养语感的最基本方法。如果英语教学中缺少这个过程，试想一下学生能学出"语言味"吗？但实际上，的确存在很多一线老师忽略了朗读和背诵的重要性。总是抱怨学生基础太差，单词都背不下来还谈什么背课文。所以，他们只是一味地让学生在没有语境的情况下去背单词和听写单个的单词。这些做法不利于培养学生的语感。长此以往，学生对英语学习也会越来越没有兴趣。

2. 仿写

英语写作能力是高中阶段学生综合运用语言能力的重要体现。然而，英语写作教学又是制约英语教学的瓶颈。多数老师采用"布置任务—学生写作—教师批改—集中讲解—展示佳作"的单一形式，对于学生来说，"写什么"和"怎么写"让他们无从下手。该怎样谋篇造句？怎样开头？怎样结尾？如何阐明观点？学生们感到无所适从，学生写得毫无兴趣，最后往往是胡编乱造，"中式英语"随处可见。这些都说明课堂上传统的写作教学效果不行。所以要想真正提高学生的写作能力，在实际英语教学过程中，要充分发挥仿写的作用，利用课本和阅读教学中经典的英语句型，先从仿写单句开始，再过渡到模仿相同体裁的文章，进行文章结构训练。学生通过不同形式的模仿训练，就能较快地熟悉不同语言风格、不同体裁、不同话题文章的基本写法，从而写起来有话可说，能说出地道的英语，能写出有条理、布满亮点的文章。慢慢地学生就找到了自信，从而想写、乐写，自然提高了写作水平。

（三）创造能力的培养

英语是一门语言学科，具有很强的实践性，这就决定了英语教学中必须更多地给学生提供接触英语和运用英语进行实际语言交流的机会，真正使学生有实践的机会以达到学以致用的目的。

杜威把教学过程看成是"做的过程"。他主张从做中去学习，从经验中积累知识。在教学活动中学生通过自身的实践活动掌握知识是不可缺少的重要环节。所以，在英语教学中，老师们要让学生动起来，从做中学。实践证明，让学生尝试自主命题是一种很有效的培养综合能力的途径。在教学中，我在所任班级中进行了"学生自主命题，感受快乐考试"的尝试，并取得了一定的成效。具体做法如下。

将班级学生分成若干小组，在生生共同合作下命制语法填空题。在学生自主命题之前，教师要给予适当的指导。自主命题的过程总体上可以分为4个阶段。

1. 学生个体自主命题

这一阶段就是让每个学生根据老师的要求命制语法填空题。学生在此阶段主要是单独命题。出题的过程正是学生自我检查、自我总结的过程，学生要想出规范的"好题妙题"，就要开动脑筋，发挥创造性和批判性。

2. 小组合作筛选考题

小组同学在此阶段相互评判、探讨、筛选出符合要求的语法填空题。学生在此阶段主要以合作学习形式为主，小组成员之间相互交流各自的试题，切磋讨论，择优选用。选题的过程是学生之间相互学习的过程。

3. 组织测试

测试过程是小组之间互换试题，全班学生的试题不是统一的，每组要做不同的题目，学生拿到哪份做哪份。（也可根据自己的情况进行选择）

4. 评价总结

测试后学生之间相互交流反馈，老师参与评价。

整个活动让学生有了实践的机会，一方面，引发了学生的学习兴趣，调动了学生学习的积极性。另一方面，培养了学生的创造性思维、提高了学习效率和实践能力。

总之，在新形势下，一线英语老师要转变观念，遵循学科特点和语言学习规律，积极探索，大胆进行英语教学改革。利用生本教育来切实提高学生素质和英语水平，真正实现促进学生的全面发展的目的。

参考文献

［1］吴松年.有效教学艺术［M］.北京：教育科学出版社，2008.

［2］广东省教育厅教研室编.普通高中新课程英语教学与评价指导［M］.广州：广东教育出版社，2006.

［3］徐火辉，徐海天.中国人英语自学方法教程［M］.北京：中国金融出版社，2011.

［4］梁平，宋其辉.这样教学生才肯学：增强学习动机的150种策略［M］.上海：华东师范大学出版社，2010.

思考着，并进步着

俗话说，教要成功，备要当先。备课的水准，直接影响教学的质量。面对坪山高级中学生源的实际情况，我们英语教师应该教什么，怎么教？这是摆在我们面前的重要课题。采用何种教学模式才能提高教学效率？怎样才能让学生学得更轻松愉悦？要解答这些难题，只有从改变备课模式开始，做到深度备课。所以首先我要说备课至关重要。接下来我想谈谈自己对深度备课的一些肤浅的认识。

首先，备课绝不是简单的"手工操作"。大家都知道，现在网络资源很发达，老师们只要上网搜索，各种相关资料和教学设计就会纷至沓来，然后很多老师粘贴一下，剪辑一下就用上了，也没有管这"拿来"的东西是否适合自己的课堂。于是，形式代替了思考，课件代替了大脑，脑力活变成了体力活，备课成了简单的"手工操作"。这种做法是不可取的。我觉得这种做法是不利于教师自身专业成长的，长久下去老师永远都不能真正理解教学的真谛。

其次，备课过程应该是创新和精心设计的过程。这就需要老师们改变备课的观念与思维方式，这是前提条件。我们要明白备课不是研究怎样讲教材而应该是研究如何用教材。不管是新授课还是复习课，所用的教材或材料仅仅是一个工具。如何用好这个工具就需要我们积极思考，动脑筋了，所以备课是一种脑力活。另外，我们要明确备课的主体应该是学生，所有的活动应围绕学生来设计。如果老师没有改变观念，那么备课时就容易走入误区，不能真正做到有效备课。所以，何为备课？用通俗的话来讲，备课就是思考在课堂上让学生做什么以及怎样才能让学生完成你想要他们做的事情。这是指导我们备课的总原则。

那么怎样做到有效备课呢？我个人觉得，细节决定成败。我平常是这样做的。

一、思考目标，确定课型

教学目标是整个课堂教学活动的起点和终点，也是教学评价的重要依据。目标的设定要考虑学情，不能超出学生的实际水平。所以，目标一定要明确、具体和适宜。换句话说，老师们必须清楚这堂课是要干什么。同时确定课型也是重要的一步。假如把上课比作开掘矿藏的过程，研究确定课型就是为开矿找寻一条路径，如果连路径都不甚明了，那么开矿的过程就会缺乏目的性。只有当教师走进课堂，对于本节课的课型了然于胸时，才能够对课堂的环节、课堂的问题、师生的互动、训练的形式有确切的把握，才能真正提高课堂的效率。

二、研读教材，合理取舍

教材是静态的，是不能开口说话的，有时只能呈现"结果"。所以，我们不是要简单地将这些静态的结果"教"给学生，而是要将这一"结果"变化为可以使学生参与的活动的过程，而这一变化过程的实现就需要我们去"研读教材"。我觉得，"研读教材"并不是意味着只备教材中的语言现象。我们要有正确的教材观，要能合理地利用教材并且能恰当地重组教材和适度地深挖教材。在这一过程中，我主要做的事情就是问问题，多问自己几个为什么。如教材呈现了哪些内容；为什么要这样呈现；哪些内容适合学生；哪些内容需要重点讲解；根据教材内容准备设计哪些相关的活动，通过这些活动要解决哪些问题，达到什么目的；如何使教材发挥它最大的功效等。这样反复思考下来，我就能合理取舍，最终确定这堂课的教学内容和教学策略了。

三、备方法要解决的是如何教的问题

这包括考虑教学目的，贯彻教学原则，选用教学方法，安排教学步骤等。这一步我主要是思考如何安排教学内容的先后顺序。我会把整个教学过程梳理一遍看看各个环节是否衔接连贯。但更重要的是我会重点思考如何做到有层次地设计教学，运用哪种方法最适合学生，从而使不同水平和不同性格的学生都有充分活动的机会，使不同层次的学生都能积极投入教学活动中。此外，如何合理分配各个环节的时间如新旧内容所占时间比例、讲解与练习所占时间比例等也是必须考虑的内容。

四、思考课后作业的设计

备课除了备教材、备学生、备教法和学法外，如何布置课后作业也是备课时需要考虑的重点内容。适当而优质的作业有助于学生所学知识的巩固、深化，有利于学生智力和创造才能的开发，是课堂教学的延伸和升华，是教师改善教学的切入点。所以，备课时我们千万不能忘记作业的设计，绝不能课后随便处理，造成作业与教学内容相脱节的现象。

当然，我们知道备课写教案是上课前的思考，是一种理想状态，但在实际上课过程中难免也会出现一些例外，所以一堂课结束后，并不意味着思考的终结，教学结束后要深入反思，将这一过程中获得的收获条分缕析地归纳总结，从中提炼宝贵的思想闪光点，并把它上升到理论的高度。

总之，备课是一件细致、费神又费时的脑力活。只要我们大家学会思考、学会创新，我们就会不断有收获、进步。漫漫取经路，漫漫修炼路。路在何方，路在脚下。

《走进英语诗歌》校本教材

Module 1 北朝民歌

A Shepherd's Song

At the foot of the hill，By the side of the rill，

The grassland stretches' neath the firmament tranquil.

The boundless grassland lies，Beneath the boundless skies.

When the winds blow，

And grass bends low，

My sheep and cattle will emerge before your eyes.

【Word Bank】

1. shepherd［ˈʃepəd］n.牧羊人；羊倌 v.带领；引；护送

2. rill［rɪl］n.细沟 v.像小河一般流

3. stretch［stretʃ］v.拉长；撑大；有弹性（或弹力）；拉紧 n.一片；一段；（连续的）一段时间

4. firmament［ˈfɜːməmənt］n.天空；苍穹

5. tranquil［ˈtræŋkwɪl］adj.安静的；平静的；安宁的

6. boundless［ˈbaʊndləs］adj.无限的；无止境的

7. emerge［iˈmɜːdʒ］v.（从隐蔽处或暗处）出现，浮现，露出；暴露

【原文】

敕勒歌

敕勒川，阴山下。

天似穹庐，笼盖四野。

天苍苍，野茫茫。

风吹草低见牛羊。

【作品简介】

北朝民歌，产生于黄河流域，歌词的作者主要是鲜卑族，也有氐、羌、汉族的人民。主要是北魏以后用汉语记录的作品，大约是传入南朝后由乐府机关采集而成存下的，传世的六十多首，以《敕勒歌》最为著名。歌词的主要内容，有的反映战争和北方人民的尚武精神，有的反映人民的疾苦，有的反映婚姻爱情生活，有的描写北方特有的风光景色。它内容丰富，语言质朴，风格豪放。形式上以五言四句为主，也有七言四句和七言古体及杂言体，对唐代的诗歌的发展有较大影响。

【比一比】

请大声朗读这首诗，看看谁朗读得最好？

【诗歌鉴赏】

1. 这首诗使用了哪种押韵手法？

2. 这首诗表达了作者怎样的思想情感呢？

【诗歌创作】

你能从这首诗中看到怎样一幅美好的画面？请为这首诗画一幅插图吧。

Module 2 唐诗

Dawn in Spring

Meng Haoran

Dawn was missed in a good sleep in spring；

Everywhere I hear birds sing.

Overnight, the wind and rain clamored；

How many flowers down did they bring?

【Word Bank】

1. dawn［dɔ:n］n.黎明；拂晓；萌芽 v.开始；变得明朗；开始清楚

2. overnight［ˌəʊvəˈnaɪt］ adv.在夜间；突然；一夜之间 adj.夜间的；突然的；很快的；一夜之间的 n.前一天的晚上；一夜的逗留

3. clamor［ˈklæmə（r）］v.大声（或吵闹）地要求；（尤指乱哄哄地）大声地喊叫，呼叫 n.喧闹声；嘈杂声；吵闹；民众的要求

【原文】

春 晓

孟浩然

春眠不觉晓，处处闻啼鸟。

夜来风雨声，花落知多少。

【诗人简介】

孟浩然（689—740），字浩然，号孟山人，襄州襄阳（今湖北襄阳）人，唐代著名的山水田园派诗人，世称"孟襄阳"。他与盛唐另一山水诗人王维并称为"王孟"，有《孟浩然集》三卷传世。孟诗绝大部分是五言短篇，多写山水田园和隐居的逸兴以及羁旅行役的心情。他善于发掘自然和生活之美，即景会心，写出一时真切的感受。

【比一比】

请大声朗读这首诗，看看谁朗读得最好？

【诗歌鉴赏】

1. 读完这首诗歌，思考此诗的主题格调是悲叹还是欣喜呢？请阐述你的理由。

2. 你能发现此首五言律诗的押韵方式是什么吗？

【诗歌创作】

请在互联网上查阅孟浩然的其他作品，选一首你最喜欢的诗歌与同学分享。

The Peasants

Li Shen

At noon they weed with hoes;

Their sweat drips on the soil.

Each bowl of rice, who knows!

Is the fruit of hard toil.

【Word Bank】

1. weed［wi:d］n.杂草，野草；水草；烟草 v.除（地面的）杂草

2. hoe［həʊ］n.锄头 v.用锄头锄地（或除草）

3. sweat［swet］n.汗；出汗；一身汗；繁重的工作 v.出汗；辛苦地干

4. drip［drɪp］v.滴下；滴水；含有；充满；充溢 n.滴水声；水滴；滴液；（静脉）滴注器

5. toil［tɔɪl］v.（长时间）苦干，辛勤劳作；艰难缓慢地移动；跋涉 n.苦工；劳累的工作

【原文】

悯 农

李 绅

锄禾日当午，汗滴禾下土。

谁知盘中餐，粒粒皆辛苦。

【诗人简介】

李绅（772—846），字公垂，祖籍安徽亳州。自幼丧父，由母教以经义。青年时目睹农民终日劳作而不得温饱，以同情和愤慨的心情，写出了千古传诵的《悯农》诗2首，被誉为悯农诗人。新乐府运动的倡导者之一。

【比一比】

请大声朗读这首诗，看看谁朗读得最好？

【诗歌鉴赏】

1. 这首诗表达了作者怎样的思想情感呢？
2. 读完这首诗给你什么启示？

【诗歌创作】

仿照这首诗歌，自创一首歌颂教师主题的诗。

The River in Snowing

Liu Zongyuan

Over mountains no birds fly high or low,

Along every road no people are on the go.

Alone an old fisher wore a straw raincoat,

He was fishing on his snowing-river boat.

【Word Bank】

1. on the go 忙个没完；十分活跃

2. straw ［strɔ:］n.（收割后干燥的）禾秆，稻草；（喝饮料用的）吸管

【原文】

江 雪

柳宗元

千山鸟飞绝，万径人踪灭。

孤舟蓑笠翁，独钓寒江雪。

【诗人简介】

柳宗元（773—819），字子厚，河东（今山西运城）人，世称"柳河东"。杰出诗人，哲学家，儒学家乃至成就卓著的政治家，唐宋八大家之一。著名作品有《永州八记》等600多篇文章。柳宗元的诗，共集中140余首。他在自己独特的生活经历和思想感受的基础上，借鉴前人的艺术经验，发挥自己的创作才华，创造出一种独特的艺术风格，成为代表当时一个流派的杰出诗才。

【比一比】

请大声朗读这首诗，看看谁朗读得最好？

【诗歌鉴赏】

1. 读完这首诗歌，此诗中用了极度夸张的手法，你能举几个例子吗？

2. 这首诗表达了作者怎样的思想情感呢？

【诗歌创作】

请为这首诗配一张插图。

On the Stork Tower

Wang Zhihuan

The sun along the mountain bows;

The yellow river seawards flows.

You will enjoy a grander sight;

By climbing to a greater height.

【Word Bank】

1. bow ［baʊ］ v.点头；鞠躬；（使）弯曲

　　　　［bəʊ］ n.弓；蝴蝶结

2. seaward ［ˈsiːwəd］ adj.向海的，朝海的

3. grand ［ɡrænd］ adj.壮丽的；堂皇的；重大的；（用于大建筑物等的名称）大；宏大的；宏伟的；有气派的

【原文】

登鹳雀楼
王之涣

白日依山尽，黄河入海流。

欲穷千里目，更上一层楼。

【诗人简介】

王之涣（688—742），字季陵，晋阳（今山西太原）人。盛唐时期著名的边塞诗人。他曾任冀州衡水主簿，被诬罢职，遂漫游北方，到过边塞。闲居十五年后，复出任文安县尉。其作品现存六首绝句。《登鹳雀楼》《凉州词》为其代表作。

【比一比】

请大声朗读这首诗，看看谁朗读得最好？

【诗歌鉴赏】

1.读完这首诗歌，你能发现此诗的押韵方式是什么吗？

2.找出此诗中描写自然风景的句子。

【诗歌创作】

按照此首诗歌押韵的方式创造一首诗。

Autumn Evening in the Mountains
Wang Wei

After fresh rain in mountains bare

Autumn permeates evening air.

Among pine-trees bright moonbeams peer；

Over crystal stones flows water clear.

Bamboos whisper of washer-maids；

Lotus stirs when fishing boat wades.

Though fragrant spring may pass away，

Still here's the place for you to stay.

【Word Bank】

1. permeate［ˈpɜ:mieɪt］v.渗透；弥漫；扩散；感染；传播

2. moonbeam［ˈmu:nbi:m］n.（一道）月光

3. peer［pɪə（r）］n.身份（或地位）相同的人；同龄人；同辈 v.仔细看；端详

4. crystal［ˈkrɪstl］n.结晶；晶体；水晶；水晶玻璃

5. flow［fləʊ］n.流；流动；滔滔不绝 v.流；流动；流畅

6. lotus［ˈləʊtəs］n.莲属植物；莲花图案

7. stir［stɜ:（r）］v. 搅动；搅和；搅拌；（使）微动；（使）行动，活动 n.（一些人感到的）激动，愤怒，震动；搅动；搅和；搅拌

8. wade［weɪd］v.跋涉，涉，蹚（水或淤泥等）

9. fragrant［ˈfreɪɡrənt］adj.香的；芳香的

【原文】

山居秋暝

王 维

空山新雨后，天气晚来秋。

明月松间照，清泉石上流。

竹喧归浣女，莲动下渔舟。

随意春芳歇，王孙自可留。

【诗人简介】

王维（701—761），字摩诘，号摩诘居士，世称"王右丞"，河东蒲州（今山西运城）人。盛唐诗人的代表，尤长五言，多咏山水田园，与孟浩然合称"王孟"，有"诗佛"之称。苏轼评价其为"诗中有画，画中有诗"。书画

227

特臻其妙，后人推其为南宗山水画之祖。存诗400余首。

【比一比】

请大声朗读这首诗，看看谁朗读得最好？

【诗歌鉴赏】

1. 读完这首诗歌，你能发现此诗的押韵方式是什么吗？

2. 找出此诗中描写自然风景的句子？

3. 这首诗表达了作者怎样的思想情感呢？

【诗歌创作】

按照此首诗歌押韵的方式创造一首诗。

Tomb-sweeping Day

Du Mu

It drizzles endlessly during the rainy season in spring,

Travelers along the road look gloomy and miserable.

When I ask a shepherd boy where I can find a tavern,

He points at a distant hamlet nestling amidst apricot blossoms.

【Word Bank】

1. drizzle ［ˈdrɪzl］ v.下毛毛雨；下蒙蒙细雨

2. endlessly ［ˈɛndlɪsli］ adv.不断地；无穷尽地

3. gloomy ［ˈɡluːmi］ adj.黑暗的；阴暗的；幽暗的

4. miserable ［ˈmɪzrəbl］ adj.痛苦的；非常难受的；可怜的

5. shepherd ［ˈʃepəd］ n.牧羊人

6. tavern ［ˈtævən］ n.酒馆；小旅店；客栈

7. hamlet ［ˈhæmlət］ n.小村庄

8. nestle ［ˈnesl］ v.坐落于；安置

9. amidst ［əˈmɪdst］ prep. 在……之中；在……气氛下；四周是……

10. apricot ［ˈeɪprɪkɒt］ n.杏子；杏

11. blossom ［ˈblɒsəm］ n.花朵；花簇

【原文】

清 明

杜 牧

清明时节雨纷纷，路上行人欲断魂。

借问酒家何处有，牧童遥指杏花村。

【诗人简介】

杜牧（803—852），字牧之，号樊川居士，京兆万年（今陕西西安）人，唐代杰出的诗人，散文家，与李商隐并称"小李杜"。

杜牧26岁中进士，先后历任弘文馆校书郎，淮南节度使幕，史馆修撰，黄州、睦州刺史等职。他的诗歌以七言绝句著称，内容以咏史抒怀为主，在晚唐成就颇高。

【比一比】

请大声朗读这首诗，看看谁朗读得最好？

【诗歌鉴赏】

1. 谈一谈清明节的习俗。

2. 中英对照，学习这首诗的翻译手法。

3. 这首诗表达了怎样的思想情感呢？

【诗歌创作】

请在互联网上查阅杜牧的其他作品，选一首你最喜欢的诗歌与同学分享。

Module 3　宋词

On the first day of Chinese New Year

Wang Anshi

The fireworks are suddenly broken out aloud,

New Year coming in, the Old is going out.

Spring breeze has home-made wine warm.

All families enjoy sunshine outside the room.

Let newly-painted peach-board lucky charm,

Replace the old amulet safely to protect home.

【Word Bank】

1. firework ［ˈfaɪəwɜːk］ n.烟火；烟花；烟火表演

2. breeze ［briːz］ n.微风；和风；轻而易举的事

3. newly-painted ［ˈnjuːliˈpeɪntɪd］ adj.新刷的，新涂的，新喷过油漆的

4. charm ［tʃɑːm］ n.魅力；魔力；吸引力；迷人的特征 v.吸引；迷住

5. amulet ［ˈæmjʊlət］ n.护身符，驱邪物

【原文】

元 日
王安石

爆竹声中一岁除，春风送暖入屠苏。

千门万户瞳瞳日，总把新桃换旧符。

【诗人简介】

王安石（1021—1086），唐宋八大家之一。字介甫，号半山，封荆国公，谥"文"，世称王文公。抚州临川人。北宋著名思想家，政治家，文学家，改革家。庆历二年（1042），进士及第，政绩显著，后官至宰相，主张变法。

在文学上，他具有突出成就，其散文简洁精密，其诗自成一家， 世称"王荆公体"。其词风格独特，开启豪放派的先声。

【比一比】

请大声朗读这首诗，看看谁朗读得最好？

【诗歌鉴赏】

1. 读完这首诗，谈谈从中反映出新年的哪些习俗？

2. 仔细品鉴这首诗，了解朱曼华翻译家是怎样通过直译和意译的手法翻译这首诗的？

【诗歌创作】

你能创造出一首描写中国或国外某个节假日的诗歌吗？

A Long Drone
Li Qingzhao

Where, how? Where, how?

So chill, so cold.

Sad, I bow; sad I bow.

The lash of early spring，

Hard, hard enow.

Just a few cups of wine，

I can't bear the harsh eve sough.

Wild geese fly while I sigh，

Which I saw last year as now.

Daisies all fall aground，

Withered now.

Which does picking allow?

Beside the sill，

In darkness I feel ill.

Th'parasol tree and rain，

At dusk drip and drip again.

Here and now，

Can I bear the disquiet, how?

【Word Bank 】

1. drone ［drəʊn］ n.嗡嗡声；持续低音（如风笛等发出的持续音）v.嗡嗡叫；嗡嗡响

2. lash ［læʃ］ v. 猛击；鞭打；怒斥 n.（作为惩罚的）鞭打，鞭梢

3. enow ［inaʊ］ adj. 足够的，充分的

4. sough ［saʊ］ v.作沙沙声；作飒飒声

5. daisy ［ˈdeɪzi］ n.雏菊（花）

6. aground ［əˈgraʊnd］ adv.（指船）搁浅 adj.搁浅的；在地面上的

7. withered ［ˈwɪðəd］ adj.干枯的；衰老憔悴的；发育不良的 v.（使）枯

萎；（尤指渐渐）破灭，消失

8. parasol ［ˈpærəsɒl］ n.（旧时的）女用阳伞；（海滩上、餐馆外等处的）大遮阳伞

9. drip ［drɪp］ v.滴下；滴出；滴水 n.滴落；滴水声；滴答声；水滴；（静脉）滴注器

10. disquiet ［dɪsˈkwaɪət］ n.不安；忧虑；烦恼 v.使担心；使焦急

【原文】

声声慢·寻寻觅觅
李清照

寻寻觅觅，冷冷清清，凄凄惨惨戚戚。乍暖还寒时候，最难将息。
三杯两盏淡酒，怎敌他，晚来风急！雁过也，正伤心，却是旧时相识。
满地黄花堆积，憔悴损，如今有谁堪摘？守着窗儿，独自怎生得黑！
梧桐更兼细雨，到黄昏，点点滴滴。这次第，怎一个愁字了得！

【诗人简介】

李清照（1084—1155），号易安居士，齐州章丘（今山东章丘）人，宋代女词人，婉约词派代表，有"千古第一才女"之称。

所作词，前期多写其悠闲生活，后期多悲叹身世，情调感伤，形式上善用白描手法，自辟途径，语言清丽。论词强调协律，崇尚典雅。

【比一比】

请大声朗读这首诗，看看谁朗读得最好？

【诗歌鉴赏】

1. 你知道这首诗描写的是什么季节吗？

2. 你能举例说明这首诗表达了作者怎样的思想情感吗？

The River All Red

Yue Fei

Wrath sets on end my hair;

I lean on railings where I see the drizzling rain has ceased.

Raising my eyes

Towards the skies,

I heave long sighs,

My wrath not yet appeased.

To dust is gone the fame achieved in thirty years;

Like cloud-veiled moon the thousand-mile

Plain disappears.

Should youthful heads in vain turn grey.

We should regret for aye.

Lost our capitals.

What a burning shame!

How can we generals

Quench our vengeful flame!

Driving our chariots of war, we'd go

To break through our relentless foe.

Valiantly we'd cut off each head,

Laughing, we'd drink the blood they shed.

When we've reconquered our lost land,

In triumph would return our army grand.

【Word Bank】

1. wrath 〔rɔːθ〕 n.愤怒

2. railing 〔'reiliŋ〕 n.扶栏，栏杆

3. drizzle 〔'drɪzl〕 vi.下毛毛雨 vt.细雨般地洒下 n.细雨

4. cease 〔siːs〕 v.终止；停止 n.停止

5. heave 〔hiːv〕 v.发出

6. appease 〔ə'piːz〕 vt.平息

7. for aye 永远地

8. quench 〔kwentʃ〕 vt.熄灭

9. vengeful 〔'vendʒful〕 adj.复仇的

10. chariot 〔'tʃæriət〕 n.战车

11. relentless ［ri'lentlis］ adj.无情的，残酷的

12. foe ［fəu］ n.敌人；反对者

13. valiantly ［'væliəntli］ adv.勇敢地

14. in triumph 胜利地

【原文】

满江红

岳飞

怒发冲冠，凭栏处，潇潇雨歇。

抬望眼，仰天长啸，壮怀激烈。

三十功名尘与土，八千里路云和月。

莫等闲，白了少年头，空悲切。

靖康耻，犹未雪。臣子恨，何时灭！

驾长车，踏破贺兰山缺。

壮志饥餐胡虏肉，笑谈渴饮匈奴血。

待从头、收拾旧山河，朝天阙。

【诗人简介】

岳飞（1103—1142），字鹏举，宋相州汤阴县永和乡孝悌里（今河南安阳市汤阴县程岗村）人，中国历史上著名的军事家、战略家、民族英雄，位列南宋"中兴四将"之首。自幼习文练武，一心报效国家。其母曾于其背刺以"精忠报国"四字训诫。岳飞是南宋最杰出的统帅，他重视人民抗金力量，缔造了"连结河朔"之谋，主张黄河以北的抗金义军和宋军互相配合，夹击金军，以收复失地。金国大将金兀术再度进攻，掳走康王二帝。岳飞领军出击，在朱仙镇围住金兵。汉奸秦桧被金人收买，怂恿皇帝下十二道金牌召岳飞回国，1142年1月，岳飞由于"莫须有"的谋反罪名，含冤而死。葬于西湖畔栖霞岭。岳飞的文学才华也是将帅中少有的，他的不朽词作《满江红》，是千古传诵的爱国名篇。

【比一比】

请大声朗读这首诗，看看谁朗读得最好？

【诗歌鉴赏】

1.你能举例说明这首诗表达了作者怎样的思想情感吗？

2.读完这首诗歌，举例说明此诗中的押韵方式。

【诗歌创作】

请在互联网上查阅宋词，选一首你最喜欢的宋词与同学分享。

Module4　现代小诗

A Grain of Sand

To see a world in a grain of sand,

And a heaven in a wild flower,

Hold infinity in the palm of your hand,

And eternity in an hour.

【原文】

一粒沙子

从一粒沙子看到一个世界，

从一朵野花看到一个天堂，

把握在你手心里的就是无限，

永恒也就消融于一个时辰。

【Challenge】

Analyze this poem in terms of literary devices and techniques.

1. The major theme of this poem is：

_____

_____

_____

2. Study the poem's rhymes.

_____

_____

_____

【Creative work】

Can you create a new poem based on the rhymes in this poem?

Rain

Rain is falling all around,

It falls on field and tree,

It rains on the umbrella here,

And on the ships at sea.

【原文】

雨

雨儿在到处降落,

它落在田野和树梢,

它落在这边的雨伞上,

又落在航行海上的船只。

【Challenge】

Analyze this poem in terms of literary devices and techniques.

1. The major theme of this poem is:

_____

_____

2. Study the poem's rhymes.

_____

_____

【Creative work】

Can you create a new poem based on the rhymes in this poem?

Friends

Breanne Franey

My friends are fun to have around

Except when thye stomp their feet and frown.

My friends like to bother boys，

But I'd rather play with toys！

My friends like to ride a bike，

But I'd rather take a hike.

But that's okay！

We're friends anyway！

【原文】

朋 友

有朋友在身边很有趣，

除非他们跺脚皱眉头。

我的朋友喜欢打扰男孩，

但我宁愿玩玩具！

我的朋友们喜欢骑自行车，

但我宁愿远足。

但是没关系！

反正我们是朋友！

【Challenge】

Analyze this poem in terms of literary devices and techniques.

1. The major theme of this poem is：

_____

_____

2. Study the poem's rhymes.

_____

_____

【Creative work】

Can you create a new poem based on the rhymes in this poem?

Never give up

Never give up, Never lose hope.

Always have faith, It allows you to cope.

Trying times will pass, As they always do.

Just have patience, Your dreams will come true.

So put on a smile, You'll live through your pain.

Know it will pass, And strength you will gain.

【原文】

永不放弃

永不放弃，永不心灰意冷。

永存信念，它会使你应付自如。

难挨的时光终将过去，一如既往。

只要有耐心，梦想就会成真。

露出微笑，你会走出痛苦。

相信苦难定会过去，你将重获力量。

【Challenge】

Analyze this poem in terms of literary devices and techniques.

1. The major theme of this poem is:

_____

_____

2. Study the poem's rhymes.

_____

_____

【Creative work】

Can you create a new poem based on the rhymes in this poem?

Facing the Sea with Spring Blossoms

Hai Zi

From tomorrow on, I will be a happy man;

Grooming, chopping, and traveling all over the world

From tomorrow on, I will care foodstuff and vegetable,

Living in a house towards the sea, with spring blossoms.

From tomorrow on, write to each of my dear ones,

Telling them of my happiness,

What the lightening of happiness has told me,

I will spread it to each of them.

Give a warm name for every Live and every mountain,

Strangers, I will also give you my well-wishing.

May you have a brilliant future!

May you lovers eventually become spouse!

May you enjoy happiness in this earthly world!

I only wish to face the sea, with spring flowers blossoming.

【原文】

面朝大海，春暖花开

海 子

从明天起，做一个幸福的人

喂马，劈柴，周游世界

从明天起，关心粮食和蔬菜

我有一所房子，面朝大海，春暖花开

从明天起，和每一个亲人通信

告诉他们我的幸福

那幸福的闪电告诉我的

我将告诉每一个人

给每一条河每一座山取一个温暖的名字

陌生人，我也为你祝福

愿你有一个灿烂的前程

愿你有情人终成眷属

愿你在尘世获得幸福

我只愿面朝大海，春暖花开

【Challenge】

Analyze this poem in terms of literary devices and techniques.

1. The major theme of this poem is:

_____

_____

2. List as many as images in this poem, and think about the effects that they bring about.

_____

_____

【思考题】

In this poem, "From tomorrow on" is mentioned for several times, what kind of feelings do you think does the author wants to express?

Saying Good-bye to Cambridge Again

Xu Zhimo

Very quietly I take my leave

As quietly as I came here;

Quietly I wave good-bye

To the rosy clouds in the western sky.

The golden willows by the riverside

Are young brides in the setting sun;

Their reflections on the shimmering waves

Always linger in the depth of my heart.

The floating heart growing in the sludge

Sways leisurely under the water;

In the gentle waves of Cambridge

I would be a water plant!

That pool under the shade of elm trees

Holds not water but the rainbow from the sky;

Shattered to pieces among the duckweeds

Is the sediment of a rainbow-like dream.

To seek a dream? Just to pole a boat upstream

To where the green grass is more verdant;

Or to have the boat fully loaded with starlight

And sing aloud in the splendor of starlight.

But I cannot sing aloud

Quietness is my farewell music;

Even summer insects heap silence for me

Silent is Cambridge tonight!

Very quietly I take my leave

As quietly as I came here;

Gently I flick my sleeves

Not even a wisp of cloud will I bring away

【原文】

再别康桥

徐志摩

轻轻地我走了，
正如我轻轻地来；
我轻轻地招手，
作别西天的云彩。

那河畔的金柳，
是夕阳中的新娘；
波光里的艳影，
在我的心头荡漾。

软泥上的青荇，
油油的在水底招摇；
在康河的柔波里，
我甘心做一条水草！

那榆荫下的一潭，
不是清泉，是天上虹
揉碎在浮藻间，
沉淀着彩虹似的梦。

寻梦？撑一支长篙，
向青草更青处漫溯，
满载一船星辉，
在星辉斑斓里放歌。

但我不能放歌，

悄悄是别离的笙箫；

夏虫也为我沉默，

沉默是今晚的康桥！

悄悄地我走了，

正如我悄悄地来；

我挥一挥衣袖，

不带走一片云彩。

【Challenge】

Analyze this poem in terms of literary devices and techniques.

The major theme of this poem is：

_____

_____

【Creative work】

Can you read aloud this poem with great passion?

Module 5 外国诗歌

She Walks in Beauty

George Gordon Byron

She walks in beauty, like the night

Of cloudless climes and starry skies；

And all that's best of dark and bright

Meet in her aspect and her eyes：

Thus mellowed to that tender light

Which heaven to gaudy day denies.

【译文】

她走在美的光彩中

她走在美的光彩中，

像夜晚

皎洁无云而且繁星满天；

明与暗的最美妙的色泽

在她的仪容和秋波里呈现：

耀目的白天只嫌光太强，

它比那光亮柔和而幽暗。

【Challenge】

Analyze this poem in terms of literary devices and techniques.

1. The major theme of this poem is：

_____

_____

_____

2. Study the poem's rhymes.

_____

_____

_____

【Creative work】

Can you create a new poem based on the rhyme in this poem?

The Night Has a Thousand Eyes

Francis William Bourdillon

The night has a thousand eyes,

And the day but one；

Yet the light of a bright world dies

With the dying sun.

The mind has a thousand eyes,

And the heart but one;

Yet the light of a whole life dies

When love is done.

【译文】

夜晚的眼睛成千上万

夜晚的眼睛成千上万，

白天的只有半双；

但辉煌的世界将一片黑暗，

当太阳灭了光芒。

脑海的眼睛成千上万，

心灵的只有半双；

但整个儿生活将一片黯淡，

当爱情熄了火光。

【Challenge】

Analyze this poem in terms of literary devices and techniques.

1. The major theme of this poem is：

_____

_____

2. Study the poem's stanzaic form and rhymes.

_____

_____

【思考题】

What does the speaker mean by saying "the mind has a thousand eyes"？

How does he use metaphors to express his love towards life and his beloved?

Leisure

W. H. Davies

What is this life if, full of care,

We have no time to stand and stare?

No time to stand beneath the boughs,

And stare as long as sheep and cows.

No time to see, when woods we pass,

Where squirrels hide their nuts in grass.

No time to see, in broad daylight,

Streams full of stars, like skies at night.

No time to turn at Beauty's glance,

And watch her feet, how they can dance.

No time to wait till her mouth can

Enrich that smile her eyes began?

A poor life this if, full of care,

We have no time to stand and stare.

【译文】

闲　暇

生活是什么　倘若充满思虑

以至无暇驻足欣赏?

无暇站在树枝底下

像牛羊一样 久久凝望

无暇注视经过的树林

松鼠在那里把果实收藏

无暇细赏 清澈阳光下

那波光粼粼的水面 仿佛夜晚的穹苍

无暇留意佳人的一瞥回眸

欣赏她的纤足 怎样轻舞飞扬

无暇等候她红唇微启

溢出笑意嫣然

生活是苍白可怜 倘若充满思虑

以至无暇驻足欣赏

【Challenge】

Analyze this poem in terms of literary devices and techniques.

1. The major theme of this poem is:

_____

_____

2. Study the poem's rhymes.

_____

_____

【思考题】

Can you create a new poem based on the rhyme in this poem?

Ballad of Birmingham

Dudley Randall

(On the bombing of a church in Birmingham, Alabama, 1963)

"Mother dear, may I go downtown

Instead of out to play,

And march the streets of Birmingham

In a Freedom March today? "

"No, baby, no, you may not go,

For the dogs are fierce and wild,

And clubs and hoses, guns and jails

Aren't good for a little child."

"But, mother, I won't be alone.

Other children will go with me,

And march the streets of Birmingham

To make our country free."

"No, baby, no, you may not go,

For I fear those guns will fire.

But you may go to church instead

And sing in the children's choir."

She has combed and brushed her night-dark hair,

And bathed rose petal sweet,

And drawn white gloves on her small brown hands,

And white shoes on her feet.

The mother smiled to know her child

Was in the sacred place,

But that smile was the last smile

To come upon her face.

For when she heard the explosion,

Her eyes grew wet and wild.

She raced through the streets of Birmingham

Calling for her child.

She clawed through bits of glass and brick,

Then lifted out a shoe.

"O, here's the shoe my baby wore,

But, baby, where are you？"

【译文】

伯明翰歌谣

（为纪念1963年亚拉巴马的伯明翰教堂爆炸事件而作）

"亲爱的妈妈，我不出去玩耍，

可不可以去市中心

在伯明翰街头行军

加入今天的自由游行？"

"不，孩子，不，你别去，
警犬都是又凶又恶，
大头棒，橡皮管，枪和牢房
对小孩子都不适合。"

"可是，妈妈，我不会单独去。
别的孩子要与我同走，
一起在伯明翰街头游行
让我们的国家自由。"

"不，孩子，不，你别去，
我怕那些枪会开火。
不过，你可以到教堂那里
在儿童唱诗班唱歌。"
她梳理好乌溜溜的秀发，
沐浴得香若玫瑰花，
白手套戴上棕色的小手，
白鞋子脚上穿踏。

妈妈笑了，知道自己的孩子
正在神圣的地方，
可那微笑竟是最后的笑容
浮现在她的脸上。

当她听见爆炸的声响，
双眼落泪发了疯。
她呼唤着自己的孩子
在伯明翰街头猛冲。

她用手在瓦砾废墟中挖掘，

随后取出了一只鞋。

"啊，这是我孩子穿的鞋，

可是，孩子，你在哪里？"

【Challenge】

Analyze this poem in terms of literary devices and techniques.

1. The major theme of this poem is:

_____

_____

2. There are sharp contrasts in the poem. Please find them out.

_____

_____

3. What figures of speech are used in the poem? How does the tone change?

_____

_____

【思考题】

1. What do the "clubs and hoses guns and jails" stand for?

2. What is the function of the colors in the fifth stanza? Is it special that the poet uses these colors instead of other colors?

3. If the mother had let her baby go to the march, would the baby still be alive?